The Praise Singer

A DISCIPLE OF MELCHIZEDEK

David Martyn

ISBN 978-1-64003-787-8 (Paperback)
ISBN 978-1-64003-788-5 (Digital)

Copyright © 2018 David Martyn
All rights reserved
First Edition

All rights reserved. No part of this publication may be reproduced, distributed, or transmitted in any form or by any means, including photocopying, recording, or other electronic or mechanical methods without the prior written permission of the publisher. For permission requests, solicit the publisher via the address below.

Covenant Books, Inc.
11661 Hwy 707
Murrells Inlet, SC 29576
www.covenantbooks.com

Preface

I have always been fascinated with the story of Melchizedek, this mysterious king of Salem and priest of God Most High briefly mentioned in Genesis 14:18 when Abram offers a tithe after his rescue of his nephew Lot. Melchizedek appears again in Psalm 110, a messianic psalm of David quoted by our Lord Jesus. The writer of Hebrews expounds on Jesus as the Great High Priest in the order of Melchizedek beginning in chapter 4 and expands to show Melchizedek's priesthood clearly as a type, foreshadowing our new covenant made by Jesus's atoning death on the cross.

Like many Christians, I believe Melchizedek may have been more than just a type for Jesus, showing a truth about Him before the incarnation, but the preincarnate Christ himself. He is identified as having no genealogy, suggesting he was not born a man. If true, I could not help but wonder about the impact he had on the people of Salem when he walked in on them and lived among them. Imagine having normal daily contact with him. For context, many Jewish commentators believe that Shem was Melchizedek.

Many writers have offered that God's revelation to man is progressive. This is clearly suggested by Paul in the book of Romans. General revelation is the evidence of God in creation and in His sustaining of creation. Special revelation begins when God enters into created order to reveal something specific about Himself. We see this as divine providence, the apparent control of the events of people and nations. Special revelation also includes prophets speaking His words under His authority. The fullest revelation, of course, is Jesus Himself, God made flesh, the Living Word of God.

PREFACE

In Romans 1:18–20, Paul makes the startling claim that in the general revelation alone, God has made plain to man all that may be known about God! It seemed to me the best person to narrate an encounter with Melchizedek was an isolated uneducated man whose only knowledge of God came from revelation. If we have no excuse, as St. Paul claims in Romans, the general revelation of God should lead us on God's path of revelation He sets out for us. This story is a fictionalized account of one man responding to God's revelation, hearing God's call, and following where it takes him, the same place His story takes each of us.

David Martyn

Note: The praise songs included are my efforts on Psalms of Ascent.

PART ONE

The Calling

Chapter One

*"You shall not pervert the justice due
to the sojourner, or to the fatherless, or
take a widow's garment in pledge."*

—*Deuteronomy 24:17*

I am become Zimri-Ruel (My Praise, Friend of God) by the calling of the Lord, the Most High God, a priest to the hill country of Khalab. This is my new name for my new identity and my new voice, a messenger for men who seek the Most High God. This, now my name, is a true identity for one who has no tribe, no clan, and no genealogy. My given name is unknown, though I have been called by many names by village masters who raised me as their slave. The Most High God did not restore my given name but gave me a better name. The Lord God took me from isolation to family, from slavery to freedom. No longer a slave to a village who show no hospitality for the foreigner, I now serve the Most High God, interceding for hill country people and bringing His message. Sing with me His praise! He has filled my heart with joy. He has comforted me in my sorrow. Hear His voice you who travel by night and shepherds of the night fold. I know your thoughts. I lived your fears.

I was found along the road to Haran and taken to a poor village in the high hills above Khalab. I have no memories of my parents. Did I have a mother who caressed me? Did my father smile at me with pride? These things I never knew. When a lamb is orphaned, it is adopted by another ewe. No village woman stepped in for my mother. No village man adopted me as his son. I was called simply Katan (little boy). Not willing to make me a son, the village elders decided Katan would be a village property, a slave to all. I was shuttled between houses and sheltered with sheep and goats. I was trained like a beast, fed when obedient, and punished until I performed. If any of the women in the village showed tenderness towards me, I was hurriedly moved to another house or barn.

I have few memories of my early childhood. I do remember painfully that I was never permitted to eat with the children of the house where I dwelt. I have no memory of sitting at the table with any other village person. It was not permitted. It was said, "It is not right for Katan to join the family table." I ate alone, I slept alone, and once taught a duty, I worked alone; I never knew of play. As I was instructed, "There is no need for Katan to play. Katan is not a child of any family. Katan belongs to the village."

Once the family had finished their meal, food would be brought to me. It was usually cold, having been left from the family table. I could not sit at the family table, even after they had finished and left. I sat outside or in a storeroom or under the cover of the goat pen. When I finished my meal, I was taught to clear the table; I cleaned the family bowls and carefully put them away. When all of the family tableware was clean, I would clean my bowl and return it to my sleeping rug. My bowl and my rug went with me when I was shuttled about the village.

Every new moon, I would move to another house and serve another family. There was no difference in my treatment. "Katan," the father would begin, "you know what is expected of you. You will sleep in the goat pen. You will eat in the goat pen, and you will do as you are told. You understand? Now put your things in the pen and return. I have a new chore for you." Each time I was moved, I was taught a new chore or expanded the work on a previous chore. My cleaning chores went from clearing and cleaning the table and bowls to fetching wood for the cook fires and then fetching water from the well.

One day was different. I had swept the dirt floor and had fetched firewood for the cooking fire. A village woman was teaching her daughter to cook small cakes in olive oil. I stood and watched as the small patties of dough sizzled in the oil.

The woman caught me watching her and said, "Katan, don't just stand there. Be useful. Go and fetch water."

When I returned with the water and set it beside the table, I saw the small cakes cooling on a wooden board. I will never forget the daughter, seeing me return, picked up a small cake and gave it to me. "Here, Katan, you earned this. They are so good when they are still warm."

"No!" the woman shouted. "Leah, take that away from him! Never give Katan anything. He is not family. He is not our guest. He is here to work."

The woman turned to me and said, "Katan, go clean the goat pen. You are never to be here while we cook. Do you understand? Go. Go now!"

That evening, the husband spoke with me. "Your work in the house is done. Now you will work only outside. You will continue to clean the stalls and the pens. I will take you to the fields tomorrow."

As I grew older and stronger, my village masters began calling me Ben Kafar (village son). My duties changed from gathering wood, carrying water, cleaning after livestock to working the full day with the men in the fields, tilling, clearing, picking, and gleaning. As was their practice, I was shown how to do a task and then left alone to work. My first task was weeding. Small fields of wheat and barley were grown on terraced hillside plots below the village. These small plots grew just enough grain to see the village through the year with just enough leftover for seed for the next year's crop. The emerging blade of wheat was dear. Every bit of fertile soil was precious. From the emergence of the first blade until the harvest in the late summer, I carefully pulled every weed to protect the grain and ensure the maximum harvest. This was lonely and tiresome work. Hour after hour, day after day, I worked hunched over beneath the burning sun, going back and forth over the wheat field, pulling everything that wasn't wheat. I was permitted to bring a small skin of water and a small cooked cake and a small raisin or fig cake to eat and drink while in the field. I was not to return to the village until sunset. Others worked in the fields as well, but I worked alone.

Working in the fields opened my eyes to a much larger world. I remember the first time I looked out from the terraced field towards the low hills and plains below. The horizon seemed like it would go on forever! My eyes could not discern the end of the land. Far in the distant east, I could see a city. They called it Khalab. I could just make out a road running along the base of the hills and people traveling the road. Occasionally, I would see long lines of men and animals approaching the gates to Khalab. From one of the remote fields, I could see the path from our village, nearly all the way down to the great road.

One day, while weeding this field, as I worked to the eastern edge, I saw one of the village men hurry from the olive grove above to the village elder returning from the path below.

"What did he want? What did you tell him?" the villager asked.

The elder answered, "I didn't ask what he wanted. I told him that he was lost and should go back down the path to the road. I said this path ends just above us, there is no road, there is nothing here for us to give him."

The villager asked, "And he turned around? He did not ask for water or a meal? He sought no hospitality?"

The elder sighed. "El (God) will not hold us to providing hospitality for every stranger who wanders up our path. El knows we are poor. We have nothing to offer a stranger, or even to offer in sacrifice to him. Let the priests of Khalab make sacrifices and present offerings to God. They are wealthy. If God honors Khalab, we will receive the blessing as well. As Khalab prospers, they will pay a fine price for our wool."

At harvest, the village men would reap the wheat and gather the harvest into bundles. They would carry the bundles to a winnowing floor, a level place with hard ground near the village, to winnow the wheat from the chaff. I was left in the field to glean. I would scour the field for any heads of grain that may have fallen or broken off during the reaping or sheaving. I would retrace every step of the trail from the field to winnowing floor, gathering every grain I could find.

I worked alone, but as always, my work was inspected. If even one head of grain remained in the field I was punished. Besides a loud and humiliating rebuke, food was withheld. Not all of my ration, and never my water, but the raisin or fig cake would be withheld. Sometimes I would be told to sleep outside the village surrounded by the sounds of the night.

Once the grain was winnowed and safely stored for the winter, the villagers would feast. I would be treated to time off, while the others celebrated. I was given freshly cooked cakes, raisin cakes, and figs. I could not join the celebration. It was always Leah who brought the warm cooked cakes to my shelter.

The grain harvest was followed by the olive harvest. The olive trees grew on the rocky hillsides. Harvesting olives was simple. Villagers spread blankets beneath the olive trees and shook the branches to free the ripe olives, which fell to the blanket below. They were very careful to shake the branches forcefully enough to free the olives but not so hard as to break a single branch. Olive harvest was also a festive event. Everyone joined in the harvest. My task was to carry the bags of the harvest up to the village. I worked alone.

The olives were pressed between two great stones. The lower stone was grooved to a channel opening where a jar would catch the pressed oil. The upper stone was turned on an axle, crushing the olives as it rotated. It was hard work turning the heavy stone and continually lifting it off to clean the residue and then adding new olives to be crushed. I would begin by lifting the upper stone, placing two handfuls of olives near the center, lowering the stone, inserting the axle shaft, and then pushing the two-handed handle rotating the heavy top stone on top of the base. After the oil ceased running into the jar, I would remove the axle shaft, lift the stone, clean out the olive reside, and carefully place it into a large jar. It would take several days to fill a jar of olive oil. At the end of each day, I would carry both the oil and the residue back to the village. I was directed to deliver the oil to the owner of the olives pressed. The olive residue was fed to the goats. The goats were happy to see me. I worked alone.

The grape harvest was another event for celebration. The whole village participated in the harvest. The whole village participated in the pressing of the grapes. My duty was to carry the grapes to the press and to carry the jars to the appointed storeroom. I was provided food and drink during the celebration, which I could enjoy on my own.

The winter was pruning time. Both the vines and trees required pruning to be truly fruitful and bountiful at harvest. I was not entrusted with pruning the vines. This was done by skillful vine dressers. I was told to carry the pruned branches to a woodpile. I removed all of the leaves, cut away the small vines, cut the branches, and stacked the remaining wood by thickness. I bound small bundles for kindling and firewood. Olive trees were easier to prune than grapevines. The small branches growing off the trunk would be cut off. The ends of branches were cut back to a prominent fork. I was young and agile, so I was sent up into the tree to prune the upper trunk and higher branches. One day, reaching high into the tree, I lost my balance and fell backwards. As I fell, I reached out and grabbed a limb. The limb creaked and bent before it broke, stripping a large portion of bark from the tree. As I landed on the ground, my fall broken at the expense of the tree, the enraged villager I was working for lunged upon me, screaming and kicking me. He kicked me again and again. It seemed he would never stop.

Hearing the commotion, the village elder appeared. "Stop! That's enough! Stop! Leave him. Leave him and go to your house. I will deal with him."

As the angry man stomped off, screaming about his olive tree, the village elder looked at me and said, "Ben Kafar, can you hear me?"

"Yes," I replied.

"Can you sit up?" he asked.

I sat up and looked at him. He carefully examined my arms and legs and then looked at my face. I saw no malice in his eyes, just a careful attentiveness. He then said, "I think you will be sore but are unhurt."

Then looking at the tree, he said, "It has not fared so well as you, Ben Kafar! But I think we can save it. Run up to the house of

Tizvi and tell him I sent you for twine. Hurry and come right back here."

I returned with the twine, and Dov, the village elder, carefully pruned the damaged limb and artfully put the bark back from where it had torn. He then wrapped the torn bark onto the trunk with the twine. "We will know in the spring if the tree lives. But it is better it happened now while the tree rests for the winter." Then looking intently in my face, he said, "He will want to punish you severely. Come with me to my house. You will stay with me until your punishment is determined."

That night, I slept in Dov's storeroom. Dov was one of the few villagers who always let me sleep inside. Most of all, I remember his house for the silence. Dov's wife died some years earlier, about the time I began my work in the fields. She was a quiet woman who rarely, if ever, spoke to me. She never abused me; it was more that she pretended I wasn't there. In Dov's house, only he spoke to me. He spoke quietly yet firmly. As I think back, I do not recall Dov after being cross with me. He just told me what was expected of me and nodded when it was done. Dov and his wife had no children. As I lay on my rug considering what had occurred and wondering my fate, Dov entered the small room. He looked down at me and said simply, "What must we do with you?" He just stared at me for a few minutes and left the room.

In the morning, all of the village men assembled outside Dov's house. I remember the anger in the voice of the man who sent me up his tree. "He must learn his lesson! His carelessness could undo us all. We cannot afford to lose an olive tree. This time, it was a tree. What destruction will he cause next? I say beat him. Beat him, and he will not forget. Never let him forget. We feed him, he belongs to us. Beat him until his back runs red with his blood!"

Tizvi spoke next. "He is just a boy. He works hard. He always has. He knows what we expect of him. He is still a boy. Yes, he should learn from this, but beat him? No, it is our duty to train him, not harm him."

Another said, "I have come to rely on him. There is always more to do. He is worth more than he eats. I would not beat my animals. Why would I beat him?"

Dov finally spoke. "It is true Ben Kafar should learn from this. It has always been our intent to train him. To make him a true son of our village, belonging to all, serving all. No, we shall not beat him, but we shall make him think upon the cost of his mistake. No, we shall not beat him, we shall bind him to the olive tree every night for a week. As he is bound to the tree he has injured, let him see his future is bound to the care of the olive tree, just as it is bound to the figs, the vines, the grain field, and flocks. I will bind him there tonight and will see he remains there every night for a week. He will be provided his cloak, his rug, water, a small cooked cake, and a raisin cake. Nothing more. He will learn from this."

I was then taken back to the olive grove. No longer allowed to prune, I carried the pruned branches up to the village and prepared them as kindling or firewood. No one spoke to me that day, not even Dov. At dusk, when the other men went back to the village, Dov led me to the damaged olive tree. He looked carefully at the torn bark now tightly wrapped back in place with the twine. He motioned for me to sit down beside the tree. I spread out my rug and sat. I presented him my hands. He put my arms around the trunk in front of me and tied my hands together at the wrists. "Lie back," he said. "Slide closer to the tree. Good, I see you can lie flat. You should be able to sleep." He paused and looked up into the darkening sky. Half to himself and half to me, he remarked, "There is little moon tonight. The stars in the heavens will be bright. Such a mystery to be found in the night sky." Then looking at me, he said directly, "Enjoy the stars, Ben Kafar." And he walked off. He stopped, looked back, and said, "Yell loudly if a great cat comes at you." And then I was alone.

The same events were repeated for seven days. On the last night, the stars were not visible. The sky was overcast, and there was a cold wind blowing from the north. I struggled to keep warm beneath my cloak on my rug. The ground was cold. My hands and feet were cold.

I curled up as tightly as I could, tucking my hands, feet, and head under the cloak. I still remember the cold.

I awoke in the morning covered with a light dusting of snow. I was cold and wet. When Dov came down to untie me, he closed his eyes and said, "Go up to my house and light a fire."

I made my way up the path to the village. It seemed everyone was out, though they were probably just beginning a normal day. But as I approached, clinging to my cloak and shivering as I slowly walked, every one stopped to watch. Then I noticed Leah coming out of her house with a blanket. I could see her mother watching her with disapproving eyes. Leah walked up to me and threw the blanket over me and around my shoulders. She said nothing. She covered me and walked back to her house. I watched her walk back. I gripped the blanket close and walked to Dov's house. I gathered kindling and firewood and lit a warming fire.

Chapter Two

"The heavens are telling of the glory of God; and their expanse is declaring the work of His hands."

—*Psalm 19:1–2*

The following spring, Dov decided it was time I learned to shepherd. Like all other responsibilities in the high hills village, shepherding had its own established routine. The sheep would spend the night in the safety of the sheepfold. The sheepfold was attended every night, all night, by one of the shepherds. In the morning, the other shepherds would go to the sheepfold and lead the flocks to different pastures higher above the village. The sheep would graze on the sparse grass in the high pastures moving about, following the grass, grazing all day under the careful watch of the shepherd. The sheep would follow the shepherd back down to the sheepfold before dark. The sheep knew their shepherd, and the shepherd knew his sheep. He knew where to find good grass. He knew his way about the high hills, and he was ever vigilant for any threat to his sheep.

There was something different about the shepherds. They each had their own way of calling their sheep. They worked well together but enjoyed their time alone in the high hills. They seemed happy. Each had his own special skill, though they were all adept at climbing the rocky hillsides. And they all were happy in their work. Rouvin was the best climber, and he could find the best way to reach any spot on the mountain. Matai had great vision, and he could spot his white fleecy sheep against the bare white rock at first glance. Jachin was skilled in reading and following tracks, and he could identify the animal and determine how long ago it passed by. Hod was just happy. He never stopped talking. He didn't require an audience; he just talked and laughed his way through the day. I almost wanted to talk to them, to know them, but no, I decided to keep my own company.

I grew strong and taller than all the other young men of the village. It came time for me to work the loneliest duty in the village, night shepherd. Already I could climb the rocky hillsides nearly as well as the mountain goat. I knew his ways, I knew his temperament, and I understood his call. Late every afternoon, I would join the village shepherds and help them herd the sheep into a night sheepfold in a cleft in the mountain. The goats would be herded to a rocky ledge above the sheepfold. I would set my mat before the gate and guard them through the night. I found refuge from the harsh inhospitality of the village. I found solitude and comfort in the mountain night. True, there was danger, and the flock was its attraction, but I would rather face the lion, wolf or bear than my masters from the village. Village men were happy to spend the nights with their wives and families in the village, and I was pleased to be free of them.

Unhurried by endless tasks and the derision of villagers, I took time to learn the night sky. You who travel by night or stand night watch know of the night sky where the mountain looks out to the desert of Aram. Always in motion, telling us the season, countless stars bright and shining, a source of wonder. Night after night, while the flocks were secure behind me, I studied the starry host. Like the sheep and the mountain, it had a voice louder and stronger than the hard voices from the village below me. It was a voice of constancy. It did not change. The voice gave me both comfort and a challenge. Night after night, I sought to understand the voice of the starry host.

In the morning, the other shepherds would come from the village. They would bring me bread, oil, fruit, cheese, and a skin of milk. They were pleased that I kept the flock safe. Their words, though few, were softer. As I climbed the rocks to herd the goats, they laughed. I heard Hod say, "You are no longer Ben Kafar. You are now Jael (the mountain goat)." By day, I stayed in a shallow cave, which was little more than a crevice in the rock. But it provided shade and shelter next to a clean running brook. When awake, I lay there pondering this mountain world beneath the starry host by night and warming sun by day.

Night by night, I lay on my rug in front of the gate to the sheepfold. The patterns of life in the village began to fade. New patterns were emerging. I felt comfortable by my small fire in front of the sheepfold. I felt comfortable with the sheep resting, making only an occasional bleat during the night. I rested comfortably during the day in the darkness of my small cave. I was escaping my life in the village, yet I was fed, and all my needs were met. Once comfortable, I began to look at my surroundings, the source of my comfort. I looked at them fondly. I noted how my surroundings so perfectly filled my need. My gaze and my thoughts began to look at my world a little further away. I considered the high pastures and the tender grass. I thought of the rocky ledges where the goats watched in safety the world pass beneath them. I thought how I could now watch the village below me safely from my rug in front of the sheepfold. Everything looked safely in its place, and I was satisfied that it was right.

As the days passed, I became more familiar with my world. I began to consider the changes in the night sky above. I knew the moon changed, but I watched it change night after night. I knew the days grew longer to summer and then shortened as the winter approached. I observed these changes and wondered at them. I noticed patterns in the seasons aligning with patterns in the night sky. I began to see consistency in the world around me. I learned the ways of the sheep and goats of the flocks—the consistent way of birth and consistent manner of the ewe with her lamb and the consistent aggression of the ram's belligerent establishment of authority. I watched the birds of the air build their nests in the spring, patiently warm their eggs, and fiercely attend their young. I watched the big cats stalk their prey and still tenderly carry their cubs. I saw how they groomed and cared for their pride. I watched the caterpillar spin his cocoon and emerge a butterfly. I saw the locust and grasshopper blow in clouds across the fields.

Over it all, the sun by day and the moon and stars by night continued in their established heavenly paths. The order of all I observed amazed me. How could such wonders be? Everything was ordered from the bleating of the sheep to the arrival of the village shepherds every morning. Who was I in this order? A shepherd slave with no father and no mother? Was something broken in this world that I sat alone by night? How could this order be? Was it always this way? A mystery. A mystery of the order I knew. This order could not come from within. This order did not come from man. For man himself was ordered. What great power put all things in order?

The season of harvest was passing. The nights became cold. The full moon rising at the setting of the sun provided a stunning light that made the village below appear close enough to touch. What beauty to behold for a slave shepherd!

One morning, as the winter set in, Hod, returning from the village, tossed me a pouch of food larger than normal. "Leah sends you an extra portion of flour and oil and another blanket should the snow come and hinder our climb to you." Leah, the most tender of the village women, never could hide her concern for me from the village elders. I guess they no longer saw the harm if I was out of the village. I was unable to answer this kindness. I did not know how to say thank you, or even be thankful.

The next night, the snow did come early. How did Leah know? There would be no fresh food in the morning. I opened Leah's pouch and found the flour and oil. I remembered watching village women make small cakes with flour and oil when I was very young before being sent to work with the men. I would need more wood for the fire to build a bed of coals for cooking. I picked up the thin jar of oil. It was cold. There was only a thin layer of oil floating above the solid frozen oil at the bottom of the jar. I looked at the brook outside the cave. It was covered with ice. I stepped out to gather wood, forgetting to put the frozen oil down. I slipped, and my feet went through the ice. I dropped the jar of oil. The liquid oil floated, but the frozen oil sank to the bottom of the brook. I quickly recovered the oil, gathered the wood, and fed the fire. As I warmed myself, I watched the oil melt as well. I pondered what happened. How fortunate I was to have a shelter and a fire to warm me. But the oil seemed to break the order I saw. The ice floated on the brook, while the frozen oil sank. Troubled, I pondered a new mystery. I considered the brook so close it provided water for me and the flocks. I depended on it. What else did I know about the brook? It provided for fish, for frogs, and certainly for flies. It provided water for the birds of the air, and even the big cats. So much depended on the water in the brook. Then I saw the order! Ice must float, or the pattern of life could not continue. The fish and the frogs would all die if the brook froze from the bottom. The flocks, birds, beast, and men could not survive the winter if the floating ice did not protect and cover the water below. Even the ice floating on the water is a pattern of life!

As I ate my small cakes, it became clear. There was no denying that the whole world and all of the heavens above must be an ordered creation. Who is the creator? If His creation is ordered and continues by design, can He be known? Does He work to maintain His patterns? If He works, He can intervene! Does He closely follow His creation, or is He far? If His creation is so carefully ordered, does that mean that He cares for it? I know the shepherd cares for his flock, the farmer cares for his field, the craftsman cares for the work of his hands. Surely, the creator must care for His creation. Who is this great maker of all things? Can He be found?

As I pondered the mystery of the great maker of all that is, I continued to observe His evidence of creation, and of all His creation, the greatest puzzle is man! Man seems set apart from all other animals. Man appears to chafe under the order and consistency of creation. Man has some authority over creation. He tends the flocks, plants, and harvests fruits and grains and crops of all kinds. But man displays a disharmony, a disharmony among tribes and clans, and even within his own family. Man is different, but he clearly is not maker of all things. I do not understand how this can be. If man has dominion and authority over other creatures and parts of creation but cannot be creator, is man between the creator and the rest of creation? The creator and maker of all things is other than everything that is created. He cannot be both the maker of all things and something made himself. Yes, He must be other. He must be greater.

There can be nothing made that is greater than the maker. Is this "other" the "great maker of all things," El (God), as spoken of by the elder Dov? Does the maker of all things have a purpose for man? How can man have dominion and authority in creation and yet fall short of order and unity? I determined only the great other, the creator, or God, as Dov called him, has the answer. Can He hear my questions? Can He answer me?

Chapter Three

*"For since the creation of the world His
invisible attributes, His eternal power
and divine nature, have been clearly seen,
being understood through what has been
made, so that they are without excuse."*

—*Romans 1:20*

As the seasons passed and spring returned, the season of storms began. One afternoon, as I helped the village shepherds herd the flocks to the night sheepfold, God sent a strong storm. The skies darkened, the wind blew hard, and the rains came with loud thunder and lightning filling the sky. As quickly as the storm came, it was over. A bow of many colors arched across the cloudy sky. I heard Hod, the shepherd, say, "At last, the rainbow! El's promise never again to destroy the world by a great flood. A sign of unchanging promise by EL Elyon (the Most High God)."

Stunned, I asked Hod, "You say there is a Most High God, and He has given a sign and a promise? How has He promised? Does He speak? Where can I go to hear Him speak? I must find this Most High God!"

"So, Jael, the mountain goat, does not know the story or Noah, his sons and their wives, how they were saved by the Most High God when all the world was destroyed by the great flood? Jael does not know our genealogy, how we are sons and daughters of Shem, son of Noah, son of Lamech? Jael does not know that the Most High God spoke to Noah and commanded he build an ark? That a remnant of every bird, every animal, every creature was carried on the ark to survive the flood? Jael, how little you know!"

Amazed, I said, "I need to find this Noah. I need to speak with the Most High God."

"Jael, Noah is buried, but his son, our Patriarch Shem, still lives. He is very old but still speaks of his salvation by the Most High God, though few have time for the tales of a feeble old man. He may be in Salem, but I don't know for certain."

I thought, *I must find this Patriarch Shem. He knows the Most High God... I must know Him too!*

As the nights passed, I would gaze up to the stars. They still spoke to me. They cried out that there was a God, a creator. And now to know he had spoken, how did He speak? What is the sound of His voice? Was it only to Noah and his family that he spoke? Does He still speak? Will He speak to me?

One night, as I made my way across the gate to the night sheepfold, I saw a dead bird. In the silence of the night, I could hear the faint squawking of fledgling birds in a craggy nest. I knew their fate. The young birds would die with no mother, just as the young lamb will perish without the ewe and lion cub will not survive the loss of the lioness. This too was created order. Is God cruel? Does He show no mercy to the orphan? But I am an orphan. I have no mother and no father. Am I a disorder in creation? Or can God save? If God saved Noah, his sons, and their wives and saved a remnant of all creatures, did God save me?

I must find Shem!

God, forgive me... I ran way.

I gathered all the wood from my camp. I lit fires across the gate of the sheepfold and all around the rocky enclosure. Every fire was fed to last through the night. The flock should be safe until morning and the coming of the village shepherds. I must go! No. I feared for the flock. I must go! I was betraying my masters. Who made them master over me? I must go!

I collected my blanket and cloaked it over my shoulder. I put all of the food in the pouch Leah had sent me, and I made my way down the mountain, avoiding the village to the road farther below. I did not know where the road led, but it led me out, and Shem and Salem were out.

I was overwhelmed with excitement as I followed the road still leading me down. I skirted the city I believed to be Khalab, which was cloaked in darkness, and returned to the road. The stars above somehow appeared even brighter. *There is a Most High God. He spoke to Noah. He rescued Shem. He must hear me.*

I walked the road by night and sought shelter out of sight during the day. Another city appeared, and again I chose to skirt around it. The road led to a ford across a wide river. The days passed. and my food pouch was empty. Still I followed the road. The road led me to a great city. The city gates were just opening as I approached it at dawn. I was gripped with fear. *Do I enter? Do I wait for someone passing and ask for direction? O Most High God, if you hear the prayers of men, show me what to do!*

I heard a man walking behind me. As he passed by me, he turned around and asked, "Young shepherd, you appear hesitant to enter our city. You look like you have been traveling all night. You must be a foreigner. Please come to my house and accept my hospitality."

"Sir, what city is this? Go with you to your house? I don't know… I never… I haven't…"

"Come with me. My name is Terah, and this is Haran. My clan and my tribe are shepherds too. We follow the grass with our sheep and goats. Our camp is to the north and the west on the plains of Nahor, my father, but I maintain an abode in Haran where we sell our wool and goat hair tents. You can tell me of your journey after you have washed, eaten, and slept. What is your name?"

"I am called Jael, but I know not if I ever had a given name. I am a 'mountain goat' with no father and no mother, a shepherd with no genealogy."

I finished washing my face, my hands, and my feet. I poured the wash water over my head and watched the now dirty brown water splash on the ground. Glancing around, I saw a clean tunic folded on the table beside me. I had never been given new clothes before. I stared at the crisp clean tunic and then reached down, picked it up, and pulled it over my head. I wrapped my old worn belt around my waist, and tentatively I went through the door where Terah greeted me. He politely directed me to a table filled with roasted lamb, cakes, fruit, and wine. I could only stare. Terah said warmly, "Sit and eat with me. Don't be afraid, we all have to eat!"

After my first meal at the table of a noble house, the hours and days of walking and the adrenalin of starting my journey wore on me. Seeing my fatigue, Terah said, "Sleep now. We can talk when you are refreshed."

I don't remember lying down. It was dusk when I awoke. Lamps were being lit in the house. Terah was seated on a cushion on a very fine rug, unlike any I had ever seen. "So, Jael, you look refreshed. Sit here and tell me what brings a lone foreign shepherd to Haran."

"Lord Terah, I am recently determined to find the Patriarch Shem. I am told he was rescued from a great flood with his father, Noah, brothers and their wives, and a remnant of all the creatures on earth. I am told that Noah has heard the voice of the Most High God. I have seen the work of the Most High God, and I am decided to find Him."

"Where, Jael, have you seen the work of the Most High God?" Terah asked.

"Lord Terah, you appear to be a great man in this great city. I live in the high hills beside the tall mountains. I see the handiwork of the Most High God in the ordained procession of the stars above by night and the sun by day. I see the work of the Most High God in the birth and care of the lamb by the mother ewe. I see the lioness care for her cub and stalk prey. I have seen the caterpillar weave a cocoon and become a butterfly. I have seen the land tilled, the seed sewn, and the harvest reaped in season. I have seen ice float above the water to protect the fish beneath and provide drink to man, beast, and crop. I have seen the order of His creation. I have determined that man is not God, but he too is a creature. I have determined that man has dominion and authority in creation but is not God, is not the creator. I see that man chafes in the world he did not create. When I heard that Noah heard the voice of the Most High God and his son,

THE CALLING

Shem, still lives, I left my master's flock and set off to Salem to speak with Shem. Can you direct my way to Salem?"

"My good Jael, you indeed are not far from the Most High God. You speak wisely for a young shepherd. Your words have more wisdom than those of many nobles. I am a distant son of Shem. I too have heard his story. He is very old and weak but still very wise. and he is no longer in Salem. He is in Damascus, a city of many days' travel from here. Yet you shall speak to him and hear his story. But now rest. Tomorrow worship the Most High God."

"Worship?" I wondered. "I will ask the Patriarch Shem what is worship."

Chapter Four

"So he said, 'Cursed be Canaan; a servant of servants he shall be to his brothers.' He also said, 'Blessed be the Lord, the God of Shem; and let Canaan be his servant. May God enlarge Japheth and let him dwell in the tents of Shem And let Canaan be his servant.'"

—Genesis 9:25–27

Several days later, a servant of Terah found me and told me to prepare for the journey to Damascus. He brought me several clean tunics, a warm cloak and blanket, shoes, head scarves, belts, and pouches. As I looked at the neatly folded clothing and articles, Terah came into the room. "The trade caravan has arrived in Haran. The trades have been made, and they depart tomorrow for Damascus. I have business in Damascus, and we will travel in the safety of the caravan."

No caravan had ever ventured near the hill village above Khalab. I walked close by Terah as his servants led several donkeys and ten camels laden with bundles far larger than anything I imagined any beast could carry. I waited while Terah talked with the caravan chief and the chief of the badraqa (trained men paid to guard the caravan).

Terah returned. "This chief was difficult. I paid far too much for a position near the front, not to mention his cost for fodder! At least, we are ahead of the herd animals. The journey is too long to chew on the dust of this caravan. He wants to travel by night until

THE CALLING

we reach Carchemish. From Carchemish to Khalab, we travel by day. From Khalab, we travel again by night across desert to Hamath. The remainder of the journey to Damascus will again be by day. For my premium, he assures me we will maintain our preferred position all the way to Damascus, even as new travelers join the caravan along the way."

I thought of all those days I walked in the wrong direction, yet how fortunate I was to be found by Terah.

As we moved Terah's camels and donkeys to the assigned area, I curiously studied all the animals, their keepers, and the obvious masters in fine attire. Most of the pack animals were camels, but there were also many donkeys and some horses. A few were saddled rather than burdened with large bundles. I noticed men in very strange robes in colors I did not know was possible for a robe. I saw head scarves of every kind under the sun. I noted some of the men were dark as night. Such a variety of men but all coming together in forming the caravan. It was established that camels, donkeys, and packhorses were assigned to groups of ten and each group, once formed, would move to an assigned place and wait. Despite all of the noise and commotion, I could see that the caravan was steadily organizing and a semblance of order pervaded.

Soon the order to move was given. The caravan chief led the way on a fine camel, but soon he swung his camel out of the line and watched with his studied glare as the caravan began to move. Also in the front, with the chief of the badraqa, were several other badraqa mounted on camels and the finely attired men riding their camels and donkeys.

"These are the nobles traveling with the caravan without trade goods who chose the caravan for safety and the benefit of an expert guide," Terah told me.

Terah had indeed purchased a preferred slot; only two groups of ten camels were ahead of us. I looked back to see group after group fall into the procession. As the end of the train of camel, donkeys, and horses fell into line, I saw several herds of cattle and sheep travel off to the side and to the rear. A line of armed badraqa fanned out behind and alongside the caravan. Quickly and without a word, the caravan chief, satisfied with the formation of the caravan, rode his camel back to the front.

As we settled on the padded backs of his riding donkeys, Terah noted, "I always found camels to be nasty animals to ride, and they won't arrive any sooner. It is so much easier to dismount the donkey to relieve yourself, an event you will appreciate more when you are my age! Well, Jael, tonight you can begin teaching me your secrets of the night sky."

The journey from Haran to Carchemish was the shortest leg of our travels. I enjoyed being under the night skies again. Terah was an excellent companion and patiently listened as I pointed out key lights among the starry host. The caravan fell into a routine, which repeated itself each night and day. I wandered about the campsites at night, but I dared not get too close and be questioned by the foreigners.

One evening, I asked Terah why it was so important to men that they know and recite their genealogy.

Terah thought for a few moments and said, "A man's genealogy tells him and everyone he meets where he belongs. It provides a link to other men. It gives his tribe and his clan and his branch and his ancestral land. It tells whether he is to be blessed or to be cursed. It can lift him up or hold him down. The one thing a genealogy cannot do is make him a better man."

"And what about you, Terah, what is your genealogy?" I asked.

Terah recited, "I am the son of Nahor, the son of Serug, the son of Reu, the son of Peleg, the son of Eber, the son of Salah, the son of Arphaxed, the son of Shem, the son of Noah, whom you speak so much of. Now Noah was the son of Lamech, the son of Methuselah, the son of Enoch. Enoch would interest you, Jael. It has been said for all generations that after Enoch became the father of Methuselah, Enoch walked with God. Yes, Enoch walked with God! And then he was no more because God took him way! But finishing, Enoch was the son of Jared, the son of Mahalalel, the son of Kenan, the son of Enosh, the son of Seth, the son of Adam, the first man created by God."

THE CALLING

"So man was created by God!" I exclaimed. "And a man Enoch, you said, walked with God, and God took him away? Where?"

"That, my inquisitive friend, no one knows for certain, but it is said he lives with God," Terah replied with a smile.

As the caravan came outside the gates of Carchemish, the various groups moved to assigned encampment areas. Some camels and donkey went into the city. Buyers and traders came out and conducted business with the various groups. Some of the groups moved to form separate caravans, and groups from other caravans arrived and joined our caravan.

"Be patient and observe, Jael. You will witness similar activity in Khalab and Hamath. Trade roads intersect in these cities, and merchants and travelers move between the caravans. As confusing as it appears, it is well organized. We will move on tomorrow." Terah explained.

"You seem well acquainted with the caravan, Lord Terah. How is it a shepherd becomes a great lord and traveler?"

Terah chuckled and answered, "It is true, I am the goat who always goes astray. For indeed—ask my sons, and they will agree—I have traveled too far and too often. Many years ago, I left my father, Nahor, and brothers, gathered up my sons, and followed the great river south all the way to Ur, city of the Chaldeans. I was drawn by the great variety of people and places under the sun of the Most High God. I lived among them, but I could never be one of them. They worship gods of wood and stone who have no eyes to see, ears to hear, or mouths to speak. They did such detestable things. My son, Haran, was born in Ur."

Terah's eyes looked down, and he softly said, "I saw my son, Haran, die. He died in Ur before my very eyes. Pray to God, Jael, you never live to see your son die. But God is merciful, Haran left sons and daughters. His line will continue."

Gathering his composure, he continued, "And I have many grandchildren. My sons, Abram and Nahor, took wives for themselves while we lived in Ur. Yet I stayed far too long. My firstborn son, Abram, was wiser than I and asked to return north. We returned to the plains of Nahor, the lands of my father. Yet Haran was not forgotten. Indeed, Haran was built by the sons of Haran, his people, and his servants. Their sons married the daughters of the land. Their daughters married the sons of the Hurrians. Haran has become a great city."

He was silent for a moment, and then his face turned sad. "But Haran is no longer an honor to his memory. The sons and daughters of the foreigners, the traders, and the merchants that do business in Haran have brought with them their detestable gods—the gods of the Hurrians and of Assur, the gods of Babylon, and yes, the gods of Ur. The people of Haran have forgotten the Most High God and practice the most evil rituals. I am glad to be away from it."

Terah paused, looked off, and said distantly, "Abram too is now a wanderer. Now he follows the voice of the Most High God. Haran's son, Lot, journeys with him."

Turning back to me, Terah finished his story. "As I told you before, I live with my family and clan. We marry from within the tribe. We seek to preserve the ways of the Most High God, as did our Patriarch Shem. It is a hard thing living near a city abounding with evil. But as I am wise in the ways of the city and merchants, I trade for the family. There are many fine things that I find for my family, clan, and tribe. I seek to make their lives comfortable, but now I see that the comfort comes from them."

When we arrived at Khalab, I was amazed that the city I had seen from the distant high hills for many years held no attachment for me. It was only another strange city.

The same caravan reorganization occurred in Khalab and Hamath. But now more of the men joining the caravan appeared different. There were more horses, and the blankets, rugs, robes, everything appeared more varied. I went to speak with a new group of shepherds but noticed I could not understand the words of these men. Though I struggled to listen, their words made no sense. I could understand the sheep and the goat but not another man?

Terah saw the confusion in my face. "These men are from Arzawa, and they are sons of Japheth, son of Noah and brother of Shem. They live far to the west and north of the Great Sea. They have a different tongue than we of Shem. The group over there are from Cush, and they are sons of Ham, also son of Noah and brother to Shem. But hold your distance from that far group. They are Canaanites. You will get your fill of them in Salem. But it was the strange tongues that you question."

Terah continued, "There is a story, Jael, you will like. Shem, Ham, and Japheth were brothers and spoke one tongue. As people moved eastward, they found a plain in Shinar and settled there. They said to each other, 'Let us make bricks and build a tower that reaches to the heaven so we can make a name for ourselves.' But the Lord God came down and saw their tower being built for no good reason. He said, 'Come let us go down and confuse their language so they will not understand each other.' So the Lord scattered them from there over all the earth, and they stopped building the city and the tower. It is called Babel because there the Lord confused the language of the whole world."

I asked, "But God can understand them, Terah, can he not?"

"Jael, nothing is too hard for the Most High God," Terah answered.

The caravan arrived in Damascus. The servants of Terah led the laden camels and riding donkeys into the city. They were unloaded in a compound with stables and storerooms. There was a pleasant house across the compound courtyard. Terah was welcomed, and both he and I were provided comfortable rooms, clean wash water, clean clothes, and a fine meal. While Terah attended his business, I pondered how large and strange the world is—much larger and more complicated than what I observed from my mountain sheepfold. Even so, despite all his cleverness in overcoming different tongues and large distances, my view of man the creature chafing under God had not changed.

Chapter Five

"Then Noah built an altar to the Lord, and took of every clean animal, and of every clean bird and offered burnt offerings on the altar. And the Lord smelled the soothing aroma; and the Lord said to Himself, 'I will never again curse the ground on account of man, for the intent of man's heart is evil from his youth; and I will never again destroy every living thing as I have done.'"

—Genesis 8:20–21

Several days later, Terah led me through the city to a noble house. Terah was immediately recognized and welcomed in. He waved for me to follow. I entered a noble dwelling with many servants, cleanly attired and moving back and forth across a shaded courtyard, which was more pleasant than shade at an oasis. Servants fanned the air, and I heard songbirds singing joyfully, which instantly made my heart long for the high hills beside the mountains. *I worry about the sheep, though less so for the goats. Is the flock safe? Surely the village shepherds now lead them safely to the sheepfold at night...* I followed Terah as he walked through the courtyard and into a dimly lit room covered above, below, and on the sides with the finest woolen rugs I have ever seen. Then I saw him—a small man withered with very old age but with bright eyes, like those of a young shepherd. His gray head and beard, slouched back, and drooping head were overpowered by the excitement and curiosity in his eyes. It was difficult even to see his rich, embroidered robe for the strength of those eyes.

A withered hand beckoned me as he softly called, "Come closer, young man, come closer. My son, Terah, has told me your story. Let me look at you. Yes. Yes. Your story is in your eyes. The Lord, the Most High God, is revealing Himself to you! Jael, is it? Well, you are one blessed mountain goat! How many men look at the night sky and see only twinkling lights? How many men farm the land and shepherd the flocks but see only meat and cakes? How many men lift their eyes to the mountains and see only a hard crossing? How many men look at God's creatures but see only stock, predators, or prey? How many men encounter snow and ice-covered paths and rivers and see only obstacles? How many men look at other men and see only kin, friend, or enemy? Blessed are you, Jael, that the Lord, the Most High God, has opened your eyes and unplugged your ears to the glory of your Creator and Sustainer!"

I could feel his eyes peer into me. He continued, "Terah knows my story well. Many times he has heard it, but he asks me to tell this story one more time. Listen, Jael, for the Lord the Most High God is never far. He knows all men. He hears all prayers and reveals His will and His commands to all who seek Him. I, Shem, and my brothers, Ham and Japheth, along with our wives and a remnant of all creatures, were rescued on an ark by the hand of God from a great flood, which covered all the earth. An ark built by my father, Noah, as he was commanded by God. Now Noah was the son of Lamech. Lamech, the son of Methuselah. Methuselah, the son of Enoch. Enoch, the son of Jared. Jared the son of Mahalaleel. Mahalaleel the son of Cainan. Cainan the son of Enos. Enos the son of Seth. Seth, the son of Adam. Now the Lord, the Most High God, made Adam from the clay of the earth and breathed life into him. The Lord took a breastbone from Adam and created Eve, the mother of all men, as a helper, companion, and wife to Adam."

Shem paused. The room was silent. I was impatient for him to continue.

At last, he began again, "The Most High God created the heavens above and the earth below and the seas and everything that is in them. But Adam and Eve were the last of all creatures, and He blessed them and gave them dominion and authority over all the birds of the air, the creatures on earth, and fish of the sea. He gave them a garden, Eden, that saw no weeds or briars or hard tilling. It never saw any bloodshed. God created Adam and Eve in the image of God. Adam and Eve were above all other creatures and lived in Eden watered by the dew. The Lord, the Most High God, declared all creation very good! They were blessed, and God walked with them in the garden. The Lord, the Most High God, gave them one command, only one condition. But they were enticed by the serpent and betrayed God and disobeyed His command. They were put out of Eden. Adam began to toil, sow grain, prune the fruit trees, and shepherd the flocks. Eve was cursed with pain in childbirth. Jael, you, a shepherd, know the ewe suffers no pain in birthing the lamb.

"Even in punishment, the Lord, the Most High God, never abandoned them. In toil, they made their clothing, tilled the fields, raised their crops, and tended herds. Adam and Eve were fruitful and had two sons, Cain and Abel. In jealousy, Cain killed Abel, spilling his blood on the ground, and sin did abound. Adam and Eve bore a son, Seth, and many more children, sons and daughters. The enemy enticed many, and sin abounded more.

"Though sin abounded, the Lord, the Most High God, loved and sustained man. He walked with many of the patriarchs, but sin grew more common. When Noah was the last of his generation to walk in righteousness with the Lord, the stench of sin—that is, pride, arrogance, idolatry, murder, and every wicked act under the sun—rose to the Lord, the Most High God. God spoke to His servant, Noah, and commanded he build an ark as He instructed him.

"Noah obeyed the Lord. He prophesized to all men that the Lord, the Most High God, would destroy all of the earth because the wickedness was repugnant before His throne on high. Men mocked Noah, but he built the ark just as the Lord told him. Noah labored one hundred years building the ark, hewing the lumber, fashioning the frames, planking the sides, and sealing its seams with tar pitch. Noah gathered food for his family and for the remnant animals."

THE CALLING

Again, Shem cast his gaze upon me. Seeing my earnest interest, he continued, "Again and again, Noah spoke God's words of repentance. None would listen. Noah gathered the creatures, and by the power of the Most High God, they entered the ark to places prepared for them. When he had loaded all the creatures, then Noah, his wife, Naamah, I, my brothers, Ham and Japheth, and our wives entered the ark and sealed the entrance as the rain began to fall.

"Man had never before seen rain, for the earth had been watered by dew. For forty days and forty nights, the rain fell. The whole earth was covered by the waters. By the hand of the Lord, the Most High God, all inside the ark were safe, and all the remnant creatures remained at peace.

"A year passed before dryland was sufficient for us to leave the ark. The Word of the Lord came to Noah. We were commanded by God to be fruitful and multiply and refill the earth. I was commanded to go east of the Great Sea. Ham was directed to go west on the south of the Great Sea, and Japheth was commanded to go west on the north of the Great Sea. We obeyed the Word of the Lord, and as God promised, we have again filled the earth."

"Patriarch Shem," I asked, "please tell me of the rainbow and God's promise."

"Yes, the rainbow. As we left the ark and gathered our wives and our remaining food and goods, a rainbow appeared, arching across the sky. Then the voice of God said, 'Now behold, I myself do establish my covenant with you and your descendants after you and every living creature that is with you, the birds, the cattle, and every beast of the earth with you of all that comes out of the ark, even every beast of the earth. I establish my covenant with you, and all flesh shall never again be cut off by the water of the flood, neither shall there again be a flood to destroy the earth.' God said, 'This is the sign of the covenant, which I am making between me and you and every living creature that is with you for all successive generations. I set my bow in the cloud, and it shall be for a sign of a covenant between me and the earth, that the bow will be seen in the cloud, and I will remember My covenant, which is between me and you and every living creature of all flesh, and never again shall the water become a flood to destroy all flesh. When the bow is in the cloud, then I will look upon it to remember the everlasting covenant between God and every living creature of all flesh that is on the earth.' Then God turned to my father, Noah, and said, 'This is the sign of the covenant that I have established between Me and all the flesh that is on the earth.'"

Shem had stopped. I asked, "God spoke to you? The Most High God speaks to men? Our creator can be heard. It must be glory! What is the voice of God like? Does He speak often? Is there hope that He may hear my prayers? Will He..."

"Jael, the voice of God was unlike any voice I have ever heard, yet it was clear and unmistakable, at once terrifying and comforting. God gives His word to whom He wills, when He wills. But be assured God hears you." He continued, "Now, Jael, Terah tells me you were on the way to Salem to find me. You must continue your journey, for there is more for you to learn. Come close to me now. Yes, young man, you are as rangy and scruffy as a mountain goat, but Lord, the Most High God, has this to say to you, 'I know your name. I attended your birth. I know your father and father's fathers to the end of generations. I know your mother and your mother's mothers to the end of generations. I raised you to be a shepherd. I have reserved a name for you if you continue to seek Me and obey the commands I have for you.'"

The Patriarch Shem motioned for me to come closer. He placed his bony hand firmly on my shoulder and said, "Jael, receive my blessing. May the Lord, the Most High God, lead you to His calling, to walk in His ways according to His will. May the Lord grant you a voice of praise to the Almighty God and a steadfast spirit to serve Him." Then he calmly said, "Terah will give you directions to Salem."

I stood there dumbfound, staring at Shem. Terah gently touched my shoulder, turned me around, and led me out the way we came.

As we walked back through the city, I was filled with questions. "I never asked Shem how to worship the Lord God. And how do I know His will? What did he mean walk in His ways? Will the Lord, the Most High God, answer these questions I have? The more I learn of the Most High God, the more questions I have."

THE CALLING

I wanted to turn around and go back to Shem, but Terah would not hear of it. "No," he said. "We must offer our sacrifice of praise, and then you must journey on to Salem." *What is a sacrifice of praise?* I wondered.

Early the next morning, Terah woke me and said simply, "Come with me."

We went towards the gate of the city and stopped at a merchant's stall. "A bundle of kindling and wood for the altar and an ephah of grain for an offering," Terah asked. Terah handed the merchant a coin and was given a bag of grain and a tightly tied bundle of kindling and wood.

A few steps further, we came upon a small pen of sheep. "Jael, choose the finest lamb, use your shepherd's eye, and be sure it has no blemish." Again, Terah provided a coin, and I lifted a fine lamb around my neck and held its feet against my chest. "Follow me, Jael."

We went out the city gate and climbed a small hill and came to a pile of stones. "Choose the round ones, Jael, and pile them here. Place the kindling on the stones and the wood atop the kindling. Now pour the grain over the wood. Good. And bring me the lamb."

Terah raised his arms high towards heaven and cried out loud, "Lord Most High God, we give you thanks for Your word to Jael, and now, Lord, accept this offering of praise from Your servants, Terah and Jael. May it be an acceptable and pleasing aroma, sweet and pure."

Terah took a knife from a scabbard beneath his robe and quickly slit the throat of the lamb. As its blood ran, he placed his hands in the flow and sprinkled the blood over the altar. He placed the dying lamb on the altar and lit the kindling. The flames leaped into the wood, and the fire burned. I was astonished and unnerved as I watched the lamb upon the altar. The sight of the blood and fire and the smell of the burning flesh both mesmerized and haunted me.

"Why did the Most High God want a lamb without blemish cruelly sacrificed on an altar of stones?" I just stood there stunned.

"You have never before offered a sacrifice, young Jael? There is a cost to following the Lord, the Most High God. You will learn that cost and gladly pay it, for grace, peace, and mercy will be yours in full measure. Shem was right. You must learn more of the Lord God. Seek Him, and He will heal all your wounds, and He will let His face shine upon you." Now we must prepare for tomorrow. You travel on to Salem alone, I cannot travel with you. There will be no caravan to escort you."

Chapter Six

*"Because Thy loving kindness is better
than life, my lips will praise Thee."*

—*Psalm 63:3*

That afternoon, Terah and his servants brought another new tunic, warm cloak, and a staff. Terah handed me a pouch of coins.

"No, Terah." I protested. "It is too much. All you have provided me before is more than ample and such generosity! Please no coins. What need have I of coins? I have never so much as held a coin in my hand, and the Lord Most High God has always provided my needs."

"At least, Jael, please take this pouch of food for your journey, some loaves of bread and sweet raisin cakes. And a skin of wine for good water may not always be available. Now I will take you to proper gate and show you the road to Salem. A healthy goat like you can walk to Salem in days."

Weighed down with the generous pouches of food and skin of wine, I confidently stabbed my staff firmly on the road and set off for Salem. Walking with the confidence of youth, I felt the excitement return. The unsettling sacrifice was pushed from my mind, and I journeyed in the hope of hearing the voice of God and understanding His word to Shem and the wonder of the blessing he gave me. That the road ahead was unfamiliar did not matter. Ahead and waiting for me was the city of Salem.

My spirit grew as I marched out of Damascus. I had a new hope. I felt something strange rising from within me. It built slowly, but I could not contain the depth of new joy welling up, and it burst out in word. Not words but a song! A song. A song I never knew. In truth, I had never before sung a song. This joyful song just bubbled up from my soul, out of my mouth and across my lips…

> I will praise You, O Lord
> For You truly deserve all praise!
> You have taught my heart to sing praises!
> You brought me joy and new life in You!
> You have saved my life when I was abandoned on the road.
> You have rescued me from injustice and freed me from slavery.
> Who is like You, O Lord?
> Who can give more than You give?
> Who is more faithful than our God?
> Your mercy, O God, I never deserved but
> will always abound for me.
> Your grace, O God, I will never fully comprehend
> You are my shelter, Your mercy keeps me warm,
> And gives me courage each new day.
> May Your name be praised by all people!
> Songs sung by faithful throngs from the ages!
> All praise to You, Lord, the Most High God!

This new song of praise had welled up from within me. The more I sang His praises, the more joy filled my heart. I could not stop singing praises to the Lord God! Over and over I sang this praise song. I became giddy as I sang, and mirth and laughter accented my voice and punctuated my praise.

I walked all that afternoon and all through the night. I was still walking and singing the next day. Soon the sun grew high in the sky, and the heat of the day bore down on me. I was still giddy from singing when I came upon a well that was sheltered in the shade of a tall rock. It was the kind of place that shepherds would bring their flocks to water in the late afternoon before herding them to the night sheepfold. Here was shade to shelter me from the heat of the day and cool water for my dry throat and dusty burning feet. The thought returned to me—I was a night shepherd. The day was time for rest. I could cover more ground traveling in the cool of the night. I drew cool water from the well, quenched my thirst, bathed my face, neck, and feet, and fell asleep on my cloak in the shade of the tall rock.

The shepherds were already watering their flocks of sheep when I awoke late in the afternoon. I considered joining them. I felt an unusual compulsion to tell them just how joyful I had become. But I did not know them, and the sun would soon set, and their sheep needed to be herded to the safety of the sheepfold. Better not to bother them, let them go about their work.

The sounds and the smells were so familiar, yet my days in the mountain watching sheep seemed so very long ago. I looked above to the heavens. One by one, the stars made their appearance, slowly filling the sky with points of light. The familiar patterns filled out, and each star followed its ordained path across the darkening night sky. I was filled with peace, and the wonder of the heavens returned like an old friend. The strange feeling began welling up from within me again. But new words flowed over my tongue and between my lips. A new song of praise was created.

> My eyes search the heavens above,
> The voice of their Maker calls out to me.
> I find my strength in my Creator!
> He alone provides a refuge for my soul!
> My refuge is found in my Creator and Protector.
> He will not permit the enemy to take me.
> His Spirit leads me on my journey.
> When I fear the trials along my pathway,
> He is my strength to go on.
> Oh, what danger can ensnare me!
> Yet He does not allow the trap to snap.
> Every footstep leads me closer to His throne!
> He protects and guards me even in the darkness
> When the robber and the lion lie in wait.

> I do not lose my way.
> My steps remain on His pathway.
> He will protect me and be my solid shield forever!

I walked and sang through the night. I sang loudly, finding and stretching this new voice within me. I sang through the sunrise. Such a sunrise called for praises to the Most High God, creator of all the earth! He orders the sun's path. He plans it along with the moon and stars. He gives it to man as a marvelous gift!

The sun grew higher in the sky. It was again time to find shelter from the coming heat of the day. Then words of praise were still flowing softly across my lips as I gently slipped into sleep safely off the road by a gentle brook in the shade of a ring of trees. As the sun fell low in the sky, I woke refreshed and hungry. I enjoyed sweet raisin cakes and a hard loaf of bread before gathering my pouch and slinging my cloak over my shoulder.

The evening was quiet with the sun now below the western horizon. As I walked along the lonesome road, I tried once again to collect my thoughts. *How did I get here? What lies ahead? Who is this singer of songs? What has become of the slave shepherd of the high hills above Khalab?* My mind was filled with questions, and again I wondered about the Most High God who speaks to men. Were the words spoken by Shem really the word of the Lord God? How did I know? What did I really know? What was this voice from inside me that I could not control? And who am I, a runaway slave shepherd, that the noble Terah and Patriarch Shem should show me such unimagined hospitality? I did not understand.

Chapter Seven

"And they said to one another, 'Were not our hearts burning within us while He was speaking to us on the road, while He was explaining the Scriptures to us.'"

—Luke 24:32

As I walked along the lonely night road, I did not notice another traveler overtaking me. When I heard gentle footsteps on the path, I turned to see a solitary traveler. His tunic and cloak appeared bright white in the light of the moon above. As he came alongside me, he looked into my eyes and asked, "Friend, do you not find it risky to travel the highway by night? Most men fear that robbers and thieves may wait in the shadows. And do you not fear the beasts of prey, the big cats, the wolf, or the bear? Why do you travel alone? Let us share the dangers of the nighttime highway together."

I said nothing; I just looked at the stranger. For some unknown reason, I did not see him as any way a threat. He appeared friendly and engaging.

Sensing my acceptance, he kept speaking. "You are alone, but did I not hear your voice as I approached? Surely something weighs on your spirit. I would hear what troubles your heart. Or if you prefer, I find a song of praise can drive away doubt from a troubled heart."

"Sir, did the noble Terah or the Patriarch Shem send you?"

I finally replied, "For truly since I left Damascus, unknown songs of praise have carried me this far. But this evening, my head is again spinning with questions. Only questions do I ponder, all the answers still elude me."

The stranger smiled. "Please, friend, tell me your story, and I will hear of all your unanswered questions."

"Do not let this fine cloak and new tunic deceive you, but I am, in truth, a slave shepherd with no father or mother and no kinsman to redeem me. I do not know my birth name, or if I even have one. My masters call me Jael, the mountain goat. I travel this road to Salem because I was called by the Most High God to seek His voice. For He made Himself known to me in the hill country above Khalab. When I heard that the Most High God spoke to the patriarch Noah and his sons, I set out to find Shem, his son, to hear of his rescue by God from the great flood—to learn from Shem of the covenant made by the Most High God, whose sign is the many-colored bow in cloud after the storm."

With the stranger silently listening, I continued, "I followed the road and came upon the noble Terah outside the city of Haran, who lavished unspeakable hospitality upon me and brought your servant by caravan to the Patriarch Shem in Damascus. The Patriarch Shem graciously told me his wondrous story of rescue by the hand of the Most High God on the ark, which God had commanded Noah to build. Then Shem spoke the word of the Lord concerning me. He knew all there is to know of me. The Patriarch Shem blessed me and sent me onto Salem to learn a new name the Lord has reserved for your servant if I seek Him and obey the word He has for me. I came to Shem with many questions, but the more I learned, the more questions filled my head. My head spins! Questions! Questions! I would have your judgment on my questions—questions no slave shepherd should ask."

"Jael, you speak so earnestly of this journey you travel. We have a long way ahead to Salem. Tell me, what put you on this journey to seek the voice of the Most High God? You say you are called. How were you called?"

THE CALLING

"Yes, good sir, I do ramble on. My story must sound strange, indeed. Patiently hear what I have to say, and then I will hear your judgment. As I said, I am a slave shepherd to a village that found me and raised me in the high hills above Khalab. I tended the village flocks by night and lived alone in a cleft in the mountain."

I looked up and pointed to the sky and kept talking. "Night after night, I studied the stars above and by day observed all the creatures of my world, both wild and flock. I observed the seasons and how life moved with them. I saw order and constancy. I realized that this order speaks to a creator. I observed my masters, the people of the village. They too are creatures of this world but with some authority and dominion over other creatures. Still man clearly has no dominion over the heavens above, the mountains and earth below. Man is no god but indeed chafes under the creator more than any other creature under heaven."

"Please go on," the stranger said softly.

"One day, while shepherding the flock to the night sheepfold with a village shepherd, a late afternoon storm ended with a beautiful colored bow arched across the sky. The shepherd remarked that Noah's rainbow was reminding us of the Most High God's promise never to again destroy the earth by a great flood. I had to find this Noah who spoke to God. The shepherd told me that Noah had been gathered to his fathers and buried, but a son, Shem, who was with Noah and witnessed all these things, still lived, and I set out to find him."

The stranger smiled warmly and said, "Jael, you rightly say that the creator God has revealed to you this truth. For the works of the Most High God have been clearly revealed to all men so that they should see them and believe, and they have no excuse! But the hardness of the heart, or as you say, "chafing against created order," dims their eyes and plugs their ears to the Lord's revelation. And, Jael, you can be assured that your creator reveals Himself so that He can be found by those who diligently seek Him. Indeed, He has called you to hear of His handiwork in the lives of men and nations. Tell me how you found the Patriarch Shem."

I replied, "Indeed, good master, I set out to find Shem, not knowing where I was or where I was going! I found a road and followed in one direction. I came to a great city and did not know what to do. I stood wondering when the noble Terah passed me by, stopped, turned, and questioned me. Master Terah showed your servant unexpected and gracious hospitality. He cleaned me, fed me, and gave me rest. He heard my story, and most amazing, he himself brought me along by caravan to Damascus and presented me to the Patriarch Shem."

The stranger affirmed. "Again, you see, Jael, the Most High God can and does order the affairs of all men. He hears the prayers and knows the heart of those who seek Him. The Lord God sent Terah to find you and direct your path. Many men chafe to rule over creation, but you chafe to find the Most High God. Those who chafe to rule this world and close their eyes to their creator turn themselves over to false gods of their own making, who are no god at all. They harden their hearts against the knowledge and revelations of the Most High God. Tell me more of your meeting with Shem."

Encouraged, I went on, "Well, good master, Terah must have sent a messenger ahead, for when I arrived, he already knew my story, but he insisted I tell it to him myself. The patriarch listened with great patience. When I finished, he, like Terah, said it is clear that the Most High God has called me to seek His voice. He told me the most amazing story of creation—of Adam and Eve, of Cain and Abel, and Seth and the genealogy of Seth to Noah. He patiently recounted how his father, Noah, obeyed the voice of God and built an ark. He told me of the salvation God provided for Noah, Shem, Ham, Jepheth, their wives, and a remnant of every creature on earth from the great flood that destroyed all the earth. He told me how God made a covenant with every man and creature on earth never again to destroy the earth by a great flood, and the colored rainbow in the cloud after the storm is the everlasting sign of this covenant. I could see in his vivid clear eyes the truth in his words. Then the wise Patriarch Shem astonished me."

"How was that?" the stranger asked.

THE CALLING

"He proclaimed a word of the Lord God to me. I remember he said, 'The Lord, the Most High God, has this to say to you. I know your name. I attended your birth. I know your father and your father's fathers to the end of generations. I know your mother and your mother's mothers to the end of generations. I raised you to be a shepherd. I have reserved a new name for you if you continue to seek me and obey the commands I have for you.' Then Shem blessed me, saying, 'May the Lord, the Most High God, lead you to His calling, to walk in His ways according to His will. May the Lord grant you a voice of praise to the Lord God and give you a steadfast spirit.' Then I was told I had more to learn and that I must journey to Salem."

"I see," the stranger commented. After stopping a moment, he looked at me, grinning. "Shepherd Jael, is not the Lord, the Most High God, good and always abounding in grace? He is ever present for those who earnestly seek Him! Do you not see that God speaks to men and through men He chooses? Through all history, He has sent his messengers who speak His words. They are His prophets called by Him to speak His very words. But men made their own gods of wood and stone, which had no ears to hear the prayers of men and no mouths to speak truth. They did not heed the word of the prophets of the Lord God. They mocked God's prophets, and some they beat, and some they killed. They were given over to every depravity, wickedness, and evil under heaven. But those who heard God's words and obeyed Him abounded in His grace and mercy. God makes His face to shine upon all those who hear His voice and obey His commands."

The stranger paused again, and his face became more determined. He could see I was listening closely. "Jael, even before we are born, God knows us. He knows all about us. He desires good for us and not evil. He can turn every hurt, sorrow, and tear into good. His love endures forever. Truly, God was with you when you were born. Truly, he raised you to be a shepherd for His purpose and is now directing your path. Truly, His plan for your life is unfolding, and you must stay on His path. Listen for His commands, which will surely come to you."

My spirits lifted, and I responded, "Master, your judgment gives me great courage and strength. But the noble Terah left me with other questions. He instructed me to worship the Most High God, and he frightened me when he made a cruel sacrifice of a lamb, though it was without malice. I am a shepherd, and my desire is to protect all the sheep of the flock. Yet he directed me to choose the very lamb sacrificed, one, by the shepherd's eye, to have no blemish. After thanking and praising God, he shed the blood of the innocent lamb, lay it on the altar of unfinished stone, and burned it. Is this worship? I do not understand how the Lord Most High God would take pleasure in the cruel sacrifice of an innocent lamb."

"I see, Jael, you have a tender heart, a love for God's creatures and a sense of justice. It is right that you ask these questions, and they are indeed joined together with truth and righteousness. Sacrifice is paying a cost that worship demands. The grace of God comes free to us, but a price must be paid to God. The two are connected. But first, you asked what is worship. You see, Jael, Terah sought to acknowledge the worthiness of the Most High God. It is right to know that the Lord God is the only God. He is the true and almighty creator. He rules over all creation and calls all who seek and follow Him to worship Him. Our worship confesses that the Lord Most High God is first in all things. He made us and provides for us all of our needs, and for this, Jael, we love Him. Yes, we show Him our love, as He has already shown His love for us."

Again, he paused. He stopped walking, turned, and looked straight into my eyes. "Jael, you say you seek the voice of God, yet you have told me throughout this night the wonderful way the Lord God reveals Himself to you. He has been speaking to you since the first night you studied the heavens above. He is drawing you nearer to Him every step of your journey. Do you not see how much He loves you? How He directs your life? Brings you to others who know Him? Does He not deserve your love? This is His purpose in creation. Did you not hear how he walked with Adam and Eve, His stewards, sharing with them the beauty of His perfect garden? His desire is to walk with each of us through all time. To worship God, Jael, is to love Him with all of your heart and soul. This is what God asks of everyone, but because He loves us, He asks for our love, and it must be ours to give."

THE CALLING

I heard a growl of a great cat off somewhere in the darkness. The stranger showed no alarm. I don't know why, but I felt safe in his presence. We began walking again slowly.

"Jael, you must learn how sacrifice is married to worship. It is good that you see the injustice and cruelty of sacrifice, for truly it points to the greatest of all injustice and cruelty possible. You told me how Adam and Eve were expelled from the garden when they disobeyed the one condition that God had laid upon them. You must learn what this means and the world-changing consequences of this one act. God is righteous always, only and forever. He can never be other than righteous and holy or set apart. When Adam and Eve disobeyed the command of God, they severed forever their own righteousness before God. This is sin, and all sin severs us from fully knowing God and experiencing Him intimately. I said God can never be other than righteous and holy. He cannot tolerate sin and unrighteousness, or He would not be God. Though Adam and Eve sinned and God could no longer walk with them in Eden, God's love, like His righteousness, cannot be changed. God's love for us cannot be other."

The stranger stopped walking again. The darkness, the danger, the sounds of the nigh were of no regard. He continued his explanation. "But God deals with this dilemma. God deals with our sin for us. Here is the consequence. When Adam and Eve sinned, they tasted the fruit of the tree of knowledge of good and evil. They had knowledge that they were naked, and they hid from God when He came to walk with them in the garden. They were expelled from the garden and began a new life of toil and labor with all of the hard consequences of life we live today. To overcome their shame in nakedness, God killed innocent animals for furs to provide clothing. This first bloodshed of creation took from the innocent to provide for the sinner. From the sin of Adam and Eve, sin passed to all men. Afterwards, when God accepted the blood sacrifice of Abel and did not accept the fruit sacrifice of Cain, Cain killed his brother, Abel, in jealousy. The sin of man grew and spread to the days of Noah as you have said. Abel's sacrifice shed innocent blood just as God shed innocent blood for Adam and Eve. It is not for clothing of skins that blood must be shed but the cost of an innocent life paying for the sin of the unrighteous."

His voice became a little more emphatic and somehow reassuring. "God in His love wants to restore each sinner to a righteous state in order that the sinner may once again stand clean and righteous before Him. Only the innocent can atone for or make clean the sinner."

Resuming his pace, he said, "So you see, Jael, when Terah asked you to choose a lamb without blemish, he was looking forward to the sacrifice of an innocent without blemish, one that is unmarked by sin, to make you clean before God so you and he could come into His presence to love, honor, and worship Him. I say looking forward because God is still working His will for all people. As men keep sinning, sacrifices must continue to atone for new sins. Taking the blood of an innocent animal is for a time an expression of that which is to come when a righteous and innocent man will of his own accord give his body and blood as an atonement for sin once and for all time. I do not expect you to fully understand this mystery, Jael. It is not yet fully revealed, but it is the greatest hope for all mankind. Now know this, our sin severs our true relationship with God, and a blood sacrifice is necessary. That is why Terah's cruel sacrifice displayed no cruelty on his part. Sin is the source of cruelty, and sacrifice is our reminder of the death it always brings and the price that must be paid for atonement. Terah saw only his love for God and true desire to worship and acknowledge God's provision to restore us as fit to walk with Him."

We walked along in silence. I looked at the beautiful night sky above. The Seven Sisters (Pleiades) somehow shone brighter this night, and it seemed Orion was watching and listening to our conversation. The bright moon was indifferent and aloof. I considered all that I heard and pondered as we walked. After a while, the stranger said, "Jael, it has been a long journey, and we are nearing Salem, but the gate will be closed for some hours. There is an inn in a small village outside the gate. Let us stop there for food and rest."

"Master, the hour is very late. Will the innkeeper open the door for two strangers?"

THE CALLING

The master, the man in white, walked confidently to the door and gently knocked. Immediately, the door opened, and when the innkeeper saw the man in white, he gasped, fell to his knees, and said, "Your Majesty, King Melchizedek! Please come in at once! You honor my humble inn and our village Emmaus. The gate of Salem is closed, of course, please let me provide refreshment, or, majesty, I can run ahead and call for the guard to open the gate, I'm sure—"

"No, but thank you. My weary friend and I have been traveling many hours. We would take rest and refreshment here if you have room for us."

"Of course, we will provide whatever you wish, majesty."

"Then please bring water that we may wash, perhaps some bread and wine and then beds for our rest."

Was it true, I spent hour upon hour speaking with a king? And he graciously listened and taught me. Should I bow to him and say something? I was speechless. I followed my companion, no, the king, into the inn.

The hall of the inn was empty, the travelers all in bed for the night. A lone candle burned on a large central table. Red and gray coals still glowed in the fire pit. We were shown to small room just off the hall. Another candle was lit and set on a small table. The water basins were set before us, and while we were washing, I looked with astonishment at my fellow traveler. Melchizedek, King of Salem! Seeing him for the first time in the candlelight of the inn, he truly looked to be a wise and noble man. There was a kindness about him, even in the light of his now revealed authority. He was kind, wise, and warm.

Sensing my glance, he smiled at me, his hands still dripping, and said, "Jael, there will come a day when man can be washed clean of sin forever and stand in righteousness before the very throne of God."

"Majesty, King Melchizedek, please pardon my forwardness on the road. I did not know, I did not recognize, I…I…"

"Jael, I did not introduce myself, I wanted to listen to your opened heart. You are on a journey at the calling of the Most High God, and I am His priest. I very much desired to hear your story. For you do not yet know the joy that is set before you, and I rejoice that the Most High God sent me to journey with you. I see the meal is set on the table. Let us take of the bread and wine set before us."

We sat down to the large table in the hall of the inn. A loaf of bread, a bowl of wine, and a jar of water and two simple wooden cups were set in the middle. King Melchizedek took the loaf of bread and broke it in two. As he broke the bread, I felt something within me snap. It was the amazing sensation of all the anxiety, worry, and tension being expelled from my body. I was left at total peace. I tasted the bread, and I felt an assurance that God knew me and loved me.

King Melchizedek took the pitcher of wine and poured it into the cups. He handed me a cup and said simply, "Drink this."

When I tasted the wine, I heard another voice, not Melchizedek's, not the innkeeper's; it was a voice unlike any voice I had ever heard before. It was unmistakable. The Most High God was speaking to me, "Jael, I know your name. I attended your birth. I know your father and your father's fathers to the end of generations. I know your mother and your mother's mothers to the end of generations. I have raised you to be a shepherd and to seek My voice. You will be My voice of praise. Now obey every word and command I give you. Listen to my priest, King Melchizedek. He will prepare you for your calling. Your praise songs will be a sign for your calling. Your praises will be a sign of a steadfast spirit to serve Me."

As the voice ended, I heard my tongue singing loudly in a strange language I had never heard and did not understand. I was a bystander to my own strange and foreign song. Although I did not understand it, I was euphoric, for I knew in the depth of my soul I was praising God and glorifying His holy name!

When my song of praise ended, my eyes opened, and I saw King Melchizedek gently smile, look at me, and say simply, "Amen!"

King Melchizedek rose from the table, gently put his hand on my shoulder and said, "Get some rest. I want you refreshed when we enter Salem."

"Rest? How can I sleep after this night?" But I lay down and immediately fell to sleep.

Chapter Eight

"God is known in Judah; His name is great in Israel. And His tabernacle is in Salem; His dwelling place also is Zion."

—Psalm 76:1–3

The next morning, the same gentle touch of King Melchizedek woke me. We walked upwards, towards the Salem city gate. The road climbed alongside a steep hill. We passed olive trees and vineyards on the sides of the hill. *Too steep for grain*, I told myself. *Not difficult for sheep and goats if the grass is good.* We walked in silence. The events of the night before were still spinning inside my head. My thoughts were broken when I heard shouts from the watchtower. "The king! King Melchizedek is coming! Open the gates for the king! Messengers, notify the royal court! Make ready, the palace throne room!"

We made our way through the narrow streets lined with stone buildings on both sides. I could not keep track of the streets and alleys without the sun or a horizon. I would not be able to find my way again. The street widened, and we entered a square. At the far end was another large gate.

We entered through a second gate into the palace hall. The center of the hall was open to the weather, but all around was covered, offering cool shade. The partial roof was supported by four massive columns, standing steadfast like giant guards, where the end of the roof met the open sky. A throng of men in robes and leather armor paced about the center hall. At one end was a large, raised, magnificent carved seat. King Melchizedek walked up and without pomp sat on his throne. I stood below him with the growing entourage as court officers brought him a fine robe of bright colors with bright stones embroidered in the smooth fabric. They placed a gold crown on his head with more bright stones, which radiated shafts of colored light with the slightest movement of his majesty. They presented him his scepter, which to me looked like a finely crafted shepherd's crook!

The king pointed to me and, in a matter-of-fact manner, told the court, "This is my fellow traveler, Jael. He will be staying with me in the palace. Please prepare a room for him. First, I wish to give my blessing to our citizen brothers and sisters today. All foreigners in the city are most welcome to attend. When all is ready for me in the square, I will come. Now is there any news or cases that require my attention?"

As messengers scrambled to announce the blessing and gather together the whole city, an officer in splendid armor stepped forward and said, "Your majesty, King Melchizedek, priest of the Most High God, we have word that several large battles occurred near our borders during your absence. The long-feared war of the nine kings has begun. The king of Elam has come from the north with his allies—the king of Shinar, the king of Ellasar, the king of Goiim, and the king of Elam—to war against the five kings in rebellion against him—the king of Sodom, the king of Gomorrah, the king of Admah, the king of Zeboiim, and the king of Bela.

"The kings of Sodom and Gomorrah fled the battle, and both Sodom and Gomorrah were sacked. All the goods of the cities were carried off. Lot, the nephew of Abram the Hebrew, and all his household and all his possessions were carried off by the four kings. One who escaped carried the news to Abram the Hebrew who was encamped with his flocks near the oaks of Mamre.

"When Abram heard that his nephew had been carried off, he called out three hundred eighteen trained men and pursued the five kings north of Damascus. He won a great victory and recovered all of the captives and goods taken by the five kings. It is reported that Abram will pass by Salem tomorrow while returning the captives and plunder to Sodom and Gomorrah. Abram has sent his messengers ahead to say that he desires to present gifts and offerings to the Most High God. Majesty, I have prepared a defense of the city, what is your command?"

"Thank you, Captain. Your diligence does you great credit. I am aware of Abram's pending visit. No defense of the city will be required. I ask that you prepare an honor guard and entourage to accept the gifts and offerings Abram will present to the Most High God. There will be many camels, cattle, sheep, goats, and donkeys. Have the city herders and shepherds accompany the entourage. See to it that corrals, sheepfolds, and pens are ready. There will be much treasure, so have wagons and carts at the ready as well. Now I understand the people are gathered for the blessing."

I followed the stream of courtiers and joined the city population in a large square at the end of the city where the city wall merged into a large rocky cliff high above a narrow valley. King Melchizedek, priest of the Most High God, serenely scaled the top of the rock, not wearing his royal robes but rather a simple but bright white robe and modest white head scarf held in place by a thin crown of woven gold, somewhat resembling a vine or wreath. No, it was somehow different. Odd, I now recognized it to be not branches but two rows of intertwined long-stemmed roses. His robe and head scarf seemed to radiate larger than its size in the sunlight. He raised his arms and lifted his eyes and spoke clearly without shouting and no audacity, yet he was still heard by everyone gathered.

"Lord God Most High, bless these your servants of the city of Salem. May the strivings and efforts of Your servants bring honor and glory to Your name. May the desires of all Your people's hearts be to humbly walk in Your ways and seek Your will. May they obey your word to us, to love You Lord with heart and soul, to love your people, and to provide hospitality to the foreigner among us. That this city of peace may be a light that cannot be hidden and that all who pass may see Your goodness and glorify Your name among the nations. We are thankful for the blessings of peace you bring to us. We beg that you forgive every transgression and lead us to joyful obedience."

Then lowering his eyes to the people gathered in front of him and lowering his arms in an open manner, as in an embrace, as if to hug everyone present, he began to speak again in what I thought to be a tenderness of voice. I watched as everyone listening prepared to receive his blessing. Everyone lowered their eyes and stretched out their arms with the palms of their hands open and facing their priest of the Most High God, and he said, "Now people of Salem, may the Lord the Most High God bless you and give you perfect peace. Go and serve the Most High God. There is no other God beside Him."

As Melchizedek climbed down from the rock, I began my return to the palace. I heard no grumblings, no talk of missed work or business lost. I saw only peace in the faces of all the people. I also saw that differences in people no longer seemed to exist. All of the city gathered together: men, women, and children. Nobles rubbed shoulder with peasants and laborers. The people moved about in small groups. The most common group was the family, but clearly there was no distinction, no places of honor, just one people coming together in their desire for a blessing.

I was met at the palace entrance by a servant who sought me out. "This way, sir, a room has been prepared for you."

As I followed him down the stone corridor, he asked, "How is it you know King Melchizedek?"

"Truly, sir," I replied, "I am just a slave shepherd on a journey. The king came alongside of me on the road by night. I had no idea who he was! I am a man raised as a slave to my village. I don't even know my given name or who my parents were. I just... I just know he is a man who walks with the Most High God."

"Yes," the servant replied. "Our king and priest of the Most High God is also a man with no genealogy. No one knows where he comes from, his family, clan, or tribe. We only know that he arrived one day when our city was torn by strife and deep division, and by the power of his person, he captured our hearts and brought about reconciliation and peace. We just trust him and have made him our king."

"Reconciliation?" I asked.

THE CALLING

"Yes, King Melchizidek brought reconciliation between the sons of Shem and the Canaanites, sons of Ham."

"I don't understand," I said as I made mental notes of where we were going.

The servant explained, "You see, this land was given by God to the sons of Shem when Noah's sons and daughters-in-laws left the ark. Now after Noah left the ark, he planted a vineyard. After his first harvest, he drank too much of the wine. Asleep and drunk, Noah lay exposed in his tent. His son, Ham, saw his father but did not cover him. When told by Ham of Noah's nakedness, his sons, Shem and Japheth, backed into the tent with a blanket and covered Noah, not looking upon his nakedness.

"For this act, Canaan, son of Ham, was cursed, and the sons of Canaan would thereafter be ruled by the sons of Shem. Now you must know that Shem was directed to fill the land east of the Great Sea, and Ham was commanded to fill the land south of the Great Sea. But Canaan coveted this land and settled here. There has been strife between the sons of Shem and the sons of Canaan ever since. Before King Melchizedek came to Salem, the sons of Shem did, indeed, rule harshly over the Canaanites in the city."

We arrived at my chambers and stood at the door. The servant continued, "When King Melchizedek came to Salem, the radiance of his presence, the wisdom of his words, and the gentleness of his spirit touched the hearts of the rulers and masters to deal justly and graciously to the servant and the laborer. Likewise, his spirit touched the hearts of the workers, servants, and vassals not to hate the master but to perform his required service fairly and honorably. Now Melchizedek rules over us by invitation and intercedes for us with the Most High God. Riches and treasures now flow into our city, even as peace and reconciliation continue to grow. We may not know where he comes from, but we would have him as our king and priest forever."

The servant started back down the hallway and then stopped, turned around, and said, "My pardon, sir, I failed to mention before. You are to eat at the king's table this evening. Someone will come for you."

The room was pleasant and cool. I surmised it was in the city wall, as a window provided a panoramic view of the valley below.

There was a small table beside the inner wall. On it were a candle, a jar of water, and a bowl. Realizing how tired I was, I lay down on the bed and fell asleep. At the king's appointed time, a servant came to escort me to the king's table in a great room with a high ceiling adorned with snow white curtains and drapes from ceiling to floor. The ceiling, as high the palace roof, was supported by great columns adorned with carved figs and palms at their height, and grape vines entwined them down to pomegranates and heads of grain at their bases. A large four-sided table filled the center of the room. The table was covered in fine linen and adorned with small palms, colorful bowls of fruit, and tray upon tray of beautifully arranged foods. As I took in the grandeur of the room, I saw that I must be late. All of the king's court were seated, waiting for the king's word to begin the feast. But I found no seat unoccupied around the great table. I turned and nervously scanned the rear and edges of the room for an ante table.

Then I heard King Melchizedek speak in his calm and measured voice, "Jael, come, you are not late. I have reserved a place for you next to me. Please come and sit."

I carefully made my way around the great table and the silent seated nobles, captains, and court officials. I tentatively settled on a cushion next to the king. He quietly whispered in my ear, "I have an important lesson for you tonight. Don't be anxious, sit, eat." In his now comforting voice, King Melchizedek blessed the food, and small polite conversations began among the men at the table.

King Melchizedek began eating and motioned for me to eat as well. In a private voice, just for my hearing, he began, "Tomorrow, Jael, you will witness an important event ordained by the Lord, the Most High God. Your eyes will see a man chosen by God to be the father of a great nation. He will be the first of a chosen nation and a chosen people who will be a living sign to all the world of God's leading and ordaining His plan for the salvation of all men."

I'm sure he saw the confusion in my face, but he knew me well by now and just continued to speak. "Today you will not understand the mystery of His plan, but He has a lesson for you and your calling as well. Your eyes will see the father of a nation called to show every nation and people under heaven how God blesses all those who love

Him and obey His word and how the disobedient are punished. God will give him a new name and establish a covenant with this nation far greater than the covenant He made with all creatures on earth in the presence of Noah, his wife, his sons, and daughters-in-law."

King Melchizedek was looking past me, looking off into the future. "From this nation will come a tribe of priests called to intercede for His people. His priests will have no other work and serve only the Most High God. The son of no other tribe can join this priesthood. This priesthood will establish the sacrifices and worship ordained by the Most High God for all people. They will be instructed in all of their ordained duties, ceremonies, and practices by the Most High God, and they will not vary in their service as priest in any word, deed, or interpretation by the mind of men. They shall make blood sacrifices for the atonement of sin and sacrifices of thanksgiving and festivals of praise to the Most High God. From this priestly tribe, God will ordain servants for His altar, singers, and musicians of praise songs and administrators to see that all these priestly functions stay true to the ordinance of the Most High God.

"God will establish this priesthood to show all mankind His gracious love and mercy, that man may know what the heart of God is for all His people—that is, to seek the Lord your God with all your heart and all your soul and obey all His commands. This priesthood will offer sacrifices daily on an altar ordained by God for generation after generation to come. But this priesthood is also but for a time."

Pausing a moment, his eyes now closed and a sad smile on his warm face, the king continued, "A day will come when the Lord Most High will raise up His Great High Priest from the nation of Abram, a priest forever, who will make a perfect sacrifice for the sins of the whole world one time and forever! This is the salvation to come when the love of God reconciles the world to Himself. A day of rejoicing when the very angels in heaven will proclaim the great victory over the grave."

Opening his eyes and looking at me once again, he said, "But, Jael, these things are to come and will be hidden from understanding until the living sacrifice is complete and God reveals His living Word."

King Melchizedek again paused for a few moments in thought, scanned the room, and looked at each of the guests one by one. He then turned, looked at me warmly, and said, "Now, Jael, the evening is late, and God has more for you to learn."

I returned to my room, exhausted. The candle on the table was lit for me. The room had been prepared for me by an attentive servant who foresaw every need. My mind returned to the overwhelming events of the evening. I tried hard to remember all that King Melchizedek told me. It was all so confusing, the details all jumbled together in my mind. I only knew that the Most High God was stepping definitively into history and ordaining the lives of men to work His will and reveal anew His love for man—His desire to save and His gift of hope and assurance. I could not begin to fathom the mind of God or why He blessed me with His voice. Nor could I begin to understand the prophecies of King Melchizedek—priests, musicians, administrators, and teachers, all instructed by the Most High God. But I began to see assuredly that God's love endures forever. As I lay in my bed, I felt a new song rising from my soul within me.

> Praise the Lord all you who sacrifice at His altar,
> Praise Him all you who come to worship,
> Praise the Lord you musicians with flute, horn, and cymbal,
> Praise our God and Creator!
> He bathes us in His grace, peace, and joy!
> He loves us as no other can.
> Shout your praises in His presence!
> Sing with joy to our God who saves us!
> His blessings kiss every face
> His blessings are like sweet morning dew on the rose.
> His loving-kindness is forever.
> Praise Him who makes our hearts, our
> souls, our love to overflowing!

That night, I fell asleep singing praises to the Lord. My songs continued with sweet clarity in my dreams.

Chapter Nine

> *"Even so Abraham believed God and it was reckoned to him as righteousness. Therefore, be sure it is those who are of faith who are sons of Abraham. And the Scripture, foreseeing that God would justify the Gentiles by faith, preached the gospel beforehand to Abraham, saying, 'All nations will be blessed in you.' So then those who are of faith are blessed with Abraham, the believer."*
>
> —*Galatians 3:6–9*

True to King Melchizedek's word, in midmorning, the watch tower guard announced the approach of large party of men driving camels, cattle, donkeys, sheep, and goats. A long train of carts followed behind, the large cloud of dust hanging over them marked their approach to the city. The noise of the animals and voices of men, women, and children grew to a crescendo just as the lead party stopped at the wall beside the gate. The gate of Salem opened, and King Melchizedek, priest of the Most High God, followed by a line of officers, brought out wine and bread to Abram and his host. As Melchizedek raised his arms, the whole host became silent, even the animals settled quietly, and he made this blessing: "Blessed be Abram by God Most High, creator of heaven and earth. And blessed be God Most High who delivered your enemies into your hand."

And Abram, in thanksgiving, presented Melchizedek, priest of the Most High God, a tenth of the cattle, a tenth of sheep, a tenth of the goats and donkeys, a tenth of the treasure carts, a tenth of everything! And Abram led his host away to Sodom.

As the tithe paid by Abram was carried into Salem, King Melchizedek told me, "Soon Abram will learn the new name God has for him and will establish his covenant with him, and he will become father of nations. I ask you, Jael, will Abram's tithe to the Most High God make Abram righteous in the eyes of God?"

His eyes fixed on Abram the Hebrew, and not waiting for my reply, he said firmly, "I tell you Abram will be made righteous by his faith and will be called the father of all who place their faith in God!"

Speaking to me softly once again, he said, "Jael, this has been a most eventful day. Come with me to a quiet place where I can pray and listen for the Word of the Lord. There are prayers you must make as well."

Melchizedek led me to a garden in a valley not far outside of the city. We sat among olive trees beside a quiet stream. Immediately, I felt at peace and remembered the quiet brook by the cleft of the mountain of my home. King Melchizedek closed his eyes and in silence sat peacefully still.

After a time, with his eyes still closed, he softly said, "Jael, there is one more thing required of you. But in prayer, you can ask the Lord the Most High God for help. Jael, God raised and ordained you to be a shepherd. God has this against you. You abandoned His sheep. What do you say to this charge?"

"King Melchizedek, it is true I left the flocks at night, but I… but I took precautions to protect them. I lit fires, large fires, that would last until morning when I knew the village shepherds would come. I believed God was calling me to seek His voice, to find Him, I… I…"

With his voice filled with authority, I heard King Melchizedek say, "Shepherd Jael, you were called to tend other sheep, the people in the high hills above Khalab. You did not love these people."

"King Melchizedek, these people raised me to be their slave and denied me my name. How am I to love them?"

THE CALLING

His voice was still with authoritative but softened. He said, "Shepherd, first you can love them by forgiving them and then by serving them."

Then he turned and looked into my eyes and softly said, "Jael, in the beauty of this garden, pray to the Lord our God that He forgive you, the sinner Jael. Pray now while God can be found."

King Melchizedek's words tore through me. How can I say I love God if I cannot love those whom He loves? Tears filled my eyes as I cried, "Forgive me, Lord God, for I have sinned. I have not forgiven my masters. I have not loved them. I have not loved any man. Give me a new heart to love and serve you and to love and serve all whom You love."

King Melchizedek again placed an arm around my shoulder. "Jael, the Lord God Most High, creator of heaven and earth, the one true God, has heard your prayer. Your sins are forgiven."

His arms, now firm on my shoulders, and his eyes looking squarely in mine, he announced, "I give you the new name He has reserved for you. You are Zimri-Ruel, 'My praise, friend of God.' He ordains you as His shepherd and priest of the hill country above Khalab. The Lord God commands you to be a shepherd and priest for His people, a voice of instruction to their ears. Intercede on their behalf."

His grasp now firmer, the king and priest said, "This is the message the Lord gives to His sheep: 'Praise God, for He is worthy to be praised. Love God with all of your heart and all of your soul, for God first loved you. Obey God, for if we love God, we will obey all of His commands. Love all men, for how can we love God if we do not love those He loves? And do not follow the ways of foolish men who serve idols and false gods, their way leads to death. Teach my people to sing praise songs and songs of joy. For the songs of my people are a sweet sound to my ear. And I will bless them for their praise with joy and peace. They shall know that my mercy endures forever.'"

As we departed the garden, tears streaming from my eyes, my spirit was bursting with unspeakable joy. King Melchizedek said simply, "Go, Zimri-Ruel, love and serve the Lord God. Intercede for His people in the hill villages until his chosen tribe of priests is ordained, looking to the day of victory when the Great High Priest atones for the sins of man once and for all time."

I did not return to Salem. I started up the road to the mountains and the hill country beyond near the city of Khalab. As I walked, a new song sprang from within me.

> How sweet to my ears is the Word of the Lord!
> His instruction rings true in my heart.
> The wisdom of men is fanciful, it tickles but cannot delight!
> It is like a tree with shallow roots
> That falls when winds of trouble blow.
> The Word of the Lord stands forever.
> His righteousness judges faithfully.
> His words of mercy know my weakness.
> His words of grace lift me above my estate.
> The Word of the Lord brings life
> And every day seeks to live within me
> Bringing wisdom and righteousness.
> The Word of the Lord brings grace and mercy beyond measure,
> His Word gives love to overcome judgment.
> Lord, let Your Word teach me to lose myself in You,
> That Your will become my will, O my Savior and my God!

PART TWO

A Changed Heart

Chapter Ten

*"And You shall love the Lord your God
with all your heart and with all your
soul and with all your might."*

—*Deuteronomy 6:5*

Somewhere above the city of Salem on the high road north, as I walked joyfully, singing, the overwhelming fullness of the day overtook me. With no plan and no thought, I stopped amid a rocky outcropping and settled my now weary body down. With my back supported by a smooth rock, I lay quietly with my eyes gazing at the star-filled sky above, my nighttime friend still there as always.

My contented thoughts morphed into softly spoken words, "O God Most High, how awesome and wonderful You are! Your goodness I cannot fathom. Your voice never stops! You speak to me in Your night sky. You speak to me in Your perfect creation in the order and sustenance of all Your creatures here below. You order the lives of men and nations. You set before my path men of wisdom, both upright and righteous, men who walk with You and speak Your words. It is all too wonderful for me! Oh, Most High God, I do love You and praise You! If nothing is too difficult for You, God, train this poor, unworthy shepherd slave to be Your servant shepherd. Teach me how to love, how to serve all those whom You love. Just as Your servant, Shem, and Your priest, Melchizedek, have spoken Your words of grace to me, speak Your words through this simple shepherd's mouth as You will. As I have been ministered by Your servants, let me minister to others. Prepare this humble servant called to shepherd Your flock to love and serve with every strength You provide me." In total peace, I fell asleep.

I awoke in the morning somewhat stiff and somewhat hungry. When I left King Melchizedek in the garden the day before, I took no thought of provisions. I had no food, no water, no cloak, no staff, just my tunic and the sandals Terah had given me on my feet. I heard voices on the road and stood up to see a man leading a donkey with a young woman riding on its back. Their conversation abruptly stopped when they saw me emerge from behind the rocks.

"Don't be afraid, I mean you no harm. Please forgive me if I startled you. You see, I myself have just awakened from my rest. I am also traveling north. With permission, I beg you, may I walk with you awhile?"

"Are you alone?" the man asked. "You have no donkey, no cloak, no provisions, no water, and you travel north?"

"Indeed, I left Salem late yesterday afternoon hurriedly, not thinking of preparing for my journey. I just knew it was time for me to leave... my name is Jael, or was Jael, and I am on my way to the high hill country above Khalab."

The young man eyed me carefully. He was much like every other man I had seen in Salem. He was average height, average build, clean, dark hair, a young beard. He had an intensity about him, but that was likely because I startled them. His clothes were clean, his cloak hung neatly over his shoulder—a good cloak but not an embroidered robe. Fine, heavy sandals were strapped to his dusty feet.

"I am Jared, and this is my wife, Abaigael. We are journeying from Salem to our home in Tel Hazor. We went to Salem to make sacrifices to the Most High God and seek the blessing of Melchizedek, king of Salem and priest of the Most High God. You are welcome to walk with us, Jael you say?"

The young man had motioned with his outstretched arm towards Abaigael seated sideways on the donkey. She said nothing and kept her eyes on the ground as her husband spoke. She was a small woman and seemed to be a fragile creature. She was wrapped head to toe in a clean cloak that appeared far too large for her small frame. Though I could not see her eyes, I thought her face very pretty surrounded by wisps of black hair showing from beneath her dark head scarf.

"Yes," I replied. "I was called Jael 'the goat' by my village masters before King Melchizedek told me the new name God had reserved for me, Zimri-Ruel. But I would like to hear your story first. I've spoken mine selfishly too often. You went to Salem. Please, I would hear every detail!"

"Should I call you Zimri-Ruel then?" Jared politely asked.

"You would be the first after King Melchizedek," I replied.

"Truly, then, it is my honor, Zimri-Ruel, for King Melchizedek is known throughout this land as far north as Hazor, as the priest of the Most High God. It is well known that he has brought peace to Salem, that he welcomes the foreigner and intercedes for all who come to worship the Most High God. He has blessed many people, and they profess that he is an upright and righteous king and priest. Truly, a man who walks with God!"

The wariness vanished from Jared's face. His eyes left me as he thought about his words. "We travelled to Salem in the hope that he would intercede with God for us. You see, Abaigael is with child, and we feared for the child's life. Our son died shortly after his birth, and our next child, a daughter, was stillborn. My kin have denounced Abaigael as cursed and counseled me to put her out and find a new wife."

We were all walking now slowly, Abaigael's donkey being led by Jared alongside him. "I could not do such a thing! Abaigael is the sweetest of women! My heart would break if she were to return to her father's house.

Abaigael kept silent, her eyes still down. "When she was again with child, we determined to go to Salem, sacrifice to the Most High God, and ask King Melchizedek to intercede on behalf of this child with God Most High. When we arrived at Salem, we were stunned to hear that King Melchizedek was away! City elders suggested we make our sacrifice and worship the Most High God and that we were welcome to wait for the king's return. We were told that King Melchizedek would come and go of his own accord, and no one knew when he would depart or when he would return. Although this behavior is most unusual, the people of Salem would only say that King Melchizedek was a most unusual man. His wisdom and righteousness could not be questioned, so why question his comings and goings?"

Jared picked up his pace and the donkey as well. "We sacrificed two white doves, sadly all we could afford after buying this donkey and provisions for the journey, and waited for the king and priest, Melchizedek, to return. When he did return, we heard his call for the people to be blessed. We made our way to the square, hoping to get close enough to get his attention. But the crowd gathered and became so large we could not make our way to the front. Even so, we received his blessing, and he even welcomed the foreigners! The blessing of such a righteous king and priest of the Most High God must surely avail!"

Jared kept his eyes on the road. He did not look at me or Abaigael seated silently on the donkey. "We tried to visit the king at his palace the following day, but affairs of state and his priesthood occupied his day. We watched from the city wall as a host appeared. King Melchizedek greeted them and provided bread and wine. He blessed the leader of the host, one Abram, the Hebrew, and blessed the Most High God for giving Abram, the Hebrew, a great victory. Then amazingly, a mighty tribute of camels, donkeys, cattle, sheep, goats, and treasure wagons were brought into the city!"

Jared kept talking, almost like he was trying to convince himself rather than inform me. "After Abram and the host with him departed and the tribute was brought into the city, we again called at the palace. A most sympathetic servant told us that the king had not returned. He said the king may be in his garden praying, or he may again be traveling. He did not know. Our money all spent, we decided to return home."

Jared paused, and I could hear the disappointment in his voice. He went on justifying this decision in his mind. "King Melchizedek had blessed us among the crowd, and we had sacrificed to the Most High God. We could only hope that God would accept our sacrifice and bless our child. We rose before dawn this morning to make the most of this day in our journey home to Hazor. We persuaded a guard to open the small door in the city gate just as dawn was breaking. As we started out, we saw a lone man walking towards the still open door in the city gate. As he approached, we could see that it was King Melchizedek."

Glancing towards his wife, he said, "I started to help Abaigael off the donkey when we heard the king say, 'No, please sit. I am afraid you caught me returning from my garden. Leaving Salem so early? Please don't go without receiving my blessing.'"

Jared, now more excited, spoke louder. "Then he said, 'O God Most High, bless your daughter, Abaigael, of most tender heart. Bless your son, Jared, of most faithful love and bless their precious child all the days of his long life! Now, Jared, Abaigael, your son shall be called Abiel, for he will grow strong in the knowledge that the Most High God is his father and steadfastly serve Him. Now go and walk in the ways of the Most High God to love Him with all your heart and soul and tell everyone you meet that His mercy endures forever! May the peace of God Most High bless you this day and every day.' King Melchizedek took an arm of each us in his hand, gently squeezed, then turned and walked into Salem."

As we walked along the dusty road and I heard this wonderful story, in every way as amazing as my own, I could not help feeling their joy in my heart. How lovely this couple, this family soon to be, were to me. I just met them, and oh, how I loved them!

I caught Abaigael now aglow with excitement. Looking up for the first time, she quietly spoke. "Husband, please permit me to speak! All that you said is true, but I must add how amazing the grace and peace we felt in the presence of King Melchizedek. We never told… he knew our names! I was covered in my heavy cloak, and there was little light. He knew I carry our child! And he spoke with such authority! And such a wonderful name for our son… it's a boy! Abiel, 'God is my father'! He will be strong! He will live a long life! He will serve the Most High God! Who could believe such good news!"

I started to say their news was indeed wonderful, but my voice just cracked in the dryness of my throat. Jared and Abaigael, together at once, said, "Why, Zimri-Ruel, you need water!"

Jared continued, "Please forgive us! Let us stop and have water and food. You must be hungry and thirsty."

We came upon a shaded area just off the road. Jared gently helped Abaigael from the donkey and took a skin of water from hanging over the donkey's shoulders and handed it to me. As I drank, he took a nearly empty food pouch as well. Opening it, he said, "We don't have much, but we can share this small loaf of bread and raisin cake. It should be enough until we reach the high fields and fruit trees this afternoon."

He broke the loaf and cake in three and handed me an equal share. After a satisfying drink of their offered welcome water, I protested. "I really should not eat the last of your food."

"You must," he said. "Our custom demands hospitality be given to the stranger and foreigner, and as I said, by this afternoon, the road will lead us down to a narrow plain to fruit trees and grain fields. There we may glean food."

"I really don't understand your custom of hospitality, and can you really glean from someone's field and orchard? I have never seen this practice in my village in the high hills above Khalab."

Jared looked somewhat surprised and said, "Hospitality has been part of our culture for as long as anyone remembers. From what I have heard from travelers, it is a practice of all people going back to our patriarchs. It can only be refused in time of war or hostility. The people of this land are sons of Canaan, son of Ham, son of Noah. Ever since the Most High God commanded the sons of Noah to refill the earth, men have been traveling, often with wives and children, seeking new pastures, new fields, and new cities in which to sell the works of their hands or all kinds of goods. Just look to the roads and see the caravan, the travelers, the clans of people on the move. It is good to remember the foreigner and the traveler, for so we have all been or may someday be. It is an obligation that cannot be denied with honor! Though many people have forgotten the Most High God, they have not forgotten their obligation to show hospitality to the foreigner. Even language is no barrier. Hospitality draws all men together. Hospitality and caring for the widow and the orphan are obligations of all people and all times."

"What are the obligations to care for the widow and the orphan?" I asked.

"Zimri-Ruel, you surprise me with your questions! These are things everyone just knows. We don't think about them, they are obligations! It is obvious that the widow and the orphan cannot survive without family or clan or tribe to help them. There are obligations of brothers if they exist to care for his brother's wife or child, and if not a brother, then parents or other kinsmen. Where none of these remain, each of us is expected to provide what we can to meet immediate needs. Would you leave your brother's wife or son to die? Would you permit them to become slaves and property no different than the beast of the field? Would you deny your brother his name in posterity? That would be not only cruel but without honor."

I did not reply. We walked along the ridge crest road in silence. After a while, Jared broke the silence. "Just as I remembered, see the fig trees? We will glean our dinner! Now Zimri-Ruel, these are the customary rules of gleaning. You may walk through the trees and take fruit to eat but only what you eat now. Take no extra for tomorrow, or even another meal later today. This is the custom for all crop food in the fields and lands belonging to others. It is a good habit to ask the owner before entering his field. These trees belong to a man in Bethel. We will thank him when we arrive."

I tasted the sweet fruit of a soft ripe fig and was immediately refreshed. Still hungry, I reached for another, but before picking it, I glanced to Jared quizzically. Jared simply nodded back to me the okay to savor another. Jared chose a few ripe figs to share with Abaigael, and we sat shaded by the trees by the side of the road while Abaigael passed around the water. Having been silent all afternoon, she now softly spoke up. "Zimri-Ruel, you remain a mystery to us. Please tell us about your family and your village. It must be so very different than what we know."

"Yes, very different. Sometimes I feel as though I were dropped into another world. A very large world where everyone knows who they are and where they belong, and I am just a goat reared without ewe or ram, the least of the beast of the field. I have no genealogy, no kinsmen, clan, or tribe. For indeed, I was called Jael, the mountain goat, by the villagers who found me alongside the road to Haran and took me in not as an orphaned son but as a slave to the village. The village is in the high hills above Khalab, never visited by the caravan or the traveler. It is a village where hospitality has been forgotten or never existed. It is the village to which I now travel! Indeed, I never knew hospitality is an obligation, although I have been blessed to receive the most gracious and lavish hospitality by a lord, a patriarch, and a king!"

I began to tell Jared and the patient, Abaigael, my story. I told of the "voice" I first heard in the skies above and the perfect creation below, about how I determined that God was the voice instructing me, and how I realized man could not be God but still has some authority and dominion over creation. I recounted the wonderful day I heard the story of the rainbow and God's miraculous salvation of Noah, his wife, sons, daughters-in-law, and a remnant of every creature on the earth. They silently listened as I recounted my meeting with Terah and the caravan journey to Damascus to hear Shem personally retell his story of the ark and his excitement at the clear memory of hearing the voice of God Most High. They listened silently, politely, as I told of my new voice from within, singing praises to God. And then I told them of my encounter with the man in white in my nighttime journey to Salem.

When I told them of the innkeepers' recognition of King Melchizedek, they both gasped and shouted, "King Melchizedek! Is it true? King Melchizedek came alongside you by night? Go on, please, go on!"

I explained how I too attended the blessing and witnessed Abram, the Hebrew, be blessed and offer his tithe to King Melchizedek, priest of God Most High. Then I told how I accompanied King Melchizedek to his prayer garden. I recounted how the king told me of the charge against me by God. The charge that I left the sheep, not the herd in sheepfold that night but the people of the village who enslaved me. He spoke of the need to love them and to begin by forgiving them. I told of my earnest prayer of confession and Melchizedek's words from God and his blessing and my new name, which God had reserved for me. Then I fell silent.

But a few moments later, I began to speak again just as Jared also started to say, "Zimri-Ruel…" He stopped as he heard me, and then I said, "No, please, you first."

He started again. "Your story, indeed, cuts me to the quick. You have truly been treated unjustly, even cruelly. Yet you confess your sin, and you offer forgiveness?"

Abaigael joined in. "I see the grace and wisdom of King Melchizedek in your account. Truly, the Most High God has called you and directed your paths. I say rejoice in His salvation for you! Take the shepherd's crook and love and serve the Most High God!"

Jared added, "You owe no tribe or clan an obligation. You are a son of the Most High God and kin to all who love and serve him! It matters not if you are Semite like Lord Terah, a son of the Patriarch Shem, or a Canaanite like us, children of the patriarch Ham. Indeed, I feel kinship to you as close as a brother."

Something just opened inside me, and I replied, "Indeed, your words are sweet to my ears, and I could not help but feel your joy and love you both as I heard your good news along the way. For this whole day, I have been considering how I will be received by my former masters upon my return. What will I say to them? Will they believe my story? I have learned that if we love the Most High God… that if we love God, we must also love those whom He loves. I realized yesterday that I have not loved anyone. I did not know how to love anyone! But today, the Most High God brought our paths together that I may learn how to love. I fear many will not be as easy to love as you are, dear Jared and Abaigael! I think loving my village masters will require much effort and determination on my part. Can a man train himself to love others?"

"Brother Zimri-Ruel, I have never met a man with so many questions! Do you never stop?"

"I stop only to sing praises to the Most High God!" A new praise song came up from within my soul.

A CHANGED HEART

Sing with me praises to the Most High God!
Join with me in giving Him thanks!
Listen as I tell of all His wonders!
I am glad and exult in Him!
He alone sits on a heavenly throne, judging righteously.
He has rebuked the nations and resets their course.
Our God is a stronghold for the oppressed!
He alone hears the cries of the afflicted!
He calls to men to put their trust in Him.
The Lord has made Himself known!
Even among the nations who forget God!
For the widow, the orphan, and the needy will not be forgotten,
For He alone is the hope of the afflicted.
Rise up our Saving God!
Let all nations be judged before You.
Let the nations know that they are but men!
Mere men but also children of the Most High God!

Chapter Eleven

*"The Kingdom of heaven is like a merchant
seeking fine pearls, and upon finding
one pearl of great value, he went and
sold all that he had, and bought it."*

—Matthew 13:45–46

We continued our way along the ridge road with its magnificent view of the western plain to the Great Sea. We passed by the city of Geba, below the high road to the east, and the city of Mizpeh, below the high road to the west, and came upon Bethel at dusk. Jared knew his way through the village and came to a modest house not far from another gate.

"This is the home of my cousin, Baram, and it was his figs we ate this afternoon. He will honor his obligation for hospitality, as he is kin. It would be even a greater dishonor to turn us aside."

He knocked on the door to the courtyard. When it creaked open, I could hear the voice saying, "Jared, Abaigael, what, you're here again? And with a stranger? Well, come in. You know it is getting late. We will see if we have something for you to eat. Come in."

As we entered his gate, we walked through an open courtyard and garden. Jared began, "Cousin, your hospitality is most kind, and I must tell you we gleaned some of your figs on our way from Salem. Our stay in Salem cost more than we planned, and then we shared the last of our food with our fellow worshipper of the Most High God, our friend, Zimri-Ruel. He too went to Salem to worship the Most

A CHANGED HEART

High God and seek a blessing and intercession of King Melchizedek, priest of the Most High God. We could not leave him alone in a strange city when we knew of the kindness of your household. But news, cousin! We have wonderful news!"

Baram interrupted. "Yes, you can tell me your good news at supper. Let's get everyone fed. I was about to sit at my table when you knocked. First we eat, and then we can talk."

Jared lovingly helped Abaigael off her donkey. Baram gave me a stern glance as he scanned me from head toe. I could overhear him say quietly just to Jared, "Really, Jared, what do you know of this fellow? He looks like a field hand to me."

Jared turned and glanced at me, smiled, and then quietly replied, "He is a most amazing man, cousin. The Most High God is directing his path! No, do not worry, for he is a humble man who will not impose heavily on your hospitality."

Abaigael found Baram's wife, Naamah, and the two women prepared for the extended supper. Baram was older than Jared, an up and coming man with fig trees, a fine vineyard, and a winepress. He was hardworking and ambitious and had two small children and several servants; feeding a few more guests would be no problem. After additional loaves of bread, more fruit, and raisin cakes were set out to supplement the roasted meat, another bowl of wine was poured, and the table was ready. After the travelers washed the dust and dirt of the road from their hands, face, and feet, they settled onto cushions around the inviting table.

Pouring himself a cup of wine, Baram asked, "Now what is this wonderful news, cousin Jared?"

Bursting with excitement, Jared nearly shouted, "Abaigael is with child! And it will be a son!" Naamah turned and gave Abaigael a hug, whispering something in her ear.

"That is good news, cousin," Baram replied, but then he added, "How do you know it will be a boy?"

Beaming, Jared answered, "That is what makes it even more wonderful. You see, we met King Melchizedek as we left Salem at dawn this morning and as he was returning from his garden. As you know, we traveled to Salem to sacrifice to the Most High God and seek a blessing from King Melchizedek. And though we made a sacrifice to God Most High and were among a crowd that King Melchizedek blessed, we had been unable to meet him. We had decided to leave without an audience when our money and most of our provisions were gone. But God be praised, the king found us as we were leaving Salem! He approached us and said, 'Leaving Salem so early? Please let me bless you.' Then he first blessed Abaigael and then me and, then he blessed our child, a son, whom he named Abiel. He knew our names and everything about us. Abiel will grow strong in the knowledge that the Most High God is his father and live a long life!"

Baram sat quietly studying Jared and then gazed at Abaigael. He finally said softly, "Jared, I know much you and Abaigael desire a son. I know you have grieved the loss of your small son and the stillborn birth of your daughter. I know that King Melchizedek is a wise leader and a great king, greatly respected even here in Bethel, but pronouncing you will have a son when Abaigael is barely showing and presumptuously giving the baby a name? I fear your hopes and desires may get the better of your judgment! Take it from me, I am more experienced than you. Take Abaigael home, let her rest, and pray to El that the child has not been injured on your reckless adventure."

"Cousin, I respect your advice. You are, indeed, more successful and experienced in the world than I am. But you were not there, you did not see the wisdom and grace of King Melchizedek. How did he know our names? How did he know Abaigael was with child?"

"That is right cousin, Baram," Abaigael bravely interrupted. "I was fully covered in my heavy cloak, and it was barely dawn, and the light was low. He knew us, and he looked at us with amazing love. Yes, love! He knew our grief and pain, our worry, and why we came to Salem. He called me Abaigael, of most tender heart, and Jared, most faithful husband, and he blessed us! I have never felt such peace! He knew our hearts, and I know his truth! He has real authority unlike any I have ever seen before. I know that everything he said will come to pass."

Baram's face hardened. "I'm afraid the both of you have been beguiled by the charms of King Melchizedek. He keeps peace in

Salem by charming everyone. He even has the shepherds and field servants believing they are somebody just so they work without grumbling. Yes, he is clever, and he claims to be the priest of El Elyon, the Most High God. And who is El Elyon? This is Bethel. The city of El, god. We worship El, creator of the earth, the first god and father of the gods. Melchizedek will not worship El. He will acknowledge no other god than his own. He is the most presumptuous charmer! You spend five minutes in his presence and you know him to have all truth? I will not hear of his schemes and mischief in my house."

"Cousin Baram, I know that you seek only good for Abaigael and me. You provide hospitality and counsel. You are right to say we spent only a few minutes with King Melchizedek. I ask you to hear the story of our friend, Zimri-Ruel. He has spent many hours, even days, in private fellowship and counsel with King Melchizedek. Hear him and then decide."

Baram turned his gaze on me. "I will hear your story of King Melchizedek. But first, tell me who you are. Who are your people that I should hear your words?"

"In truth, Lord Baram, I have no genealogy. I was found along the road to Haran and raised a slave to the villagers who found me. I was a humble shepherd whose duty was to guard the sheepfold by night while the village shepherds slept in their beds…"

"A slave! Even worse, a shepherd!" Baram interrupted. "Am I to take counsel from such an unworthy man?"

"Cousin, please just let him speak and then decide. Do you not hear the reports of your field servants before making a judgment?" Jared replied.

I continued my story. "The villagers called me Jael, the mountain goat. I do not know my given name, or if I have one. I lived alone in the high hills above Khalab. My only company were the sheep and goats. Villagers would tend the flock by day, and I would join with them in the afternoon to herd the flocks to the sheepfold surrounded by the mountain. I would spend the night in front of the gate to sheepfold. I lived in a cleft in the rock near the sheepfold. This life permitted me to observe the sheep, the goats, the birds and beast of the mountain, and the star-filled heavens above. I observed creation and creatures and discerned that God has revealed Himself in the heavens above and all the earth below. His revelation was to me a voice calling for me to seek Him and to hear His voice more clearly and fully.

Baram scoffed. "A shepherd, God speaking to a worthless shepherd!"

I just kept speaking. "I had many questions for God! One day, a rainbow appeared following a brief storm, and I heard a villager say it was the sign of the covenant God made with Noah following the great flood. I asked after this Noah and was told he is buried, but his son, Shem, still lived and had been saved on the ark with Noah. I determined to find Shem and hear of this God who saved him. I lit large fires all around the sheepfold to burn through the morning to secure the flock, and then I ran off in the night, skirting Khalab, and eventually I arrived in Haran."

"Not only a slave but a runaway! Can your testimony get any worse?" grumbled Baram.

"I was taken to Damascus by caravan in the company of Lord Terah of Haran…"

"I know of Lord Terah, he is an honorable man." Baram asserted.

I continued, "Lord Terah introduced me to the Patriarch Shem, who knew my story. He retold for me his experience on the ark and how he, to this day, clearly remembers the voice of God, a voice unlike any other, clear and unmistakable! The Patriarch Shem insisted that the Most High God had called me and was directing my paths. The Word of God came upon the Patriarch Shem. God's words were, 'I know you. I attended your birth. I know your father and your father's fathers and your mother and your mother's mothers to the end of all generations. I raised you to be a shepherd.' Shem blessed me and urged me to go to Salem, where the Most High God would reveal a new name reserved for me. He prayed that I would become a voice of praise to the Most High God and steadfastly serve Him. Indeed, after I left Damascus on the road to Salem, a voice emerged from within me I have never before known. It was a voice of song. With no thought or intent on my part, I heard myself singing praises to the Most High God."

"This is true, cousin." Jared interjected. "We have heard him sing stirring songs of praise as we walked the road today."

"So the mountain goat can sing," replied Baram. "But what about Melchizedek?"

"It was my habit to travel the road by night. It was cooler, true, but really, I was uncomfortable with people, and the night sky is my old friend and a constant reminder of the voice of the Most High God. I had finished singing a song, and my mind was again filled with questions. Why was I on this journey? Where did this voice within come from? How was all of this happening? I did not notice a lone man dressed in a white robe that shone brightly in the moonlight overtake me on the road. He asked to walk along with me and to listen to my story."

"Only a shepherd would be so foolish as to walk the road alone by night," Baram said, shaking his head.

Ignoring his comments, I continued my story. "I told him everything that occurred. And as I told each event, he would comment on why such things must be. It was as if he knew the questions I had for the Most High God and wisely answered. He told me about worship and sacrifice. He told me the Most High God created the heavens and the earth and how the Most High God walked with men in Eden. He told me how sin came into the world, how God himself shed the blood of animals for skins to clothe man, and how man was put out of Eden and was made to toil. He told me how man sinned again, that Cain killed his brother, Abel, and sin abounded more. He explained that God no longer walked the earth alongside men and sin grew. He said that when the wickedness of men rose as a repugnant odor to His throne above, God destroyed the world by a great flood, saving only Noah, his wife, his sons, his daughters-in-law, and a remnant of all creatures on earth. He told me that the Most High God cannot abide any sin but that He made provisions for atonement. He taught me that innocent blood could atone for a sin and why sacrifices must be made to the Most High God. He told me that man, alone in all creation, has dominion and authority in creation but that man chafes under the authority and holiness of the Most High God. He agreed with the Patriarch Shem that the voice of God was calling me and directing my paths. We talked for hours and hours. I was amazed at his wisdom and grace. It was not until we stopped at an inn near Salem and he was recognized by the innkeeper that I learned that he was King Melchizedek, priest to God Most High!"

"King Melchizedek, walking alone on the road at night with no guard, no officers, and conversing hours on end with a shepherd? A runaway slave?" Baram exclaimed, "And you believe this story, Jared?"

Jared responded, "Please go on, Zimri-Ruel. Tell us what happened next."

"King Melchizedek asked me to accompany him to the palace, claiming he had more to teach me. The events in Salem were just as Jared has said. He blessed the citizens, and even the foreigners in the city. He met Abram, the Hebrew, outside the city wall, returning from a great victory. He blessed Abram and the Most High God for giving Abram the victory. Then Abram presented a tithe, a tribute of one-tenth of all the camels, all the donkeys, all the sheep, and all the cattle and one-tenth of all the treasure Abram had seized in his victory over the kings. He told me at his table the night before special things, secret things about Abram. He spoke of a father of nations, of a new tribe of priests who will serve the Most High God. These priests will intercede for all people as the Most High God will instruct them. He will call some to be musicians and some to oversee the priesthood, that no priest veers from the instructions of the Most High God to the left or to the right. Only this priesthood will offer acceptable sacrifices to the Most High God. But King Melchizedek mysteriously added that a day will come when God will send a great high priest who will atone for all the sins of man once and forever! He was adamant that only the Most High God is God, there are no others. It is the hardness of men's hearts that stop their eyes from seeing the revelation of God in His creation and their ears from hearing his voice calling out for all to seek Him. King Melchizedek explained what God asks of man—that is, to love God with all of your heart and your soul and to love others as yourself."

Now Baram just sat there, huffing and shaking his head.

"After Abram and his host departed, I accompanied King Melchizedek to his garden. The king prayed and then told me what God has against me, that I had abandoned his sheep. It was not the flock he referred to but to the villagers in the high hills above Khalab. He sent me back to serve them as priest, to intercede for them until the priesthood of Abram's nation is established. He taught me to pray and to seek forgiveness. He taught me how to be thankful for all His many blessings. And most of all, he gave me my new name, Zimri-Ruel, as a sign of my new life in His service. I immediately left for Khalab, not returning to Salem, with no provisions, no cloak or staff, just a new song on my lips."

"That is my story. Jared and Abaigael woke me with their conversation as they walked by the rock behind, which I had been sleeping. Do you not see, good Baram, the truth of the Most High God that has been clearly revealed? The truth of Adam, the truth of Noah and Shem, the truth of the covenant forever testified by the rainbow? The truth in creation in the paths of the stars and the procession of the seasons? God reveals Himself to us always if we but look and seek! The Lord, the Most High God, is our creator and sustainer. His mercy endures forever!"

Baram sat silently with an angry, grimacing face. Finally, he said, "Naamah, bring me the household gods."

Naamah meekly got up and silently went as told. She came back with a finely worked wooden case with intricately carved figures, which she carefully handed to Baram. He carefully picked up the figure in the middle of the case and said, "This is El, creator of the earth, first among the gods. He lives at the mouth of the two rivers where heaven meets earth. El does not often interfere in the affairs of men, more content at ruling the gods above in the heavens. Bethel is his city. We worship him for his authority and for his protection when the other gods rule over the earth."

He carefully put El back in his place in the case. He chose another, a female figure with large full breasts. "This is Athirat, or some call her Asherah, 'walker of the sea,' wife of El, and mother of the gods. She is a goddess of fertility. Her sexual unions bring fertility to the earth."

Baram placed Asherah back in the case and chose another figure with an outstretched arm. "This is Baal, son of El and Asherah and who strives with his brother and sister gods for dominance. He is the god of male fertility, virility, and energy. It is his copulation with his mother, Asherah, that provides fertility to the earth below. He made himself a warrior god. He exercises power over the other gods, bending them to his will. He must be appeased for the earth to be fruitful."

Replacing Baal, he chose another. "This is Dagon, who contends with Baal and is also a god of grain fertility."

Now he was pointing at other gods as he named them. "Eshmun, god of healing. Ishat, goddess of fire. Anat, virgin goddess of war and strife. Kotharat, goddess of marriage and pregnancy. Kothar-wa-Khasis, god of skilled craftsmanship. Nikkal-wa-ib, goddess of orchards and fruit. Qadeshtu, goddess of love. Yam, the river god. Shachar and Shalim, twin mountain gods of dawn and dusk. And Sydyk, god of justice. There are many more gods. They strive between them for authority, and the earth feels the pain of their strife. We must appease them, for we never know which god may overpower another."

Returning the case of idols to Naamah, Baram continued, "Goat shepherd, you do not understand the gods at all. They have no desire for mercy. They do not seek our love. They do not rule for righteousness. We appease them for peace and continued fertility for the crops of the fields, fruit of the land, and children by our wives. Priests help us to influence the gods to fulfill their duties so our lives can be blessed. That is why the temple prostitutes perform ritual sex acts of every imagination to entice the gods above, for Baal and for Asherah, for Dagon and Ishat and Kotharat to copulate and make our land fertile."

Turning to his cousin, he said, "Jared and Abaigael would be better served worshipping our gods, sacrificing to Kotharat than traveling to Salem, worshipping El Elyon, whose very denial of all other gods is a hard affront. Pray they did not observe this affront. Melchizedek may be king of Salem, but his priesthood does not interest me at all."

A CHANGED HEART

Jared shot back, "Do the temple prostitutes seek to influence the gods, or do they just meet the desires of a wicked and lustful people, men and women drunk on wine and overcome by lust and desire doing unspeakable sex acts in the name of worship? It is a wonder anyone knows who his father really is!"

Baram shouted, "Enough! This conversation has tired me and unsettled my stomach. I will hear no more of it. To bed."

The next morning, the conversations were subdued and cordial. A breakfast was offered, and Baram presented pouches of food containing loaves of bread, dried figs, cheese, and raisin cakes. Several skins of wine and water were strung over the shoulder of the saddled donkey. A new cloak was brought forward, and Baram presented it to me, saying, "I have met my duty to provide hospitality. Go in peace."

As he began to turn away, I spoke up. "Lord Baram, you have, indeed, more than fulfilled your obligations to the foreigner, and I thank you. I would ask you to humbly consider the beauty and the mercy the Most High God offers you. You care very much for the richness of your crops and quality of your wine, how much more then would the God of creation care for his world? Would he not love it and nurture it as you love and nurture your children? Why serve hostile and unpredictable gods when the Most High God can, by reason, be the only God and one worth serving? May His voice call out to you. I leave you in peace, Lord Baram."

Walking to Jared, Baram spoke out. "Cousin Jared, do you too have a lecture for me?"

"No, cousin. You know where Abaigael and I stand. We will follow the Most High God and trust in His word. We will wake every morning and resolve to love the Most High God with all our heart and all our soul. We will learn to love all whom He loves. Cousin, thank you for your gracious hospitality. You will always be welcome in our home."

Jared then lovingly helped Abaigael onto her donkey. Until this time, she had been silent, not speaking a word all morning. Clearly, something was troubling her. It was much more than the heated talk of the night before.

"I have to say something;" she said. "I had a dream last night, but it was more real than any dream I have had before. I saw a man, I think it was a man, though he shone too bright for me to see his face. I had to squint my eyes and cast my view down. He said, 'Abaigael, you are a woman of tender heart in whom no bitterness can be found, as a mother crying over her lost children. I bring you a message from the Most High God, "The sin and wickedness of Canaan land has reached my throne as in the days of Noah. I will curse Canaan. I will destroy this nation and give this land to a new nation that will be my people. But I am a merciful God and will spare every Canaanite who turns from whoring after false gods and returns to me. The day will come when this city, Bethel, will be destroyed and every man, woman and child here will be put to the sword. But all those who repent will know that My mercy endures forever."'"

Abaigael looked at Naamah and then Baram. "I was too frightened to say this earlier, but I couldn't leave you without sharing this message. Please know I love you all and pray to the Most High God this does not befall you."

Naamah ran forward and hugged Abaigael. Not another word was spoken as we left Bethel.

Chapter Twelve

"How lovely on the mountains are the feet of him who brings good news, who publishes peace, who brings good news of happiness, who publishes salvation, who says to Zion, 'Your God reigns.'"

—Isaiah 52:7

We set out of Bethel in silence, once again on the high road north. Abaigael's prophecy and Baram's offense at our total determination to follow the Most High God and trust completely the words of King Melchizedek, priest of the Most High God, weighed on our minds. How different this morning was than our joyful walk of yesterday. I considered my new friends, how strong they were! Jared was respectful of his elder and more successful cousin but would not be intimidated. He stood his ground, firm in his commitment to follow the Most High God. He really did know in his heart that the Most High God had been revealed to him. He must be following the voice. And Abaigael, her silence and her tenderness existed beside a fearsome strength! She would be heard! This morning, when she spoke of her dream (or was it a vision?)—what courage! She certainly heard the voice, and she would carry the message. I thank the Most High God for bringing them across my path and teaching a lonely shepherd how to love.

Then I remembered Naamah. She seemed so frightened and vulnerable. Clearly, there was a bond between her and Abaigael, and that gave me great hope. Surely the Most High God, whose mercy endures forever, must love Naamah. How could I not love Naamah? Now Baram, he was prideful man, maybe even arrogant. But he met his obligations of hospitality and desired to be an honorable man. I think he saw the ugliness and cruelty of the Canaanite gods and the almost pointless efforts and rituals to appease them, but he couldn't seem to let go and trust that the Most High God is the only God—a God of righteousness, mercy, and love! The only God who could be creator. Oh, I do love Baram as well and pray one day he would walk away from his deaf and dumb idols and, with Naamah, follow the Most High God. Oh, that he would hear His voice!

We had been walking quietly for an hour when Abaigael gently placed her hand on her stomach bump and smiled. Jared, beside her and leading the donkey, caught her smile in the corner of his eye. Smiling, he gently laid his hand on top of hers, leaned over, and gave her a gentle kiss on her cheek. Then they both lightly and quietly laughed. Canaanites may bow before idols and perform some of the most wicked practices, so much so that the day is coming when God, on his throne, will give the land to another people, His people. But today, this Canaanite husband and wife knew that He, in His love, had blessed them and would give them a son, and that joy could not be denied. Their love lifted my spirit, and I sang.

> I will sing of the great mercy of the Lord!
> And I will ascribe to Him all glory forever!
> I will follow Him only and serve Him with gladness!
> For He has planned my path
> He has attended my birth
> He knows each day of my life
> And He decides the future while we are still in the womb.
> He sees when we depart from His path.
> Our God is a forgiving God, always full of mercy
> He welcomes us when we return from our straying.
> Help me, my God, to walk with integrity in my heart.
> Let no worthless thing be set before my eyes.
> My eyes shall be upon the faithful of the land,
> May they dwell with me,

A CHANGED HEART

> And we shall serve You together
> That we may give heed to the blameless way.
> I will sing of Your loving-kindness and justice,
> To You, O Lord, I sing praises!

We walked on north, stopping at Shiloh, Shechem, and Beth-Shan, where we followed the River Jordan north again. We followed the western shore of the Sea of Chimnereth to the city Chimnereth where the road went north to Hazor. Jared and Abaigael had become the family I had never known. As we entered the city, I knew I would have to travel onto my village and my commission in the high hills above Khalab alone.

My thoughts wandered; I worried about what awaited me at the end of my journey. I became conscious that Jared was speaking. "Brother Zimri-Ruel, now you will taste of our hospitality! There are so many people you must meet. They must hear your story and ours too! And singing, you must teach our family and friends your songs of praise to the Most High God. Look, it is my father and brother at the door to our home. Come, it has been such a long time, and so much has happened. Come."

Jared led Abaigael on her donkey through the door of a compound. Inside was a neat courtyard with a shop on one side filled by a great oven, troughs of water, large flat stones, tables, piles of charcoal, and sacks leaking a stone gravel. Next to the shop was a small stable and storeroom. Across was a row of small apartments—three apartments to be exact.

Jared's father and brother both approached, removing heavy leather gloves as they walked. Both were wearing heavy leather work aprons. Jared hugged his father and then his brother, and then he helped Abaigael from her donkey.

"Great news, Father, and for you too, Obed. Abaigael will deliver a boy, and he shall be called Abiel, for he shall grow strong in the knowledge that the Most High God is his father! We have been blessed by King Melchizedek, priest of the Most High God. We have so much to tell! It is indeed so good to see you, Father. You look well. You too, Obed. It was beyond what we hoped. So amazing…"

"Jared, Abaigael," said Zadok. "God be praised you are home safely. We will hear all about your news. And this… your friend?"

"Yes, Father, our dearest friend and fellow traveler, Zimri-Ruel. I have promised him our hospitality for his stay. Zimri-Ruel, this is my father, Zadok, and my brother, Obed."

"Welcome, Zimri-Ruel. Please, all of you wash and rest. Be refreshed, and we shall hear all of your news at supper."

Obed led the donkey to the stable and showed me to his apartment while Jared and Abaigael went into theirs. After washing, I lay down and fell asleep to the sound of heavy hammers striking metal.

I was gently awakened about dusk and led next door to Zadok's apartment. A sturdy but rustic table was set for dinner. The tableware was fine copper and bronze, and even the cups were finely worked metal. The food was simple but hardy: bread, cheese, lentils, and lamb. A large bowl of wine was set in the center with an intricately worked ladle set alongside. Abaigael was helping her mother-in-law, Shifra, with the final preparations. Zadok was seated at the center of the table with Jared across from him. Obed signaled for me to sit beside Jared as he sat beside Zadok. Shifra and Abaigael settled down at the end of the table.

Handing Jared a loaf of bread, Zadok began, "Now before Jared tells us everything that happened, is it true I will have a grandson who will be called Abiel?"

Zadok, Obed, and Shifra all patiently listened as Jared retold all the events of their visit to Salem. Abaigael could not help but add to Jared's account in describing the grace and loving authority she observed in King Melchizedek. Jared went on to tell of his visit to Baram and the obvious offense Baram took to the priesthood of Melchizedek.

Zadok replied, "Your cousin Baram always expects to be first in all things. He wants to be honored, and he considers himself better and wiser than others. don't let him upset you. He did provide you every hospitality, I trust?"

"Yes, Father, but he seemed most upset when Abaigael spoke of her dream as we were leaving."

"Abaigael, what was this dream?" asked Zadock.

Abaigael spoke quietly. "I dreamed, but it was more real than a dream, like I was awake. I saw, I think, a man, and he shone too bright for me to see his face. I had to cast my view down. He said, 'Abaigael, you are a woman of tender heart in whom no bitterness can be found, as a mother crying over her lost children. I bring you a message from the Most High God, "The sin and wickedness of Canaan has reached my throne as in the days of Noah. I will curse Canaan. I will destroy this nation and give this land to a new nation that will be my people. But I am a merciful God and will spare every Canaanite who turns from whoring after false gods and returns to me. The day will come when this city, Bethel, will be destroyed and every man, woman, and child here will be put to the sword. But all those who repent will know that My mercy endures forever."'"

Zadok began, "Abaigael, do you believe these words to be those of the Most High God?"

"Father Zadok, Mother Shifra, I believe the Most High God is the only God and that King Melchizedek is His priest. I believe that he has blessed Jared and me and will direct the path of your grandson, Abiel, as his servant. My husband, Jared, and I will serve only the Most High God all the days of our lives. And if the Most high God chooses His maidservant to speak His words, I will do so. His mercy endures forever!"

Jared responded, "The Most High God has blessed Abaigael. She is trustworthy and true. We will follow only the Most High God, walk in His ways, and let Him direct our paths. Our friend, Zimri-Ruel, is of like mind. He has become as our brother. The Most High God has directed his path in the most amazing manner. I beg you to hear his story."

Once again, I told my now familiar story. In telling it, I could not escape the realization that my life before hearing the voice was now only a distant memory. My new life lay before me, unknown but exciting. God was directing my paths in a mysterious and most wonderful way. When I finished, I could see Obed and Shifra looking at Zadock with questioning eyes, and Jared and Abaigael were also looking to him but with excited and joyful faces. Zadock glanced at each one in the room.

Then he turned his gaze on Abaigael and said, "I have known my daughter-in-law before your journey to Salem, and I see her now. She left in fear for the baby she carries and with a heart broken in the loss of two other children. I see now a woman of strength and determination. I am convinced that what she says is true. This house will follow the Most High God! Zimri-Ruel, the Most High God has directed your path here. You will teach us to worship the Most High God. We ask that you offer sacrifices of thanksgiving for this house and our grandson."

Turning to Jared, he continued, "Jared, we must invite our relations, friends, and neighbors to celebrate with us the blessings of the Most High God. Obed will help you in the preparations."

Zadok's voice changed to a matter-of-fact tone, and he went on, "Now, Jared, you must hear of what has happened while you were away. The troubles in the court of Egypt have worsened. The Egyptian governor has returned to Memphis and has left only a small garrison in Megiddo. The kings of Canaan have been emboldened by the absence of the governor and the restraint of his army. There has been much raiding. As you know, there has been a war between the five kings against the four. Abram, the Hebrew, came and rescued his nephew, Lot, carried away with the spoils of Sodom and Gomorrah. In addition, bands of raiders have come from the north—the Sea People, the Horites, the Hurri, the Hittites, and the Mattani—seeking new cities as well as spoil. Without a strong Egyptian presence, the kings are increasing their armies. There is much tension and distrust. We have seen new weapons from the fallen of these raiders and invaders, much finer weapons than those of the Egyptian garrison. The Egyptians rely on their bows to rain down arrows on their enemy from afar, and only if necessary do they use their spears and hand axes with flint heads. The men from the north move swiftly, many on chariots, wielding swords of bronze and spears with bronze ax heads that can pierce even the heaviest leather. All the kings of Canaan seek these new weapons. And now Jared, Obed, and I are making them! Obed, please bring a new spearhead and shaft to show your brother."

A CHANGED HEART

While Obed went to fetch the new spearhead and shaft, Zadock continued, "Hazor has been a center for metal working for many years. As you know, many of our neighbors work in bronze, copper, and tin as we do. We have always relied on traders to bring us copper from the royal Egyptian mines in Sinai and tin from the mines above Tarsus. The demand for copper and tin here in Hazor has made the price double since you left! Ah, thank you, Obed. Now, Jared, look at this spearhead. See the balance between the piercing tip and the slashing ax head? And look at the base. This spearhead does not simply fit in a slot in the shaft to be bound by a leather tang. No, see how the casting extends to an elongated cup with the hole sized to fit the shaft. Now the shaft can be inserted into spearhead and riveted in place with bronze nails. This spear is far stronger, both in thrusting and slashing, than the spear of the Egyptian army. We can sell every one of these spearheads as quickly as we can make them. We perfected the molds and the casting method. It is the material that is our problem. One of us must move to Damascus where we can secure our copper and tin directly from the trading caravans. I would hope that you and Abaigael would consider this responsibility. You are an experienced traveler, and you have a good way with people of different lands, while your brother and I are gifted in the forge. Please consider this."

Zadok paused and looked at the puzzled faces of his family. The he quietly said, "The night is now late. We will speak more of this later."

I spent the night in the courtyard under the sky above, my constant reminder of the watchful eye of the Most High God. My thoughts turned to my host's request to teach them to worship and to lead them in a sacrifice of thanksgiving. If I am to become a priest to the hill people above Khalab, perhaps I should prepare for this calling. And sacrifice, yes, I too should sacrifice to the Most High God!

The courtyard awakened, as all courtyards do, early in the dawn, while those in the house still slept. The cocks first announced the new day, and then the stable animals began to stir. I again found solace in the patterns of God's creation. It occurred to me that I had no money. How could I make a freewill sacrifice if I could not pay even for a dove? I remembered turning down the coins Terah offered me when I left Damascus. "What need have I for coins?" I insisted. "I have never so much as held a coin before, and God has provided for all my needs." Maybe coins could be useful after all. I decided I must focus on simply trusting the Most High God. He had directed my path so far, why should he not continue now? I had so much to learn!

At breakfast that morning, Abaigael stayed close to Shifra, talking quietly back and forth concerning the preparations to be made for the feast to come. They were not about to leave it to Obed and Jared to arrange.

As we finished breakfast, Zadok reached out and handed me a small pouch of coins and said, "A priest should be paid for his service. Take this as payment for teaching our household and interceding for us with the Most High God. I ask that you arrange for the sacrifice of thanksgiving to be held tomorrow morning. At dinner tonight, you shall teach us what is expected of us in sacrifice. Now Obed and I will be in the forge. Jared, you are to join us when Zimri-Ruel dismisses you."

Jared showed me the way to the market, and sure enough, the animal pens were next to the temple, a massive temple to Baal. I told Jared, "We will select two sheep without blemish by a true shepherd's eye."

Jared asked, "Why two?"

I replied, "I must make a sacrifice of my own before we sacrifice your lamb. I will explain this evening."

We each slung a lamb over our neck and held the feet closely against the chest and walked back to the compound. With the lambs safely in their pen, I told Jared he could join his father and brother in the foundry. I decided I needed a time to pray just as Melchizedek had prayed in his garden some weeks ago. I walked out of the city to a shaded area on the shore of Lake Merom, and I sat starring at the calm waters of the lake. A few fishermen could be seen casting and hauling their nets. I tried to collect my thoughts; nothing left in my life was of my own plan. Events and directions from above had taken total control. I tried to tell God how overwhelmed I felt.

"Most High God, I thank You for calling out to me. I thank You for the signs and revelations that you clearly set before my eyes. I thank You for the counsel and encouragement of those who walk with You and share their wisdom with grace and love. I thank you for making me a shepherd, for learning to care for the flock. I thank You for showing me how we are to love and be loved. I thank You for opening my heart to Jared and Abaigael, to learn from them total trust. I know, Most High God, that You are my Father, God, that you hear my prayers. For every question I ponder, You provide an answer. My every need, You have met to overflowing. Your word to me by your priest Melchizedek still overwhelms me. You who have all power grant that I may grow into the servant and shepherd You have called me to become. Enlarge my heart to love and serve You. Grant me wisdom to shepherd the flock you set me before. Challenge me when I depart from Your path and set me back in the way. May my intersession for your sheep be acceptable to You. May the sacrifices I bring atone for every confessed sin, and may Your sheep thrive."

As I walked back to Hazor, I went over every word Terah, Shem, and Melchizidek shared with me regarding worship and sacrifice. I remembered their teaching about sin and the need to shed innocent blood. I remembered the need for atonement, and I remembered that night at the banquet table of Melchizedek his foretelling of God's new plan for a new priesthood to come. And I remembered his prophecy of a high priest who will make one sacrifice for all man's sin once for all time. Surely, our Most High God is a loving God, who acts in loving-kindness despite every wickedness man can imagine. Our Most High God is worthy of our praise! We must know that his atonement comes at a price, but it is a price that He himself pays! I must make it clear that we sacrifice to demonstrate our need for atonement, and we worship because He is worthy to be praised!

That night after dinner, all of Zadok's household was gathered, and we sat in his modest but comfortable room. I began with the story of creation—how all was very good and how God walked in the garden among His creatures with Adam and Eve. I told of Adam and Eve's first sin in the garden. I told of the first shedding of blood when God took the life of innocent animals for theirs skins and how

God Himself made the first clothes for Adam and Eve. I told of the cost of sin, how Adam and Eve were put out of the garden and were required to toil for food, and the pain Eve would suffer in childbirth. I recounted the story of how Cain killed his brother, Abel, in a jealous rage over his unaccepted sacrifice, and this story caused worry to cross the face of Zadok. I explained how sin had gained a foothold among the children of Adam and Eve and grew and multiplied, even as the children of Adam and Eve grew and multiplied. I told of God's righteousness and holiness and that He can be no other. But I also told of God's love for each and every man, how His heart was towards walking with man that they may know His heart, His will, and His love. I told of how a patriarch, a man called Enoch, walked with God and was no more. Then I told the story of Noah, another man who walked with God and, in fact, the last man of his generation to walk with God. I told the story of the ark and God's salvation of Noah, his wife, his two sons and their wives, and a remnant of every creature on earth from the great flood and that the rainbow was the sign of God's covenant with all the earth, never to destroy all life by a great flood. I told how I had found the patriarch, Shem, himself saved by God on the ark, who heard the voice of God clearly and unmistakably.

Zadok interjected. "Yes, I have heard of this Shem, a man of very great age who told of a great flood and the message of the rainbow."

Jared interrupted. "You say the Patriarch Shem lives in Damascus? I so very much want to meet this man!"

I continued my teaching. I told of how Terah taught me to sacrifice grain and a lamb. I told of how all sin required atonement (atonement was God's provision for sin) and how God, who is all righteousness and holiness and cannot tolerate any sin, can again allow men to walk with Him and know His love. I explained that without the shedding of blood, there can be no forgiveness of sin. The purpose of our sacrifice is to use God's own provision to apply undeserved righteousness to us in the innocent shed blood of a spotless, unblemished animal—unblemished being a reminder of having no sin—and being atoned, we become company fit to walk with the Most High God. The grain sacrifice was made in thanksgiving for all of the blessing we receive from our God, the fruit of His love for us. Having been forgiven our sin and made righteous in the eyes of God and company fit to walk again with Him, we worship Him! We worship Him with hearts of love for His mercy for us, for all the goodness that He is, and for the grace He brings to us as we walk in peace and joy with Him!

Then I said, "King Melchizedek, priest of the Most High God, taught me the true key to worshiping the Most High God. From him, I learned that I must know my own heart, that I must see my own sin, that I must come before our God humbly, seeking His forgiveness, and apply His atoning sacrifices within my own heart. It is a conscious act of the will to approach the Most High God with a contrite heart, to examine oneself carefully, to hear what God has against me, to see myself as I am and seek His forgiveness, and to change my way. This is repentance. God calls all men to repent, to give up our sinful ways and walk with Him. King Melchizedek taught me that if we love God, we must also love those whom He loves. And God, our creator, loves all of His creatures!"

I then added, "I must tell you that today, while you toiled in your forge, I walked to a quiet place by Lake Merom and prayed to God as King Melchizedek taught me to pray in his garden outside Salem. I find this a most helpful practice. It is good to always pray. And prayer can be short and instantaneous, but it should be a time set aside, a time alone just to consider our God and our own heart and a time to not only feel His grace but also hear his complaint against us. This is a most helpful way to prepare for sacrifice and worship. It prepared me. The Most High God can reveal the most marvelous things when you set your heart to hear His voice. Yesterday, I did not know how to intercede as your priest, but after my time with Him, I am ready to do His calling. Tomorrow, we will make two sacrifices—first, I will make a sacrifice to the Most High God so that we know that I am righteous before Him when I make a sacrifice on your behalf. I ask you now to consider all these things. Seek the heart of the Most High God tonight. Listen for His voice and know what is required of you."

The next morning, the whole household gathered in anticipation. I asked Jared to gather kindling and wood, all that the donkey could carry. I asked for an unlit torch, flint, sharp knife, and the two lambs we chose yesterday. We then made our way through the streets of Hazor to the north gate. Hazor is set on a tel, a small raised hill of rock and stones overlooking Lake Merom. I asked each member of the household to gather the largest stone they could carry and place them in a pile for the altar. I told them to choose only rough stones as a reminder that not even the altar is of man's craftsmanship, merit, or earning. God provides the altar stones. We erected two crude stone altars. The stone altars were covered by the kindling and then the wood.

I lifted my arms towards the heaven above and called, "Most High God, accept this sacrificial offering from your humble servant. Forgive my sin and cleanse me from all unrighteousness, prepare me as an instrument of Your will to intercede on behalf of these your servants and people of your flock. May it be pleasing unto You."

I then lifted the lamb onto the altar and cut its throat. I captured the blood flowing down and sprinkled it over the altar. I then lit the torch and from it the kindling.

I then repeated the sacrifice of the second lamb on the second altar and lit the fire. Zadok and his family stood silently watching the fire consume the lambs, facing the household of Zadok. Again, I lifted my arms and spoke. "Most High God, accept the sacrifice for the household of Zadok. Make them clean and righteous before Your eyes. Bless them and bless Abiel the child to come. Open their ears to Your voice and walk with them in mercy and grace. Direct their paths, keep them close to your heart, heal their wounds, and strengthen their walk with You."

The silence was broken when Zadok shouted, "Blessed is the God Most High, creator of heaven and earth!"

Jared spoke up next. "His mercy endures forever!"

Shifra called out, "Our God brings comfort to the afflicted and remembers the widow and the orphan!"

Obed, usually silent, shouted, "God gives strength to the weak and lays the proud man low!"

And finally, Abaigael spoke authoritatively. "The Most High God appoints all our days before we are born. He establishes justice on the earth and judges the nations. Our God calls to all His people and bids them to come walk with Him and receive His love. Blessed be His holy name!"

Then we altogether spontaneously sang this song:

> The Most High God calls out to His people.
> His voice summons His sheep to His fold
> To walk with Him in the sunshine of His face
> To hear Him and know the safety of His presence.
> The Most High God gives an abundance of food to eat.
> He grants us peace to sleep at night.
> The Most High God blesses our children
> And our children's children, our joy in our old age.
> Oh, lay out my path, Most High God,
> Wash me clean this day, my God
> And keep me in Your ways forever!

Chapter Thirteen

*"You shall not follow other gods, any of the
gods of the people who surround you."*

—*Deuteronomy 6:14*

Guests began arriving at Zadok's home for Jared and Abaigael's celebration. The entire courtyard had been covered with a trellis of poles across where tent cloths and rugs hung. Several tables were set with every available fruit, dried figs, raisin cakes, fresh loaves of bread, fish, and roast meat. Bowls of wine were spaced across each table in easy reach of each guest. Abaigael's family, Zadok's relatives, neighbors, friends, and fellow bronze and metalsmiths mixed with each other, freely sampling the good wine. Several of the leading men of Hazor and the heads of households praised Zadok for preparing such a grand feast. When asked the reason for the celebration, Zadok would only say, "We will share our good news and the reason we feast once all have eaten. Soon you will hear, and I pray you will rejoice with us!"

Once all the guests were comfortably seated and enjoying the extravagant table and fine wine, Zadok rose from his seat of honor. Speaking from his heart, he said, "My dear kin, family of my beloved daughter-in-law, friends, and fellow craftsman, we are honored that you came today and shared in our celebration. Most of you know the pain that Jared and Abaigael have suffered in the loss of their young son and the stillbirth of their daughter. In despair, they traveled to Salem to sacrifice to the Most High God and seek the blessing of

King Melchizedek, priest of the Most High God. Today we celebrate their safe return and their good news! Abaigael is again with child, and they shall have a son, and his name will be... but I prefer they share the joy of their news themselves. Jared..."

Jared squeezed Abaigael's hand, gave her a peck on the cheek, and rose to speak. "Yes, thank you all for coming, for doing us the honor. As my honored father, Zadok, has said, we have recently returned from Salem and want you to share in our joy. King Melchizedek has, indeed, most graciously and unexpectedly blessed us, even as we were departing the city before dawn. It was as if he had planned the whole encounter. He knew everything about us before we met. He knew our names, and he knew our loss and the pain in our hearts. He knew Abaigael was with child, even though she was covered in a heavy cloak and the light of the day had not yet appeared. He blessed us, and he blessed the child Abaigael carries. He said his name shall be Abiel, for he will grow in the knowledge that the Most High God is his father. He will serve God his long life! We have known only joy and the peace of the Most High God since that moment. God has brought before our path our good friend and brother, Zimri-Ruel, who instructs us in the wisdom of King Melchizedek and intercedes for us with the Most High God. He leads us in sacrifice to the Most High God and teaches us to worship only Him. We want each of you to know the joy we know and to rejoice with us! Celebrate that we will have a son! He will live a long life and walk with the Most High God!"

One of the honored guests, an elder of the city and respected craftsman of bronze, rose to speak. "To Jared and Abaigael, we share your joy in the news that you, Abaigael, again carry a child. We saw the pain you have suffered. The joy you have found has lifted your spirit, and Abaigael's smile is once again seen in our city. I very much hope that for your sake, you do have a son. You will call him, what was it, Abiel? Yes, and that he grows strong and lives long. I just don't understand why you made such a risky trip to Salem when the temple of Baal is here in Hazor and the Asherah poles are in the pleasant fields along the lake? If Zadok hasn't provided you Baal's image or Asherah's image, I have them to give to you. But welcome home to

Hazor! Raise your family here, and, Jared, once again hone your skill in bronze."

Zadok again rose to speak. "Thank you for those kind words, but we have more to celebrate! On the testimony of my daughter-in-law and the word given to her by the Most High God, the house of Zadok from this day forward will walk in the ways of the Most High God. We will serve Him only. For we sacrifice to Him only and worship Him only. The joy we celebrate today is the joy in knowing that the Most High God is God! He has made us, and He calls out to us to follow Him. We desire for all of you to know the joy that we know. To have the peace that we now have. This is the good news that we share with you!"

There was only a soft murmuring among guests. No other guest rose to speak. They enjoyed the feast and shared pleasant and polite remarks with Zadok. Many encouraged Abaigael in her pregnancy, offering advice to ensure all would be well.

Abaigael's father approached Zadok and privately said to him, "I am grateful to hear of the respect you hold for my daughter. I had heard rumors that Jared would put her away as his wife and send her back to me. Such a dishonor would have devastated her and, indeed, be an affront to our house."

Zadok looked squarely in his eyes and replied, "Do you not know your own daughter? Jared could never put Abaigael away. Never have I seen such a marriage! I have heard it said that the two shall be one flesh. And for certain, Jared and Abaigael are one flesh and also one mind and one soul! No one will ever set them apart! And now I have seen that the Most High God speaks His words through her. Abaigael is the heart and soul of my household! We shall never give her up!"

The guests enjoyed the feast and drank all of Zadok's wine. They left merry and cheerful. They all wished Jared and Abaigael well. None made inquiry to Zadok's invitation to follow the Most High God. None offered any interest in the blessings and prophecy of King Melchizedek. None had any question for the stranger, Zimri-Ruel.

A CHANGED HEART

The next day was a festival day of Baal. Bulls would be sacrificed on the altar to Baal, and the entire city would gather at his temple. Zadok had no intention of attending this festival. He would follow only the Most High God. He had made his sacrifices, and he was under the instruction of a priest ordained by Melchizedek. So when Jared announced that he and Abaigael would go to the temple, he was completely taken aback. Abaigael would only say that she had that night again heard the voice in the light too bright to look upon, that she received a word from the Most High God for the people before they make another sacrifice to Baal.

When Jared, Abaigael, and I arrived at the temple, it was surrounded by Asherah poles. The priests of Baal were already performing ritualistic sex acts with the temple prostitutes. The people of Hazor were calling out to the priests and the temple prostitutes for more and more unspeakable behavior.

In the midst of this public debauchery, Abaigael climbed the steps of the temple and shouted out, "People of Hazor, hear the word of the Most High God. The sin and wickedness of Canaan has reached my throne as in the days of Noah. I will curse Canaan. I will destroy this nation and give this land to a new nation that will be my people. But I am a merciful God and will spare every Canaanite who turns from whoring after false gods and returns to me. The day will come when this city, Hazor, will be destroyed and every man, woman, and child here will be put to the sword. The Most High God has judged all the cities and all the people of Canaan. All will be destroyed, and those who survive will be put into the service of my people for generations to come. But all those who repent will know that My mercy endures forever."

The crowd shouted back to her, "Join the temple prostitutes, woman! Yes, let the blasphemer join the temple prostitutes! The priests of Baal can provide what you need now!"

Jared ran up the steps and pulled her back with him before any violence could occur. The crowd was more intent on wine and sex than the words of a young prophetess. I helped Jared push our way through the taunting crowd, and once safely back to Zadok's house, we barred the door behind us.

When Zadok heard all of what happened, he told Jared, "You must immediately take Abaigael and go to Damascus as we discussed. It will not be safe here for her or the child. Zimri-Ruel, go with them to Damascus and keep them safe. It is on the way to your village in the high hills above Khalab. Intercede for them with the Most High God. Give them strength and assurance that the Most High God is with them."

Zadok and Obed hurriedly packed provisions for our journey to Damascus. He placed the provisions and a saddle on Jared's donkey for Abaigael to ride, and a second donkey was laden with baskets filled with gleaming bronze spearheads. When you get to Damascus, seek the house of Keshet. He will introduce you to the arms merchants and direct you to the dealers of tin and copper. Once you sell the spearheads, buy as much tin and copper as you can and send it back here. Look for adequate space for a forge and notify me of the prospects of moving our work to Damascus. Do not forget to find a good house for your wife. She must be comfortable! And for a midwife, ask Keshet where to find a midwife! You must look after Abaigael. Shifra would never forgive me if any harm comes to Abaigael or your son, Abiel. Leave once it is dark, when the city is quiet."

As we waited for the light of day to dim into dusk and darkness, I encouraged Zadok. "Zadok, indeed, you are a faithful man and true father to your house. You have shown me more than hospitality. Your uncompromising faith in the Most High God has set a great example and will enable Shifra and Obed to share in your strength. You know what is expected of you, to love the Most High God with all of your heart and soul and to love all those whom our God loves. You know this will be a difficult walk, but you will not walk alone. The Most High God will direct your paths. Listen for His voice. You know how to sacrifice to the Most High God for the atonement of your sins. You know how to worship and love the Most High God, knowing He is worthy of our praise. You do not need another priest to make sacrifices for you or to lead you in worship. You may do these things as long as your heart is humble and contrite and your love for the

Most High God is true. The Most High God will accept your sacrifices, and He covets your worship. Learn to pray and listen."

When darkness finally settled in, the tearful goodbyes were said. Hugs were exchanged, and words of hope that all would soon be reunited were spoken. Zadok, taking it all in, finally commanded, "It is time. Go. Go in the safety of the Most High God."

Chapter Fourteen

"A just balance and scales are the Lord's; all the weights in the bag are His work."

—Proverbs 16:11

It only took a few days to arrive safely at Damascus. We arrived as the caravan from Egypt was being met by traders. Heavily laden camels were going into the city while equally laden camels and donkeys were coming out. Other caravans would come and go from the coast, making the city an important transfer city. Because the north-south trade routes intersected here with the east-west trade routes, everything and anything traded from the east, west, north, or south could be found in the crowded markets of Damascus. And if supplies were low today, another caravan would be arriving soon. As important as Damascus was in commerce, Jared explained the city was just outside of the control of Egypt to the South, which controlled Canaan, the Hittite and Hurrian kingdoms to the Northwest, and Sumer and Babylonian kingdoms to the east. The city was convenient and open to the competing empires, and for the time being, it benefited the competing kings to leave the city unaligned and unconquered.

As we entered the gate and began our inquiries after the house of Keshet, both the wisdom and difficulties of Zadok's interest in establishing a market presence here immediately became evident. He was certainly correct concerning the availability of supplies of copper and tin and the markets for weapons, but the city was crowded—

very crowded. I had not taken note of this when I came here with Terah. Finding a house, not to mention space for a forge, or even a market stall, would be difficult. Again, Zadok had thought things through very well. Keshet was well known in the city, and his house was very near the center of the market.

We easily found the compound of Keshet and entered the outer courtyard, lined with stalls and storerooms. Jared was led to another door and told to enter and wait. Soon, all of us were beckoned into an inner courtyard. It was a world apart from the crowded, noisy streets outside. Keshet appeared wearing a fine but not ornate robe. He walked forward as he spoke. "Jared, son of Zadok! You are welcome. So your father has finally taken my advice! Come in, please. Refreshments? You must be tired from your journey. Your wife, Jared? Please, if she would follow my maidservant. She must surely rest."

Once Abaigael was out of the courtyard, Keshet asked, "And who is this?"

"Master Keshet," Jared began, "this is my friend, Zimri-Ruel, a priest on his way to the hill country above Khalab. We have been traveling together since leaving Salem."

"Salem?" said Keshet. "Then he is no priest to Baal! Not if he was welcomed by King Melchizedek!"

"No, he is no priest of Baal. And that is why we come in such haste from Hazor. I must warn you, we have offended the priests of Baal in Hazor, and my father, Zadok, saw this as opportunity for establishing his market here. I was instructed to seek your aid in finding a market for new bronze spearheads after the fashion of the raiders from the north. We will need to buy tin and copper for more bronze weapons. I also seek a small house for my wife—oh, she is with child, so she will need a midwife soon. And then I am to look for suitable space to set a forge here in Damascus."

Keshet replied, "Yes, I know your father's plans. I have discussed them with him at some length. He has long hoped that you would establish his name in Damascus once you were ready and your family was settled. He has very high hopes for you. But come wash, refresh, and I will send for you later to sup with me. May I examine one of your spearheads in the meantime?"

"Of course!" Jared replied.

That evening, we were invited to eat at Keshet's table. He was head of a large household with three sons and their wives, daughters, and relatives. He welcomed us graciously, inviting us to sit near him. Jared was seated to his right. One of Zadok's spearheads was on the table in front of him. Once we were all seated and wine was poured, Keshet picked up the spearhead and said, "Your father, Zadok, is not the first bronze smith to try and copy the spearheads of the raiders from the north. It is really very delicate work to achieve a perfect balance with this design. But where others have failed, Zadok has excelled! Yes, I can sell these, or should I say I will put you in contact with the right buyers. All the kings of Canaan and, indeed, some of the Egyptian commanders are looking for the right arms. Did your father name his price? No, I expect he has not. I know he is looking for lasting trading relationships, and the price must be negotiated. I will help with your permission, Jared, of course."

Jared was surprised and unprepared for the apparent negotiation taking place. "My instructions were to sell, buy more tin and copper, and look for space in the city for a forge. He did not mention price or selling to you. He just said to seek you out."

Keshet smiled and said, "Your father, Zadok, and I have done business before. As I said, I know his plan. You see, Jared, this is what I do. I match special buyers with special sellers. You are, of course, free to open a stall in the market and wait for interested buyers where you will compete with other bronzesmiths whose work may not be as good as this fine piece, but their price may be lower. You see, Jared, the best buyers buy only from sources they know, sources who deliver the best quality at an agreed-to price and agreed-to delivery date. It becomes an issue of trust. While trust can be earned over time, the trust of a known third party may vouch for the product of a new producer. Did you have any trouble finding my compound? I am sure you did not. People know who I am and where to find me. I am the man in Damascus whose business it is to know who to know."

Jared asked, "Do you then set the price and the terms? And how are we to be paid? And you must be paid as well. I don't know these terms."

A CHANGED HEART

"Your father and I have come to terms on my payment already. You will learn how these negotiations occur, I have agreed to teach you. Tomorrow we will visit buyers. There are many interested, so you can be assured of a good price. There is time for this tomorrow. Now let us eat before this food gets cold."

While we were enjoying our meal, Jared asked, "Master Keshet, my friend, Zimri-Ruel, has told me the most wonderful account of his recent meeting with the Patriarch Shem here in Damascus. We would very much like to meet the Patriarch Shem, not interfering with your business on our behalf, of course."

Keshet turned and studied me up and down and said, "The Patriarch Shem is very old, and his health has taken a bad turn recently. It would be difficult to see him."

Staring directly at me, he asked, "Tell me of your visit to the patriarch. It is a rare and honored event."

I recounted to Keshet how I met Terah, who, with the most gracious hospitality, took me in and heard my story. I told of the caravan trip to Damascus and how he personally escorted me to see Shem. I could see his intense interest when I recounted Shem's words to me and his blessing.

When I mentioned that Shem said I had more to learn and that I should continue my journey to Salem, he interrupted me. "Of course! He was sending you to Melchizedek! Yes, Zimri-Ruel is your new name, and King Melchizedek sent you back as a priest to your people. Yes, of course, your name, Zimri, 'my praise,' certainly a priestly function and Ruel, 'friend of God.' You must have had a very special encounter! What was your given name, may I ask?"

"I don't have, or I don't know my given name. I was found on the road to Haran and raised by a village in the hills above Khalab as their slave, a shepherd. They called me Jael, 'the mountain goat.'"

Keshet chuckled. "Do you not know, Zimri-Ruel, that Zimri can also mean 'goat'? It appears your shepherding days are not over!"

I answered, "Now that you mention it, I was told that God had this against me—that I left his sheep. But Melechizedek told me the sheep God was referring to are the people in the hill country, not the village's flock of sheep and goats."

Keshet then shifted his gaze to Jared. "And why do you wish to visit Shem?"

Jared then told of his and Abaigael's visit to Salem, how they made their sacrifice in the absence of Melchizedek, and how they were among the crowd for his blessing. He recounted the scene from the wall as Abram, leading his host, was blessed by Melchizedek. He told of the magnitude of the tithe Abram presented to King Melchizedek. Jared recounted in great detail the special encounter with Melchizedek outside the gate. He emphasized the grace and authority of Melchizedek as he blessed them and announced the name for their son to be born and of his prophecy over Abiel. He described how he met me, sharing with me his walk and prayer with Melchizedek and his shared determination with Abaigael to serve the Most High God. He told of Abaigael's visions and duty to warn the Canaanites to repent, leave their idols, and follow the Most High God. He went on to say he was not prepared for the rejection of their good news by all except by his own family at the strong leading of Zadok.

"From the testimony of Zimri-Ruel," finished Jared, "it was the word of the Most High God given to my friend that directed his path to Salem. It was the word of Shem that told him a new name was reserved for him. And only Shem still lives among those who were saved aboard the ark. And it is Shem who still recalls hearing the clear, unmistakable voice of God. Abaigael and I seek Shem as one who speaks the word and knows the voice of the Most High God."

Keshet responded solemnly, "I do know Shem. He still follows the Most High God. And Abram too I know. Abram came to Damascus several years ago with a host of men, camels, and flocks. His wealth and power were overwhelming. He could have stayed as king. He too visited his Patriarch Shem, whose son he is by Terah. When he departed, it was widely rumored he was following the voice of the Most High God. He journeyed south throughout Canaan to Egypt, and even into the deserts. He has grown stronger and richer. I heard how he rescued his nephew, Lot, who was taken captive from Sodom in the battle of the kings. I too have heard of his great victories and his blessing by Melchizedek at Salem. I know he camps at the Oaks of Mamre. I often hear of his acts. My brother, Eliezer, is his steward. Ask Shem how he took my brother and convinced him to leave our family and chase after the voice of the Most High God. Yes, he left our business to live with and serve Shem in his desire to know more of the Most High God. And how did Shem repay him? By sending him to Abram as his steward."

Jared asked, "Then you will take us to see Shem?"

Keshet exhaled slowly and said, "As you wish. I will arrange it."

Abaigael, silent until now, spoke up tenderly. "We thank you, Master Keshet, for your hospitality, for helping the house of Zadok, for offering to teach Jared your skill. We thank you for honoring our request to meet Shem, which must weigh on you as you view the service of your brother, Eliezer, as a grievous loss to your house."

Keshet smiled at Abaigael and replied, "Perhaps after you visit the Patriarch Shem, you can convince me that the Most High God is directing our paths and that this is all, in some way, for the good."

The next morning, Keshet announced, "Time to meet some customers. I would estimate that you brought somewhat more than one hundred spearheads, yes?"

Jared replied, "One hundred sixteen, to be exact."

Keshet studied the spearhead. "How long did it take Zadok and your brother, Obed, to make these?"

"With the current forge and molds, they produce ten a day, but then with additional copper, tin, and molds, I believe twenty a day might be made, but then there is also the finishing work, the pounding, the sharpening, and the rivets, of course. Some of the less skilled work might be hired out..."

Keshet cut Jared off. "Now you are thinking like a Damascus merchant! Here is our first buyer, listen and answer when I ask."

We entered the courtyard of a fine house, and Keshet announced his name to a servant. In a short time, an Egyptian entered briskly. "My good friend, Keshet, what have you found for me today?"

"Just a sample today, but I'm sure you will find the quality unmatched, even in the best market stalls of Damascus. I have heard of a few unfortunate encounters of the Pharaoh's Canaan garrisons with raiders from the north armed with a particularly effective spear.

A spear with a head like this one." Keshet opened a pouch and handed the Egyptian the spearhead.

The Egyptian replied, "I can readily find spearheads like this in the market. You should know this, I have complained about them in the past."

Keshet went on, "Not like this. Bring a spear shaft and a hammer, and I will show you."

A servant was sent off for the shaft and hammer while we waited. Keshet took the spearhead back from the Egyptian, placed two fingers inside the base, clearly not touching any of the sides of the base, and, holding up his hand, demonstrated perfect balance. The spearhead didn't so much as wobble.

When the servant returned with the shaft and hammer, Keshet gave them to Jared and asked him to show them how to rivet the head. Jared placed the end of the shaft in the spearhead and hammered in the rivets, alternating from opposite sides until all were affixed. He then tossed the spear to the Egyptian. He wielded the spear with skill, balanced it in his hand, and let it steady.

Keshet said, "You may keep that one. Let your guard test it, though I can see it is not the first spear you wielded." After a pause, he continued, "Jared, you come from Hazor, long known for its fine bronze work. Tell me, do you have difficulty in obtaining enough good copper in Hazor?"

Jared answered, "The raids have made it difficult to obtain enough fine copper. The craftsman of Hazor have seen a great demand for bronze swords for the armies of the Canaanite kings. We have even used up our supply of finished copper and tinware. Not enough copper can be found from the merchants coming from Damascus. What we do find is very dear in price. Even unprocessed ore is difficult to find."

Keshet then turned to the Egyptian and said, "We can provide one hundred spearheads today, but I know you have need for many times that number. With access to fine copper from the royal mine in Sinai, we can provide you, say, four hundred spearheads a month as a start. If your garrisons find them to their liking, I'm sure something can be worked out."

Keshet paused again and then said, "I come to you first, my friend, but I also meet with buyers for the kings of Tyre and Usher, who have expressed an urgent need."

The Egyptian said, "Is not Tyre offshore of Usher, the import city of tin?"

"Just as you say," Keshet replied.

The Egyptian asked, "Jared, what is the ratio of tin to copper in your spearhead?"

Jared responded, "This is a stronger bronze, harder to make. It is six weights of copper to one weights of tin."

The Egyptian said to Keshet, "Go to your Tyre and Usher buyers, and tell them if they guarantee best price and access to the tin of Tarsus, they may buy fifteen out of every one hundred of any spearheads you make. Do you have any spearheads left for them?

Keshet replied, "We still have fifteen for them today, and we could provide them eighty a month."

The Egyptian smiled and said, "Of course, price will be established based upon my copper and Tyre's tin."

"It will be the best for all of us!" Keshet replied.

After a similar and equally successful visit to the buyers representing the kings of Tyre and Usher. We walked back to Keshet's house. When we arrived, he asked a servant to bring wine and fruit refreshments. He looked at Jared and said, "Our business today was successful because we met the needs of all parties. This is the second most important rule in trading."

Jared looked a little confused. "The second? You were masterful in knowing each party's need and putting it together perfectly? I don't understand? What then is the most important rule in trading?"

Keshet looked at Jared and me and said softly, "My older brother, Eliezer, who taught me everything I know, always maintained the first rule is trust. Without the trust of the Egyptian or the buyers for the kings of Tyre and Usher, do you think we would have had an audience? Without trust, you can at best sell to total strangers in a market stall. But even then, your business will die. Eliezer is nothing if he is not completely trustworthy, and I resist any temptation that will damage the trust my buyers and sellers have in me. Trust may take years to earn but one day to destroy. Learn from this always to be trustworthy."

A servant then walked up to Keshet and whispered in his ear. Keshet nodded, and as the servant departed, he said, "Shem will see you tomorrow."

Chapter Fifteen

"And it shall come to pass afterward, that I will pour out My Spirit on all flesh; your sons and your daughters shall prophesy, your old men shall dream dreams and your young men shall see visions."

—Joel 2:28

The house of Shem was just as I remembered it. The same busy servants crisscrossed the courtyard. And as before, once we were announced, Jared, Abaigael, and I were told to wait. Only this time when we were brought into the apartments, we were ushered into a bedroom. The Patriarch Shem was propped up in his bed, covered in fine blankets, his white head covered in a woolen cap. He looked much older and far more frail than I remembered.

"Is that you, my friend, 'the goat'? Come closer, Jael. And who is that with you? Come closer all of you. My eyes and ears fail me at such a distance."

As we approached, I said, "Patriarch Shem, yes, it is me, Jael, and these are my dearest friends, Jared and Abaigael. We have traveled together from Salem, and I have told them of your gracious hospitality towards me, of your word from the Most High God, and of your wonderful blessing. All of it happened in Salem just as you said. We have all encountered King Melchizidek, priest of the Most High God, and received his blessing. These, my friends, were anxious to meet you as one who has heard the voice of the Most High God, who speaks His word and walks with Him."

Shem quietly responded, "It brings an old man great pleasure to hear the stories of those who follow the voice of the Most High. It is a great encouragement to know that the Most High God still calls to men and that some still have open hearts and ears to listen. You must tell me everything that has happened! Hearing your story will bring me joy and help me to forget my current weakness."

I began, "As soon as my feet touched the road to Salem after leaving Damascus, a strange and wonderful thing happened. I heard sounds I never heard before. Not words but a song—a song coming from inside me and not of my own will. It crossed my lips and came from my mouth as strange to me but still my own. It was a song of praise to the Most High God! I sang halfway to Salem! I remembered your prayer for me, to be a voice of praise to the Most High God. As I walked the road by night and pondered all that had happened, a man in white approached me on the road. We walked together, and I told him all of the questions that raced through my mind. He answered each one, explaining why they must be. I learned later when we stopped at an inn and he was identified that the stranger was King Melchizedek! I spent hours and hours with King Melchizedek. He brought me to the palace. I attended a blessing he gave to everyone in the city. I sat by him at a wonderful banquet, and he shared with me events to come. He said I would see a man called by the Most High to be a father to nations. He said that Abram, the Hebrew, would be the father of a new nation, who will be a people of the Most High God. And from this people will come a tribe of priests—priests who will offer sacrifices to atone for the sins of His people. These priests would be instructed by God Himself in the sacrifice for atonement, in sacrifices of thanksgiving, for leading the people in worship with music and with appointed leaders to ensure no priest varied to the right or to the left but held fast to the teachings of God."

I paused for a moment, and Shem said to me, "Go on, I'm listening."

I continued, "The very next day, Abram, the Hebrew, appeared with his host outside the city wall. Melchizedek blessed Abram, and he blessed the Most High God for the great victory God gave him over the kings of Canaan who had sacked Sodom and Gomorrah and taken Abram's nephew, Lot, captive. Abram gave a tithe of one-tenth of all the spoil—a very large number of camels, donkeys, cattle, sheep and goats, and wagons of treasure. After Abram and his host left for Sodom, I went with King Melchizedek as he prayed in his garden. He told me God has this against me, that I left His sheep. King Melchizedek explained that it was not the sheep in the mountain fold but the people of the village that enslaved me. He told me I should love them and serve them. That to begin to love, I should forgive them. He said that the Most High God, first of all, desires that we love God with all of our hearts and soul and that we love all whom He loves. He made it clear that the Most High God loves all men and longs for them to return to Him. King Melchizedek told me the new name God had reserved for me, Zimri-Ruel. He commanded me to return to the village in the high hills above Khalab and be a priest to serve and intercede for His people. I immediately left and am on my way back to the village now. All the way, the Most High God has sent people in my path to teach me. He is teaching me how to love, for truly I have never loved anyone else before. And He is teaching me how to serve. I met my dear friends here, Jared and Abaigael, after I left Salem. But it is better if they tell the rest of the story."

The Patriarch Shem smiled and said, "The Most High God is God, and His mercy endures forever! All praise to Him! Jared and Abaigael, please tell me your story."

Jared began, "Patriarch Shem, Abaigael, my wife, and I are Canaanites from the city of Hazor. We had heard of the wisdom and righteousness of King Melchizedek, priest of the Most High God. We went to Salem to sacrifice to the Most High God and seek the blessing of Melchizedek to bless and protect the child Abaigael now carries. We had a son who died shortly after birth and a stillborn daughter. Some of my kin counseled me to put her away, send her back to her father, and marry another woman. This I could not do, for I love her so. We were consumed by our grief. When we arrived at Salem, King Melchizedek was away. No one knew where he was or when he would return. We sacrificed two doves to the Most High God and waited for King Melchizedek to return. Just as our money was almost gone, the king returned, and we tried to gain an audience.

We attended the blessing just as Zimri-Ruel described. We watched the blessing of Abram, the Hebrew, from the city wall. But when King Melchizedek did not return, we decided to leave, as our money was gone. We trusted that the blessing we received in the crowd and the sacrifice to the Most High God would avail. We left the city just as dawn was breaking and immediately encountered King Melchizedek returning from his prayer garden."

Shem nodded his head in understanding.

Jared went on, "The king questioned as to why we were leaving so soon and asked to receive His blessing before we went. He blessed us by name! He blessed our child and said Abaigael will bear a son and his name will be Ariel. He assured us that Ariel will grow in the knowledge that the Most High God is his father and that Ariel will steadfastly serve God his whole long life. It was after we left King Melchizedek and traveled the high road north from Salem that we awoke Zimri-Ruel with our conversation…"

Abaigael interrupted. "Husband, you did not tell him how Melchizedek knew everything about us. He knew our names, he knew of our reason of coming to Salem. He knew I carry our child despite my heavy cloak and the dim light. You did not speak of the authority of his presence, the love in his eyes, or the peace and grace he brought upon us."

Jared replied, "Yes, Abaigael is correct in all that she adds. Please, Abaigael, tell of your dream in Bethel."

Shem smiled at Abaigael. "Yes, please do continue."

Abaigael began, "We were at cousin Baram's house in Bethel. We had joyfully told Baram and his wife, Naamah, our wonderful news, but Baram would not hear of it. He brought out his household idols and denied the Most High God as an affront to the gods of Canaan. He loves no god but only seeks to appease the uncaring and unreliable gods of Canaan. That night in bed, I dreamt, or maybe saw, a man too bright to look in the face. This man, I think him a man, spoke to me. He said, 'Abaigael, you are a woman of tender heart in whom no bitterness can be found, as a mother crying over her lost children. I bring you a message from the Most High God, "The sin and wickedness of Canaan has reached my throne as in the days of Noah. I will curse Canaan. The day will come when this city, Bethel, will be destroyed. I will destroy this nation and give this land to a new nation that will be my people. But I will spare every Canaanite who turns from whoring after false gods and returns to me. I am a merciful God, and all those who repent will know that My mercy endures forever.'"

Shem motioned with a withered hand for her to go on.

Continuing, Abaigael said, "After we had returned home to Hazor, the night before the festival of Baal, the man too bright to look upon appeared again. He reminded me of the message I heard in Bethel. He said the same message is sent to Hazor."

Jared interrupted. "On the insistence of Abaigael, we attended the festival to urge no sacrifice be made to the false god, Baal. Abaigael climbed the steps of the temple of Baal and shouted the message she heard, intending for the people to repent. But they, being drunk on wine and aroused by the unspeakable sexual rituals of the priests of Baal and the temple prostitutes, shouted her down. 'Give her to the temple prostitutes. Let the priest of Baal have their way with her,' they shouted. I rushed to bring her to safety and, with the help of Zimri-Ruel, got her back to the house of Zadok."

I felt compelled to explain. "Outside of the household of Zadok, Jared's father, I know of no followers of the Most High God in Hazor. Zadock, an upright man and quick to believe the good news of Abaigael and Jared, is a man strong in faith and desires to walk with the Most High God. Concerned for their safety in Hazor, he asked me to accompany Jared and Abaigael to Damascus. We were to find Keshet and establish a trading house in bronze safely outside of Hazor. Keshet too is an upright man who is helping Jared and Abaigael. It is he who agreed to arrange our visit, though he believes you took from him his most loved and esteemed older brother, Eliezer. Keshet greatly respects the desire of Jared and Abaigael to seek the counsel of the patriarch who knows the voice of the Most High God and speaks His words. A man who walks with God and whose blessings God makes known."

Shem finally spoke. "Truly, the Most High God is working His will in all these things. It is a great blessing to watch as the Most High

God calls His remnant to Himself. At all times and of all peoples, God has made Himself known, and there has always been and will always be those who follow Him."

Shem gazed intently upon Abaigael and said, "The man too bright to look upon is the angel of the Lord. His words are the words of God, ever true and ever faithful. You were right to share them! You should rejoice, for you are a chosen vessel. Be vigilant to do all that he asks. Speak every word he gives but never attribute to the Lord any word that He has not given to you. You may seek Him in prayer and petition, but wait for His word."

To Jared, he said, "You have done well! Love your wife and be a strength to her, even as she submits to your authority. You are of one flesh and one soul, and it is the one True God you both serve."

Shem turned his gaze upon me and said, "You, Jael, now Zimri-Ruel, have you truly learned to love? Can you forgive? Do you love the people of Hazor? God has judged Canaan and truly will destroy the Canaanites. The people of Bethel and Hazor will fall by the sword, every man, woman, and child in these and many cities of Canaan. God shall surely destroy them because of His righteousness and their wickedness. Yet does He love them and long for them to repent of their wicked ways and walk with Him. There are many sheep and few shepherds. The shepherd must stay diligent day and night!"

Shem continued, "There are other things you should know. God is working His will. Abram, the Hebrew, is my son through his father, Terah. Abram follows the voice of God. As King Melchizedek has rightly said, he will be the father of nations. His people will be God's people, they will inherit the land, and from his family, a tribe of priests shall come who will establish a way of atonement for the sins of the people. They will be instructed by the Most High God in sacrifice and worship. They shall not turn to the left or to the right from the practice of their priesthood. They will teach the people of all that God requires of them, to love God with all of their heart and all of their soul and to love those whom God loves. This priesthood shall make known to all men their sin and that death is the consequence of all sin. They show that God Himself provides a way to atone for sin, the blood of the innocent and the righteous, for the sin of guilty and undeserving. This shall be a lesson to all people until the great day when God will raise up a great high priest and a sacrifice for all the sins of man once and for all time!"

Closing his eyes for a moment, Shem said, "I also know of Keshet. A good man. I know his brother, Eliezer, who came to me in his desire to walk with the Most High God. Eliezer too follows the voice of God. Eliezer is a man of great ability. He is a man with a servant's heart. Eliezer puts his trust in the Most High God, and it was the Most High God who called Eliezer to be a steward to Abram, to see that his host, his camels, his flocks, his trained men, and all who serve him are fed, clothed, and equipped as they follow the voice of God. Eliezer is called to serve Abram, as his paths are directed by the Most High God."

Looking intently, Shem spoke. "Now, Jared and Abaigael, hear the word of the Lord concerning your son, Ariel, 'He shall steadfastly serve the Most High God in the manner of Eliezer before him. He shall serve the sons of Abram as Eliezer serves Abram. Prepare him in the ways of the steward of the father of nations.'"

"To you, Zimri-Ruel, hear the word of the Lord, 'The thief and robber will come and scatter your sheep. But your sheep will know your voice, and you shall shepherd them safely to a new fold.'"

"And to you all I say, I will soon walk with my fathers, Enoch, Noah, and the Most High God. Give my blessings to your father, Zadok, and to Keshet. Pray for Keshet, I know his eyes, ears, and heart are open."

When we returned to Keshet's house, he was sitting with a cup of wine. He announced in a matter-of-fact voice, "I believe I found a foundry compound with a large oven, good storerooms, and comfortable apartments. It had been let to the former armorer to the royal Egyptian representative. I have taken the liberty of sending a messenger to your father, Zadok. How was your visit with the Patriarch Shem?"

Jared looked at Keshet with compassionate eyes and replied, "It was all a bit overwhelming. I need some time to collect my thoughts. Could we discuss it this evening once we are all refreshed?"

Jared and Abaigael went off to their room, and I went off to mine. We all fervently petitioned the Most High God that Keshet would yet hear His voice.

Later that evening, while Jared clearly and coherently related all that occurred with Shem, Keshet listened politely. When Jared spoke of Shem's account of Eliezer coming to him and obeying the voice of the Most High God by serving Abram as his steward, I could see the apprehension in his face.

I carefully added, "Shem too saw in your brother a man of great ability and a man who valued trust in every relationship. Do you not see, Keshet, that your brother trusts that the voice he follows is the voice of the Most High God? He chose his path. By his own choice, he follows God. You say Eliezer taught you that the first rule is to develop trust. Can you not trust the choice he has made? Can you not show him that honor? You are an upright man, Keshet, it does you honor. But you must also know that the Patriarch Shem commands us to pray for you as I am certain he himself does. You are a man with open eyes and open ears. Perhaps it is time you looked through your eyes and hear through your ears anew for the revelations and the voice of the Most High God."

Kashet got up and said, "I need some air."

He went out into the outer courtyard and looked at the heavens above. I followed a few steps behind. Looking up, I prayed, "Most High God, call out to Keshet. He must hear your voice."

Quietly, in front of me, I could just overhear Keshet speak. "Most High God, are you there? If only You would give me a sign."

A lonely but bright meteor shot across the clear night sky.

PART THREE

Learning to Serve

Chapter Sixteen

"And He said to him, "You shall love the Lord your God with all your heart and with all your soul and with all your mind. This is the great and first commandment. And the second is like it: You shall love your neighbor as yourself."

—*Matthew 22:37-39*

Walking the road north towards Khalab alone, challenged by what lay ahead and encouraged by what lay behind me, my heart was bursting with praise for God. It amazed me that the Most High God would choose to reveal Himself to me, a simple shepherd, and then use this same unworthy shepherd as His servant as God works His will and His plan for His people. I saw how God had been preparing me every step of the way. My only task now was to trust Him and to listen to His voice when He calls. It was so evident that the amazing events that occurred around me were of the Most High God. They certainly were not of me! If the Most High God could change me so completely, He must be able to change everyone else! I pondered why some people open themselves to this marvelous reshaping by the love of the Most High God and others remain frozen in the insecurity of a life unfulfilled by the richness of the knowledge of God. They choose to chafe in a halfway world with some authority and some dominion but apart from the freedom of knowing that this is His world. He has gifted it to us to enjoy as His special creatures, to see it through the beauty of His love, to walk with Him in amazement at all that He provides us. My thoughts of the love of the Most High God once again turned to song.

> O God Most High, who could know You and not praise You?
> You who cannot change have changed your servant.
> You have opened my eyes to see Your works.
> You have taught me with Your knowledge.
> It is by Your wisdom my path is laid before me.
> You have remade my heart within me!
> My heart was once dead to all others,
> And I chafed under the rule of men,
> You have shown me Your love
> And planted a new love in my heart.
> You live and move within me
> And bring forth Your praises across my lips.
> O God Most High, You rule in righteousness and love!
> O God Most High, my God, reshape your
> servant by Your loving hand.

As I walked along, it occurred to me that another change had come over me. I felt the pain of being alone. I missed my friends, my new brothers and sisters. I never before felt this strange sweet sorrow of happiness for dear friends now absent. I knew they were safe. I had rejoiced with them as Zadok, Shifra, and Obed joined Jared and Abaigael in Damascus in their new compound with all the new opportunities that the Most High God had opened up to them. Zadok became a most righteous head of his house. The whole house worshipped the Most High God led in worship and sacrifice by Zadok. Shifra and Jared fussed over Abaigael as Abiel grew within her, and Abaigael was certain that the Most High God had called her to be His voice.

Most of all, I was surprised, though I shouldn't have been, that after all the years of skepticism, Keshet too now followed the voice of the Most High God! He spent hours every day with the Patriarch Shem just as his brother, Eliezer, had years ago, learning the truths of the Most High God. And the Patriarch Shem, no longer confined to his bed, again spent his day recalling everything the Most High God told him in His clear and unmistakable voice. Keshet joined Zadok and his household in worship and sacrifice. He compelled his sons to attend, but they still needed some prayer. Keshet had taught me that not everyone responds to the call of the Most High God immediately; the times belonged to the Lord, not to us.

It occurred to me that the joy I found in being loved by the Most High God and in loving Him was connected to my love for my friends and enjoying their love for me. And when I was open to this mutual love, all of my old chafing under authority went away. It was as if the burdens of my servitude were lifted, yet I would gladly do anything any of my friends or the Lord would ask. In fact, serving them would only bring me joy! I would have to think about this. I must think of all that King Melchizedek, priest of the Most High God, taught me about love and serving.

Walking on confidently, remembering how I first heard the voice of God, it occurred to me I was drawn by the order of His creation. I had observed how all of creation fit together perfectly according to the plan of the Most High God. Only man chafed under this order having some authority and dominion over creation but still himself a creature. I learned from the Patriarch Shem and King Melchizedek that this chafing was the result of sin, man's rebellion against the perfect plan and creation of the Most High God. I remembered how God walked with man in the garden. God walking with man, walking alongside His creature in friendship and love, this was the will and the plan of the Most high God for mankind! Adam did not chafe under God's authority in the garden! He walked in love and friendship with God! This is God's will for man! If man seeks God's forgiveness of his sin, he can once again walk with God in love and friendship. And this is still God's plan for man, to walk in love with Him and with all those whom he loves! Yes! Of course! Love God with all of your heart and all of your soul and love all those whom God loves! This is what makes us all brothers and sisters. This is what stops us from chafing under authority! This is what lifts the burden of painful servitude and calls us to joyfully serve those whom He loves. I was not made to live alone on the mountain. I was made

LEARNING TO SERVE

to live in a loving relationship with the Most High God and all those whom He loves! By sending me back to the village in the hills above Khalab, King Melchizedek was not sending me back to repay for my sin, but he was sending me back that the pain of my old servitude would be lifted and I would be granted freedom and the full joy of serving in love!

> Walk with me, O God, my Father!
> Walk beside me every day of my life.
> Laugh with me as a young child chasing the spring lamb.
> Instruct me as I learn to shepherd the flock.
> Encourage me as I hone every new skill.
> Walk alongside me and tell me the mysteries of the night sky.
> Smile with me as I behold the wonders of Your creation.
> Lead us when I walk with our friends.
> Walk with me, and I can bear any burden.
> Walk with me when I face danger.
> Squeeze my hand when the darkness hides Your face
> Let me know that You are always with me.
> Sit beside me when I am old and cannot walk.
> Whisper your wisdom in my ear.
> Do not let me miss any hidden mercy.
> Tell me of every transgression and show the path of obedience.
> How I love to listen to Your voice singing over me!
> Walk beside me and listen to my love song to You.
> Walk beside me, O my Father, that I would
> always delight in Your will.
> Walk with me, my saving God, this day and forever!

How unlike any other man is King Melchizedek! He knew the needs of my heart. He understands the will and plan of the Most High God. He interceded on my behalf and instructed me wisely on my path in life. Who is like him? Who is like this man of mystery? No one knows where he came from, or where he goes. They only see his wisdom, grace, and connection to the Most High God. What was it Abaigael said of him? Authority! His authority was undeniable and unquestionable! The Patriarch Shem certainly hears the voice of God, but he sent me to King Melchizedek! King Melchizedek must be greater than the Patriarch Shem. Yes! In every way, he is greater than Shem. The patriarch speaks of what he remembers. He repeats what God spoke, and he listens for the voice of God. King Melchizedek is the priest of the Most High God, knowing God's will before asking or waiting as others who hear the voice. He is so different than any other man! King Melchizedek never spoke of himself. He never spoke of his past or his family. He never claimed authority or bore any trappings of kingship. He never justified his priesthood. He just is the priest of the Most High God! He is not only different than any other man, but he is different than any other king. There can be no other answer—King Melchizedek is sent by the Most High God! He puts all of God's revelation together! He demonstrates what the Most High God reveals about Himself and confirms what the Most High God asks of us! He knows our weakness and sin and leads us to repentance, intervening and leading us back to the will of the Most High God. His grace is amazing. He does not lecture, he does not condemn, he just opens our eyes and unstops our ears to the truth that we intimately know in our hearts to be true. If I am to be a priest to the hill people above Khalab, I must follow King Melchizedek's example. I must ask myself: what would he do? I must remember everything he taught me. *I pray, Most High God, that you would help me to remember the words and example of your priest, Melchizedek. Lead and guide me to serve and intercede for your sheep in the hills above Khalab to your glory and according to Your will.*

Throughout the days that followed, I rehearsed every conversation I had with King Melchizedek, repeating them aloud over and over, burning them into my memory. I knew I could depend on his words to refresh and renew my spirit in the days ahead. I knew I faced hostility and condemnation when I returned to the village. How would King Melchizedek address the villagers? He would be warm. There would be no condemnations or accusations. There would be accountability for sure. Then I remembered something one of his servants said about King Melchizedek while showing me to my room in his palace. He said, "He arrived one day when our city was torn by strife and deep division, and by the power of his person, he captured our hearts and brought about reconciliation and peace. We just trust him and made him our king."

I too must trust him and make him my king. And I must seek reconciliation with the villagers. Reconciliation—I must be reconciled with my village masters and they with me.

Chapter Seventeen

*"But when I say to the wicked, 'You will surely die,'
and he turns from his sin and practices justice and
righteousness, if a wicked man restores a pledge,
pays back what he has taken by robbery, walks by
the statutes which ensure life without committing
iniquity, he will surely live, he will not die."*

—*Ezekiel 33:14–15*

The road followed the base of the hills fronting the mountain range. The city of Khalab, with its massive fortress rising from a high rocky outcropping, appeared to the right and grew larger and larger as I traveled along. As the road turned away from the hills towards Khalab, I found the narrow path leading up into the hills. It had been many months since I came down this path at night, not knowing where I was going but determined to find the Patriarch Shem and hear of his account of the voice of the Most High God. Looking up the path, I could only see the dry, brown, rock-strewn hillside. I began to climb and pray, "O Most High God, walk beside into the village, strengthen me, and grant me Your peace and grace as I seek forgiveness and reconciliation with my former masters. By your grace, let them accept me as their humble servant."

After two hours climbing the narrow path, the village came into view. I saw it like I never saw it before—small and without even a hint of a wall for protection. And what was there to protect? Houses that were little more than hovels and made of stone, clay, and straw and with a few crude pens for animals with parched straw over sagging poles and a well in the center surrounded by jagged stones mortared with mud. The only sounds were the buzzing of flies and the occasional bleating of a sheep or a goat. Not knowing where to go, I simply walked to the well in the center of the village, drew water, and washed the dust from my face, hands, and feet. I drank slowly but deeply of its cool refreshment.

As the heat of the dusty path and the dryness of my throat were relieved, I heard a voice behind me say, "Is that you, Jael?"

And then someone said, "Look! Jael has returned?"

And another voice spoke. "He would not dare to show his face here again after the way he deserted us. It must be someone else!"

"No," said the first voice. "It is Jael. He has come back!"

I turned and saw the entire village circling around me. They looked surprised as they talked among themselves. Finally, the village elder, Dov, spoke. "So, Jael, you come back to us. Do not expect us to help you after you deserted us and left our sheep unprotected. We took you in. We fed you and raised you, and how do you repay us? You run off in the dark of the night like a thief and the scoundrel that you are! Why have you returned? To beg from us? To steal from us? Why are you here?"

"I have returned to seek your forgiveness and to serve you," I replied. "Not as I served you before but how I have learned to serve—faithfully, joyfully, placing your well-being above my own. I am no longer the Jael that snuck away in the middle of the night. I have followed the voice of the Most High God. I know that the Most High God is God. He made us for Himself. He put me in the path for you to find. It was by His will and His design that you raised me to become a shepherd."

I could see the surprised look on each face. Afraid to stop, I kept explaining. "Though I knew no love from you and, indeed, had no love for you, the Most High God meant all these things for the good. I preferred your sheep and your goats to all of you in this village. I found peace and solace in the mountain nights alone. With no distractions, I watched the night sky. I observed the ways of the creatures of the mountain and the pattern of the seasons. And I saw each of you, unhappy, fighting everything in God's creation, hoping to make your will prevail against the earth, the sky, the seasons, and other men."

I paused for only a moment. I could see confusion in their faces. Quickly, I continued, "All that I saw made me understand that the Most High God created this world and that all men are creatures of His creation having some dominion and authority over creation, but clearly no man is a god, and all men chafe under the authority of our creator. It was when young Hod told me that the rainbow is the sign of the covenant God made with the earth following the great flood and that Shem was saved on the ark with Noah that I determined to find Shem and hear of his story of hearing the voice of God. I have followed that voice all these many months and was commanded by Melchizedek, king of Salem and priest of the Most High God, to repent of my sin against you, to return to you, and to serve you."

Finally pausing for breath and looking into the eyes of each one present, I continued, "It is a good thing that you are all here. I come to seek your forgiveness for not loving you and for not serving you with all my heart and all my soul. Forgive me for loving your sheep and goats more than you. Forgive me for seeking isolation rather than your company. Forgive me for not sharing what the voice of God was speaking to me. I have repented before the Most High God for my sin and now ask each of you to forgive me as well. I will serve you as you need me. I will shepherd your flocks with you, I will work your fields with you, I will dig wells, I will repair pens and houses. I will do whatever you ask with you. But I will no longer dwell apart. I will be one with you, and I will share with you the wisdom of the Patriarch Shem but mostly the teaching of King Melchizedek. I will make sacrifices to the Most High God for you and teach the richness of praising Him in song. I am no longer a slave with no passion for work but a free man choosing to serve you with love."

I finished speaking and stood waiting for a response. Dov just stared at me, cold-faced and silent. Then Leah approached, took my hand, and said, "Come, Jael, you must be hungry. Come, I will make you something to eat."

LEARNING TO SERVE

As I followed Leah, I heard Dov shout out, "Jael, this is not settled! I will have more to say on this!"

As I meekly followed Leah, I could think only to say, "Thank you for the blanket and food pouch. I got them just in time for the first freeze and snowfall."

Leah smiled and replied, "Come, I will make you cakes and see what else I have." She studied me for a moment and said, "You have grown into a man. Where once your chin was soft and clean, now you wear a beard, almost full! The clothes you wear are not those of a shepherd. They are much finer than any to be worn in this village. You walk differently and speak so boldly! Yet it is indeed you, Jael, and I am happy that you have returned to us safely."

I sat on a thin rug on the dirt floor in the home of Leah. There was but one room with a small oven and fire pit in one corner. Another rug lined the opposite wall with blankets rolled up at one end. Even so, it was tidy and inviting, reflecting the warmth of Leah herself. I watched as she made the simple flour cakes and cooked them in the olive oil. It brought back memories of watching the women cook them when I was very young. As she poured a little more olive oil, I recalled the olive oil she sent to me before that first hard freeze. I remembered how the frozen olive oil that sank as I dropped it cemented in my mind the perfect order of God's creation. I thought how God had used the kindness of Leah to reveal the perfection of His creation. The Most High God could order the smallest things and events to draw us closer to Him.

I said, "Leah, sitting here, I am reminded as a little boy of watching the village women cook their cakes. I imagine you were one of those I watched."

Leah chuckled. "Jael, I am only a few years older than you. I was perhaps helping but certainly not allowed near the hot oil! But it is sad, I remember you never played with the other children. You were always kept separate. How much that must have hurt."

After an awkward silence, it occurred to me that Leah must live alone. "Forgive me, Leah," I asked, "but do you live here alone? I would not want to bring dishonor on your name."

Leah replied directly, "I am a widow. This was the house of my husband. We married about the time you ran off. He died from a fall chasing after the goats on the mountain."

"I'm very sorry to hear that. I should not have left the sheep…"

"It is not your fault," she replied. "Honi, my husband, was bored working the small stand of olive trees and grain field he owned and loved climbing the hills. He was adventurous and a bit careless. It is not your fault. And as for my honor, I will spend the night with my sister and her husband. There is no harm in giving you a meal. Let the tongues wag. I am already a widow."

"Leah, your hospitality is more gracious than that of Lord Terah of Haran, or even the Patriarch Shem. You will pay a price for helping me. I must find other shelter tomorrow. For your sake."

Leah paused from her cooking and then said, "There is no empty house in the village, and it is not likely you will be welcomed in another home as another mouth to feed. But there is the roofed pen for my animals, which now houses only one goat for milk. Part of it could be walled off and made fit for you and still leave room for my goat. You are a strong man. Gathering rocks and mortaring with clay, you could do that. And I cannot work the olives and grain field alone. I must pay a portion of my crop for your help. I would provide food and space from the pen in return for your work. The work is not hard and varies with the season, and you will have time for other work as well."

Her face changed again, her mood lifted, and she said, "I have never left this village, while you have traveled far. Tell me of everything you saw, everywhere you went. Who is this King Melchizedek? And the voice you speak of, the voice of the Most High God, tell me, please. I would gladly hear of it."

Leah listened patiently and attentively as I told her all that I learned and experienced since leaving the village.

The next morning, I began gathering stones to wall off the far end of the pen. I wanted to ensure a respectable distance from Leah's house. The stones and clay mud would be easy, and finding new poles for the roof would require me to climb the hills to the forest above outside of the rain shadow of the mountains. As I worked, I saw many of the villagers walking back and forth watching me work, looking but saying nothing.

Finally, Dov came by and said, "So you intend to stay after all. Looks like you are making it comfortable for yourself and convenient to Leah as well."

I stopped my work and faced Dov. "As I said yesterday, I have returned to serve you. I would not be a burden on anyone. Do you want to feed and house me?" I looked around at the villagers standing by. "Do any of you want to feed and house me? I thought not. I will live in my own house and work for Leah, but I will also serve you. Any of you. All of you. I am not your slave, but I will serve you and not burden you. Ask me. Try me and see if my word is true."

Once again, there was silence. Then I said, "Leah is a good and honorable woman. All of you know her kindness. I will not dishonor her."

That evening, as I ate the simple fare Leah could provide, she said, "You must understand Dov. He is a good man, and he wants to do well. He leads not because he is wise or strong but because no one else will accept the responsibility. Dov cannot stand indecision. He decides because no one else will. He makes decisions so we can get on with life. But know this, he is unsure of his own decisions. He decides and then worries that he has decided rightly. He must be encouraged when deciding rightly. You are a great puzzlement to him. He doesn't know what to do about you, and it is greatly troubling him."

I nodded and then replied, "Tonight I will sleep in the pen. It will be good for me to sleep under the stars one more time. Soon the roof will be finished and my shelter complete. You must show me my duties in the olive grove and grain field."

That night, as I lay under the stars, I thought about all that had happened since I returned to the village. I thanked the Most High God for the kindness of Leah. I considered Dov; he is certainly cautious and perhaps skeptical of my intentions, but no one else has spoken to me. I thought of how Melchizedek came alongside me on the road to Salem, and he asked me what weighed upon me. He listened—he listened patiently. I must be patient. I must be willing to listen. But how do I get anyone to speak?

The next morning, I went back to work on my hut. The walls were complete, but I would need to set poles across the top to support the roof. As I went to the well for more water to finish the last of the mortar between the flat stoned walls.

I asked one of the villagers, "Who now tends the sheep at night?"

He replied, "We take turns. Each of us takes his turn."

Then I asked, "Does Dov take a turn?"

"Yes," he replied.

"Do you still work together to gather the flock in the afternoon?"

"Of course, they don't gather themselves, you know."

"Then I will ask Dov if I can help you this afternoon. Where do you gather?"

He looked at me and said, "Meet us here two hours before sunset."

As we completed our conversation, Dov arrived. Before he spoke, I said, "With your permission, I will help you gather the flock this afternoon. I understand that each of you must now take his turn watching the flock by night. Since you are the elder, Dov, I would like to take your duty. You already serve the village as leader, let me do my share. When is my night? I am off to gather poles for my roof, but I will return in time to help. Is that acceptable to you?"

Dov just stared and said, "Yes, that will do. Be here two hours before sunset."

I managed to cut, trim, and bring back three long poles before the appointed time that afternoon. I waited as the shepherds gathered. I recognized Hod, of course, who first told me of the rainbow. And there were Jachin, Rouvin, and Matai as well. As we walked up the mountain, I asked if anything has changed with the flock since I left.

"No, but the grass is now scarce near the sheepfold, and the flock grazes higher up the mountain," Rouvin replied.

Matai added, "We saw the prints of a large cat recently, but it has not been seen near the sheepfold."

I then asked Hod, "Your story of Noah and the rainbow meant so much to me. Where did you hear it?"

LEARNING TO SERVE

Hod thought and then replied, "I overheard a traveler in Khalab speaking as I waited to deliver wool to a merchant. The man was a servant to a great lord traveling with his flocks, men, and many carts to Canaan. He was telling the wool merchant that he learned of it from the Patriarch Shem. He was a follower of the Most High God and steward to his master who, he claimed, was following the voice of the Most High God."

Jachin and Rouvin both replied, "It is just as Hod says. We were there. It is not often we meet great men when taking our wool to Khalab."

"Do you follow the Most High God?" I asked.

"We only know what we just told you," Hod replied. "We know that the people of Khalab worship many gods. They make sacrifices to their gods."

"Have you ever sacrificed to the Most High God?" I asked.

"No, we have never sacrificed to any god. We are poor people, we have no priest. We cannot afford to sacrifice one of our sheep."

After thinking a moment, Rouvin asked, "Should we sacrifice to the Most High God? Certainly, Dov has never told us to make a sacrifice. Does God command sacrifice? Will he punish us for not making a sacrifice?"

I answered, "Certainly, it makes no sense to sacrifice to an idol or to a false god. The only benefit is to the priest and his belly. And it does not make sense to sacrifice to a god you do not know. But if you know the Most High God, if you know His commands and obey Him, then you will follow Him and worship Him. Then you will know He is worthy of your praise and sacrifice not because he demands sacrifice from you to earn His goodwill but because He is holy and cannot abide the sin of man and has made a way to atone for this sin by sacrifice. But look, we are at the sheepfold. I will speak of this later. We should divide here to gather the flock."

Within an hour, each shepherd returned with a noisy flock of sheep. The shepherds would continuously call out and talk to his sheep. The voice of the shepherd brought a measure of calm and assurance, and the sheep followed willingly to the sheepfold.

Once the sheep were safely in the fold, the four shepherds anxiously talked among themselves. "Yes, I saw the prints too," I heard Hod say.

"They were very fresh," Matai added.

"The largest I have ever seen," said Jachin.

"I will light a large fire tonight," Rouvin replied.

"You have a great cat nearby?" I questioned.

Rouvin answered, "It has been in the area for the last several days, but it is coming closer to the sheepfold, and the tracks are very fresh."

"Let me stay the night with you tonight. If the great cat attacks the fold, at least one of us can raise the alarm in the village," I offered.

"I would like that," Rouvin answered.

"Please let Leah know I will not need supper tonight," I told the group. "Leave me a crook for the night," I said as the others started to leave.

As the sun set in the mountain sheepfold, darkness came quickly. I helped Rouvin light a large fire at the entrance to sheepfold. We hoped the steep rock walls behind us and the fire in front would deter the cat from coming too close. I took a torch and worked my way above the sheepfold to gather more firewood. My eyes moved continuously from side to side, and my ears listened for any sound. I know the silence of the great cat, but any hint of stirring, any out-of-place sound, would be enough to alarm me. The night was still and warm; I saw nothing and heard nothing. I could only hear my own uneasy breathing as I returned to sheepfold. This was not a night to ponder the heavens above or consider the perfection of God's creation. It was a tense night. We talked little. We sat in silence behind the wall of flames and listened. As I sat beside the fire, I heard myself singing softly my song of comfort.

> Walk with me, O God, my Father!
> Walk beside me every day of my life.
> Lead us when I walk with our friends.
> Walk with me, and I can bear any burden.
> Walk with me when I face danger.

LEARNING TO SERVE

Squeeze my hand when the darkness hides your face
Let me know that You are always with me.
Walk beside me, oh my Father, that I would
always delight in Your will.
Walk with me, my saving God, this day and forever!

Chapter Eighteen

*"Leave your offering there before the altar, and
go your way; first be reconciled to your brother,
and then come and present your offering."*

—*Matthew 5:24*

When Rouvin and I returned to the village the next morning, Dov was waiting for us. "I am glad to see you both return safely. Any sign of the great cat during the night?"

Rouvin shook his head and answered, "No. I think the fire and the steep rock walls are adequate protection at night. But we must keep careful watch both day and night until the danger is past."

Dov then looked at me and said, "Jael, I don't understand why you came back. You are different now. Not only are you no longer a boy, you are now a man but a most unusual man. You speak of the Most High God. I hear from the other shepherds you speak of priests and sacrifices. You say idols are false gods and their worship only enriches their priests. I am glad you stayed with Rouvin last night. Get some rest, and we will talk more."

When I went to the yet unroofed house I was building, Leah was waiting for me. "I have prepared something for you to eat. Eat first and then sleep."

When I finished eating, I got up to go out to my house. Leah spoke up. "Stay here, you won't sleep well in the bright sunlight. I will go and tend my orchard. It will be all right. My sister will go with me, so no one will question you being here."

LEARNING TO SERVE

I stretched out on the rug and immediately fell asleep. I slept deeply for hours. I awoke in the early afternoon to muffled voices and banging of wood. I got up and went outside and saw Hod, Matai, and Jachin lifting poles across the roof of my new house.

Matai smiled and said, "Jael, you may be a good shepherd and you may hear the voice of God, but you do not know how to set a roof pole. It must be set into the rock and mortared in place. Your poles would have blown off in the first wind!"

"It is my first roof. Thank you!" I smiled back. "Will the walls stand?" I asked.

"Yes, the walls are fine for an unskilled builder. You did not lay out the fire pit and oven. It should be in this corner, opposite the door. We will make sure it is done right."

Then Jachin said, "Go to Dov. He asks after you. We can manage here."

I found Dov in his house waiting for me. "Jael, come and sit. I would hear your story. You are a different man, changed in every way. I would hear how you have changed. What makes you a new man. Tell me everything, hold back nothing. I do not condemn you. I want to know this new Jael."

"Elder Dov," I began, "I had no love for you or anyone in this village. I had no family and no genealogy. I was alone. I was raised a slave to all—the only slave. There was no one like me. Alone, I was unloved and little more than a beast, valued only for what service I could provide. What you saw as service, I saw only as a means to survive. I served you only for the food and few clothes and blankets you gave me. I was not thankful. Happy was the day I could leave the village and live on the mountain among the sheep and goats. They gave me comfort. They heard my voice and followed after me."

Dov interrupted. "I was wrong. I know that now. We were all wrong, but it was my decision to raise you with no family. I thought we could all raise you. We could provide you all you needed. We would all be your people. I allowed no one to get too close so you would have no favorites. You would serve all of us together. I saw you were provided all the food you needed. I saw that you had clothes and a blanket. I thought that would be enough. I thought you would find that enough to live among us and work as one of us. I was wrong. I never considered the love of a mother and the guidance of a father. I gave no thought to the importance of a genealogy, of knowing who your people are, where you come from, and who will always accept you as their own. I thought you would see us as your people, that you were one of us. I was so wrong in every decision. What can I do now?"

"Elder Dov, you must open your eyes and unplug your ears. You must hear the voice of the Most High God. He knows your heart. He calls out to you to repent of your sin and seek Him. His command to you, His desire for you, is simple—'Love the Most High God with all of your heart and soul and love whom He loves.' The first step in loving someone is confessing your sin against them and seeking forgiveness. I forgive you and everyone in this village, but I did not forgive you when I left. It took time. I had to follow the voice of the Most High God. You see, He had a plan for me all along. All that you did to me prepared me. It was by His will that you found me and raised me. It was by His will that you made me a shepherd. But let me resume my story, and you will soon understand."

Dov replied, "Yes, yes, I would hear more."

I continued, "Living on the mountain, I was able to see the work of the Most High God. His work, His order, and His creation spoke to me. The night sky and the seasons all revealed His perfect order. The ordered life of the sheep, the wild beasts, the birds, and the fish all spoke of a creator. It was men that puzzled me. Men have some authority and dominion over the earth and all other creation, but men are not gods. Men too are creatures—creatures fighting all other creation, trying to subdue it and control it. Men seek to make creation serve them. Men must not hear or perhaps ignore the will and plan of the creator. The creator must care for all of His creation as men do for the work of their hands. And if the creator cares, He has revealed Himself, and then He must communicate His will to men. That is why when Hod told me of Noah hearing and obeying the voice of God, I had to leave. What was there to stay for? I determined to follow the voice of God."

Dov nodded his head in acknowledgment. I could see his eyes and his heart were open.

Going on, I said, "As I told you, I followed the voice of the Most High God. I had heard that Shem was in Salem, so I set out at night, not knowing where I was going. God led me to Haran to meet Terah, a son of Shem and Noah. Terah follows the Most High God and told me that truly the voice of God was calling me. He told me to worship the Most High God. At the time, I did not know what worship was and did not ask. Terah took me with him by caravan to meet the Patriarch Shem in Damascus. Now the Patriarch Shem was very old, but his memory was keen, and his eyes shone as he told me his story. He told me how the sin of man was repugnant to God. He told how sin grew among men and the stench of it reached the throne of God in heaven. Shem spoke of how God determined to destroy the earth with a great flood. God spoke to his servant, Noah, a righteous man, and commanded Noah to build an ark. Shem was with his father, Noah, his mother, and his brothers and their wives, and a remnant of every creature on earth on the ark, and God saved them from the flood. He confirmed everything that Hod had said about the rainbow. It is God's covenant with the world to never destroy it again by a great flood. Shem told me to go to Salem, that here was more I needed to learn. He also said that in Salem, I would learn the name the Most High God had reserved for me if I obeyed His commands. The Patriarch Shem blessed me and prayed that I would be a voice of praise for the Most High God. Before I left for Salem, Terah led me in a sacrifice of praise to the Most High God."

Dov quietly commented, "So it is true. The rainbow is God's covenant, not just a story told by old men."

He thought for a moment and then asked, "Will you teach us to make sacrifices of praise to the Most High God?"

"That is why I returned, but listen as I tell you of King Melchizedek. I must tell you the most amazing thing happened as soon as I left Damascus on my way to Salem. I heard a voice singing. It surprised me to learn it was my voice. I was singing. I have never sung before! But I was joyfully singing the praises of the Most High God in words that… in words that came not from my head but from somewhere within me. Words I knew but did not compose. It was a most wonderful thing! And to this day, songs will come to me, and I will sing praises to the Most High God! After hours of singing, my voice and body exhausted, I considered all that had happened to me. Questions, so many questions!

Dov interrupted. "You mentioned King Melchizedek?"

"Yes, I was about to say. I was traveling alone at night. True, it was cooler at night, but I had become accustomed to being alone. I like the solitude, and to be honest, I had found the company of our village painful. As I said, I was walking and questioning out loud as I walked. I did not notice a solitary figure, a man in white, come up beside me. He asked what troubled me as I walked. And as I shared with him my many questions, he answered them one by one, telling me why things must be. He even knew my questions, and he knew that it was the voice of the Most High God leading me."

"This man was a seer, a prophet of God?" Dov asked.

"Yes," I answered. "I never thought of him as a prophet, but yes, indeed, he must be. Well, we talked and walked all night. I learned amazing things. He taught me the Most High God, though He loves us, cannot abide any sin. Sin creates a great gulf that separates us from God. God, who walked in the garden with Adam and Eve, has cast all men from the garden to live and toil in hardship. But in His mercy, the Most High God made a way for the sins of man to be atoned that He might walk with them again. The sacrificial blood of a spotless, innocent sheep can atone for the confessed sin of a man. And once our sin is atoned, we again walk with God and worship Him, for He alone is worthy of worship."

Dov asked, "Why must the sacrifice be a blood sacrifice? Why not fruit or grain or anything else of value?"

"He explained that atonement for sin cannot be bought. The Most High God cannot be paid off like a corrupt official. When Adam and Eve were disobedient to the only command God gave them in the garden when they ate the fruit of the tree of knowledge of good and evil, they hid from God because they were ashamed they were naked. But in love, God provided for them. God killed blameless animals to make clothes of fur for them. Innocent blood was spilled. In God's wisdom, he provided atonement for their sin. So when we make a sacrifice to atone for a sin, we make a blood sacrifice to remind us that all sin results in death. It is not the sacrifice alone that the Most High God desires but a heart seeking forgiveness. That is why God accepted Abel's sacrifice and did not accept Cain's. God accepts all of our sacrifices when they are made with a thankful heart. That is why we can make sacrifices of thanksgiving with grain or the first fruits of all our harvest. But we must always remember that there is a cost to sin, and the cost is death. A price must be paid, but we will never have the means to pay the price ourselves. We must come to God, creator of all things, and it is He who pays the price on our behalf."

"I know nothing of sacrifice and worship," Dov said.

"I will teach you, but there is more to my story. When we stopped at an inn late at night before reaching Salem, the innkeeper was astonished and fell before my companion, King Melchizedek. I had no idea my seer, or my prophet, was King Melchizedek! He was such a wise and warm man, so unlike a king, so unlike any man I have ever met. We supped together, and after a brief rest, we entered Salem, and he had me stay with him in his palace. His authority was unquestioned. It could not be denied, yet he was always kind and gentle. The people of Salem made them their king not by birth or by right of conquest but because he came to Salem and brought the city peace and reconciliation between the quarreling factions. They told me they knew nothing of his past, where he came from or his genealogy, and they did not care. It was for his wisdom and grace and his own authority that they made him their king. He himself declared that he is priest of the Most High God. I witnessed his rule. He invited me to his table and honored me to sit beside him. He told me I would witness an important event. He told me the Most High God was not through with me."

Dov looked at me with a slight smile. "Lowly Jael, a shepherd boy from our small village sitting at the table of a king! It is almost unbelievable, yet you, Jael, you prove to us it is true by the new man you have become!"

"Truly, Elder Dov, I thought as you think! It is too amazing to believe, but it is true! Let me continue. I saw an amazing event. I saw a great lord, Abram, the Hebrew come to Salem with a host of trained men. He presented a tithe to King Melchizedek in thanksgiving for his victory in rescuing his nephew, Lot, and the people and belongings of the cities of Sodom and Gomorrah from the war of the nine kings. King Melchizedek made a prophecy concerning Abram, the Hebrew, that from him will come a tribe, a people of priests who will lead in making sacrifices on behalf of the people of the Most High God and lead them in worship and praise—a tribe of priests and musicians and teachers of obedience to God. But even these priests will serve but for a time, until a Great High Priest will come and will make atonement for sin one time forever."

"This Melchizedek then is a most remarkable man. At once a great king, a prophet, and priest of the Most High God! A man who speaks the word of the Most High God. His voice is true and must be heard! Truly, Jael, the Most High God has blessed you." Dov avowed.

"It is just as you say, I have been blessed. King Melchizedek told me there was one thing I lacked, the one thing God had against me: I abandoned His sheep!"

"And that is the reason for your apology when you returned!" Dov exclaimed.

"Yes, he spoke not of the flock in the mountain sheepfold. He spoke of you and everyone in the village. I confessed I did not love you. I did not love any of you. I did not love anyone. I did not know how to love. I tearfully confessed my sin to God. King Melchizedek told me God heard my confession and forgave me. He told me to return here and intercede for you. To be your priest and teach you to trust God and obey all of His commands for you. Then Melchizedek told me the name the Most High God had reserved for me. I have become Zimri-Ruel, my praise friend of God. It is my new name for my new life. Now hear, this is what the Most High God asks of you—you shall love the Most High God with all of your heart and all of your soul. And you shall love all whom the Most High God loves."

Dov looked at me thoughtfully and spoke. "Welcome, Zimri-Ruel. Be a priest for us and intercede for us with the Most High God.

LEARNING TO SERVE

Teach us His ways. Teach us to love Him, to worship Him and to sacrifice to him for the atonement of our sin. We are pleased that you have returned to serve us. Praise to the Most Hight God!"

A new song came from within me.

> I will sing of the glory of the God who made me!
> I will shout from the mountaintop that He alone rules!
> The valleys will echo with the sound of my rejoicing!
> I will proclaim Him as my Savior before the thrones of kings!
> I will not hide His righteousness from the humble.
> Or be silent before the shepherds in the fields by night.
> Listen all who hear me!
> Hear my story of the Most High God!
> He called unto me and set me free.
> He taught my heart to sing His praises!
> His Spirit sends praises across my lips.
> His mercy surrounds me like a blanket on a cold night.
> His love warms my heart.
> His grace lifts my soul!
> Listen once more, I will repeat His works of kindness.
> His story never grows old!
> Let me tell again of His love for me!
> I will sing of His mighty saving arm and His tender calling voice.
> O let me sing His praises now and forever!

Chapter Nineteen

"If we say that we have no sin, we deceive ourselves and the truth is not in us. If we confess our sins to Him, He is faithful and just to forgive us our sins and to cleanse us of all unrighteousness."

—*1 John 1:8–9*

The next morning, Dov gathered all the villagers and, in his authority as village elder, spoke. "Brothers and sisters, you have all have had an opportunity to watch and listen to Jael who has returned again to us. It is clear to all that the Jael who has come back to us to serve us as he claims is not the young shepherd Jael who ran off in the dark of night. This man, now among us, has all the skills of a shepherd, but he is a wise man with a true servant's heart. I have watched him since he returned. I have listened to his story at length. He has been received by Lord Terah, taught by the Patriarch Shem, and honored at the table of King Melchizedek in Salem, priest of the Most High God. Yet he is humble and has confessed his sin against us and asks for our forgiveness. He speaks of worship and sacrifice to the Most High God. Such things we do not know. He follows the voice of the Most High God and carries God's message and commands to us. He comes to serve us, to be our priest, and to intercede for us. His words to me ring true. No, this man is not the same bitter Jael who ran off. He returns a new and changed man just as the Most High God has given him a new name reserved for him before his birth. He has become Zimri-Ruel, my praise and friend of God! We will learn from Zimri-Ruel to follow the Most High God. To learn His will, to obey His commands, and to make sacrifices to God and praise and worship Him! Tomorrow, Zimri-Ruel shall make sacrifices to the Most High God to atone for our sin. For surely we have sinned against Jael. We made him a slave. We cut him off without a mother's love or a father's guidance. I ask that today you fast, that you eat nothing the rest of this day, and pray that the Most High God speak to your heart and show if there is any wicked way in you. Confess to the Most High God and tomorrow come to the sacrifice."

I could feel the eyes of the villagers on me as they walked away from the meeting. They murmured among themselves, but I did not sense any hostility or animosity. I sensed that the villagers agreed with Dov, that this time he got the decision right. Their mood was a combination of curiosity and introspection. No ovens were lit for dinner that evening.

I returned to my now roofed house. True to their word, Hod, Jachin, Matai, and Rouvin had finished the job nicely. I noticed a rug was unrolled, and several blankets were folded neatly in a corner—gifts from I know not whom—and I could not stop my tears when I saw them. The thought occurred to me that this was my first room in a home in a village where I belonged. The mountain cave was shelter but never a home. It did not match the rooms provided by Terah, Beram, Zadok, Keshet, and certainly not the palace of King Melchizidek. But it was my room, my house, my home. I have been welcomed indeed. Now I must serve them as I promised. Serve with all of my strength. Tomorrow I will intercede for them as their priest. I will make a sacrifice for them to the Most High God. And yes, I believe I can love them. *Please, I pray, Most High God, send me Your voice, that Your people here in this village earnestly offer their sacrifice. Speak to their hearts. Prepare them and prepare me.*

When all of the people were gathered by the well in the center of the village, I lifted my hands and motioned for their attention. "Brothers and sisters, it was by God's plan that you found me and raised me to be a shepherd. It was His voice that spoke to me in the silence of the mountain night. He revealed to me that He alone is God and creator of the heavens and earth. He revealed to me the perfection of His creation, the order that brings life and sustains all creatures on earth. Of all creation, only man chafes against God's order. Man alone, among creation, has some authority and dominion. But man is not God. In following the voice of the Most High God, He has taken me to lords, patriarchs, and to Melchizedek, king of Salem and priest of the Most High God. This priest of God is one sent by the Most High God. He showed me how all these things come together. We chafe because we lost what the Most High God gave us when we were created. We lost companionship and friendship with our maker. When God created man and woman, they lived in a garden. A perfect garden watered by the dew and home to every fruitful tree and plant. The Most High God walked with man and woman in the garden in fellowship and love.

"But we no longer live in the perfect garden. The Most High God does not visit us and walk beside us as He once did. We now toil in the land, scratching and digging, fighting weeds, thorns, and drought. How did this come about? Did the Most High God abandon us? Never say such an evil thing! No. Man and woman sinned. They disobeyed the one and only command given to them in the garden. Know this—the Most High God is a righteous God. He can be no other! God cannot abide any sin. It is abhorrent to Him. It is fully contrary to His nature. But know this as well—the Most High God loves you. He loves every man and woman and child who has ever lived or will ever live. The Most High God is all wise and all powerful. By His will and His perfect plan, He can restore us unto Himself by removing the sin that He cannot tolerate."

The people of the village listened patiently. I was different. They recognized I had changed. They found my story was worth listening to.

"The sin of man and woman in the perfect garden led to death. Man and woman ate from the forbidden tree and knew they were naked. They hid from the Most High God when He came to walk with them. They hid from the God who made them and loved them! What pain and sorrow they brought to our maker! But God, in His love for them, took the life from innocent animals for fur to make clothes for His disobedient creatures. Their sin brought death, and death is now with every one of us. Never forget, brothers and sisters, that the result of sin is always death! God took the blood of the innocent to pay for the sin of the guilty. That is why we are here today. We will shed the blood of an innocent to pay for the sin that we here today confess to the Most High God. A spotless lamb has been chosen, one without blemish, as a sign of innocence. This sacrifice is a reminder that our sin is ever before God until it is atoned. Atonement cannot avail unless your confession comes from a contrite heart.

"Come with me now outside the village. We have prepared an altar on which the sacrifice will be made and presented to the Most High God. The stones of the altar are unhewn rock. The handiwork of man does not play any part in the atonement for sin. Rocks as the Most High God has made them form the altar."

Each villager followed silently behind me as I led them to a rocky outcropping overlooking the village. While Dov quietly led the lamb, my shepherd friends carried kindling and firewood. Hod brought a lit torch. When we reached the altar, the kindling and firewood were placed on top. I waited until everyone was gathered around, and then lifting my arms towards heaven, I spoke. "Most High God, may this sacrifice atone for the confessed sins of Your people."

I then took the lamb from Dov and led it to the altar. As I walked, I unsheathed the fine bronze knife Zadok presented to me before I left Damascus and quickly slit the throat of the struggling lamb. I placed my hand in the gushing blood and then sprinkled the blood over the altar. I placed the now bloodied, lifeless lamb on the altar and lit the fire. I again raised my hands towards heaven and loudly prayed. "Accept this sacrifice and restore all these whom You love to stand before you clean and forgiven. Walk with us again, Most High God." I lowered my arms and spoke to the gathered villagers. "The Most High God hears every confession made from a pure heart. Now go, and with this blessing, may you love the Most High God with all of your heart and all of your soul and may you love all whom the Most High God loves. Go in peace."

As the villagers slowly walked back to the village. I approached Dov, who was standing with his eyes fixed on the burning lamb. He spoke to me as I stood next to him. "Every sin leads to death. Every sin? I have so many. And the innocent must pay for the guilty. That helpless, spotless lamb sacrificed for my sin? I never realized how much a little sin mattered."

"Elder Dov," I answered, "what you say is true, but consider also that the blood of this lamb can atone for every evil you can imagine. God wants you back close to Him, He desires only good for you. You must know both the cost and the reward."

We both reflected upon the impact of the atoning sacrifice we had just witnessed, and after a few moments, I spoke again. "Come let us return. I have so much more to teach our people. Today we learned to sacrifice for atonement, but worship is more than sacrifice. After the harvest, we will make a sacrifice of praise. Yes, we will learn together to worship and praise the Most High God."

"Yes," Dov responded. "We must learn to worship and praise. Oh, I should hurry, tonight is my turn to night watch the sheepfold."

"Elder Dov," I replied, "We spoke of this before. You are the village elder, you serve the people well. Let me, your servant, take your turn at the sheepfold. I came to serve you, and I intend to serve wherever I am able. I am still a shepherd, am I not? I will go tonight."

Back in the village, Leah was standing outside of my new house, once her goat pen. "You must be hungry after the fast, I know I am. Come, I will make us some cakes. I have a little meat today in payment for my early olives. Soon the olive trees will be ready for harvest, and I will press them for oil."

I quickly responded, "Yes, and I must help you! I must learn your work and share your toil. I must not forget what you do for me."

Leah answered, "I do not say this because you have forgotten me. I just tell you to let you know."

As I sat and ate with Leah, she commented, "I see you and Dov are becoming close. This is good. You can help each other. No one should bear the burdens of leading alone. I see his confidence growing, and he supports you before the people."

"Yes," I replied. "And Dov is hearing the voice of the Most High speak to his heart. He is, indeed, a righteous man. Please let me accompany you to the olive grove and show me what I must do. But tonight, I stand night watch at the sheepfold in place of Dov. I desire to serve in every capacity I can. I am a shepherd, and I am glad to help in shepherding. And soon I will be an olive picker and oil press worker!"

I paused and looked deeply into Leah's eyes. "Thank you once again, Leah, for your kindness. You were the first to make me welcome, and now as I recall, you have always provided for me."

Leah lowered her eyes and softly said, "Enough talk. Sit and eat."

As I joined the shepherds in gathering the flock and leading them to the sheepfold, I carefully looked for fresh tracks or signs of the great cat and saw none. Once all of the sheep were safely penned in the sheepfold, each shepherd made the same report. No fresh prints, no sign of the great cat.

"Perhaps the great cat has moved on to a less protected area," I offered. "Perhaps tonight, I can once again ponder the Most High God's starry host."

"All the same," Hod replied, "keep a careful watch."

"I will. God's peace be with you until I see you again in the morning," I answered.

The night wrapped the mountain in its cold embrace just as it had countless times before. I was comfortable with the fire set before the sheepfold gate and my rug laid behind it. I settled back and looked contentedly at the heavens above, filling with stars as the sky darkened. Familiar constellations appeared, and I named them as my eyes traveled across from the darker east towards the faintly lighter west. They once were my only friends and companions, and I sighed in contentment. It was as though we were being reacquainted after my long journey. It was good to linger again in their presence! One thing had not changed: the night sky still made me ponder my maker—to seek what He revealed of Himself. It was in the night sky that I first heard the voice of the Most High God, and He still spoke to me through it but in so many more ways. It occurred to me that even Melchizedek came alongside me in the night like a bright star with a new revelation from the Most High God. How peaceful this night was. How good to know the love of the Most High God.

As my thoughts drifted peacefully, I heard a faint snap. I thought it was a snap. Did I really hear something? Maybe not. Perhaps it was a snap from the fire? I listened intently. I heard nothing. *I need to be more attentive*, I thought. *Let me check to be sure.* I got up from my rug behind the fire and stepped forward a few paces. I listened intently and waited for my eyes to adjust to the darkness. With the fire now behind me, I searched the area in front of the sheepfold. I knew the glow of a great cat's eyes. I slowly and carefully searched. I saw and heard nothing. Assured for the moment that nothing was out there, I returned to my rug behind the fire. I instinctively picked up my shepherd's crook and held it upright beside me.

I was turning back towards the fire, just about to sit down, when a great force slammed my body against the rock. A massive paw had pinned my left shoulder against the rock. The lion was immediately upon me. Another paw was swinging towards me. Now I could clearly see the great cat, its mouth opened wide in a loud roar. Its eyes were large and bright. The fangs were just above my head. I shifted my body around the rock and managed to tear loose of the paw. The great cat quickly lunged, and as he did, I propped the crook against the rock. The shaft of the shepherd's crook impaled the cat as he came down upon me. I heard a scream from the great cat unlike anything I have ever heard before. He was on top of me, his great claws flailing and tearing into my body. My right hand managed to find my bronze knife under my belt. Quickly, I had it out and plunged it into the cat's neck and slid it forcefully across the throat. I was covered in the blood of the great cat. As the lifeblood drained from the lion, all of my strength was drained from me.

Chapter Twenty

*"He who finds a wife finds a good thing
and obtains favor from the Lord."*

—*Proverbs 18:22*

I remember the brightness. The light was too bright to behold I could not look upon it, so I kept my eyes closed. I heard a voice coming from the brightness I could not shut out. "You have done well, Zimri-Ruel. You are a good shepherd to the flock." I knew that voice, though I hadn't heard it in some time now, but I knew it. "My lord, King Melchizedek!" I cried.

"I am here, my friend. You have obeyed the command of the Most High God. You shepherd His flock with love and faithfulness. The hearts of men are hard to win. You have learned that if your heart remains faithful and you follow the voice of the Most High God, trusting in His will, He will direct your path. He will honor your work. He will show the faithfulness of your message and convict the hearts of men. Your service will be hard. You will find it easier to face the jaws of the hungry lion than to persevere the troubles ahead. You will recover from your injuries. Remember, your flock will be scattered in the days ahead. But you will gather them once again. Be aware, that serpent, Satan, will attack the shepherd to separate you from the sheep. Remain steadfast! They will hear your voice and follow you. The Most High God will be with you. Even in the darkest night, you are not alone. In His strength he will protect you. His love will never depart from you. But you should not be alone. Do not fear to take Leah for your wife. She completes you, and you complete her. Together you must prepare the sheep of my flock. May the grace and the power of the Most High God be a shield over you until you are called to walk alongside Him forever."

With my eyes still closed against the brightness shining all about me, my soul began to sing.

>The brightness of the glory of the Most High overwhelms me!
>Who can look upon Him and not be blinded by His light!
>His righteousness is beyond my power to comprehend.
>He is my shield and defender.
>He stops the mouth of the lion.
>He leads me in paths only He knows.
>His love will never depart from me.
>He is my constant companion,
>He will keep me ever in His sight.
>I will serve the Most High God with my whole heart.
>I love Him because His love delivers me from all danger.
>I love Him with a pure heart, but His love will always be greater.
>Oh, praise the Most High God with me!
>He alone is worthy of all our praise!
>Oh, that I may walk with Him forever!

I once again tried opening my eyes. The bright light was gone. I saw only the concerned face of Leah watching over me. It hurt to smile, but I could not stop from beaming at her face. "How fine you look, Leah," I quietly said. I saw a tear fall from her eye. She did not wipe it away, so I caressed her cheek as softly as I could. I will never forget the first time I felt the tenderness of her face.

"Oh, thank the Most High God you have come back to me! You have come back to all of us!" She smiled and cried. "I see color coming back to your face. I thought I had… we had lost you. Don't try to move." She scolded. "You were very badly mauled. Your wounds will take time to heal. You are wrapped tightly in bandages and herb and spice leaves. You must not lose any more blood."

LEARNING TO SERVE

I looked at her with warmth, and I was overwhelmed by the beauty I beheld. I finally was able to say meekly, "I am too weak to move, but it is pleasant just to look upon your face. Come close and sit beside me."

Leah leaned over me and said, "I heard you singing. Just now, just before you opened your eyes, you were singing. You always surprise me. You are on the edge of death after being mauled by a great cat, and you sing?"

I replied, "It must have been my dream. I clearly remember seeing a light too bright to behold. I had to keep my eyes closed. And then I heard the voice of King Melchizedek, priest of the Most High God. He spoke to me. He said I would recover from my wounds. He told me that troubling times are ahead and that I must, we must, prepare for them. He gave me a word concerning you."

"A word concerning me?" Leah asked.

"Yes, concerning you. And after his voice departed, I began to sing. Surely you know how I love to sing praise songs to the Most High God?"

"Yes, yes, I know you sing," Leah replied. "Aren't you going to tell me the word he spoke? I too was told a word concerning you by a stranger who came to see you two days ago. But first tell me the word you heard."

My words stumbled out. "It is hard for me to say. Not undesirable hard but hard because I do not know what you will say. I do not want to be disappointed."

"What was the word?" she gently asked again.

I hesitantly told her, "King Melchizedek told me not to fear taking you as my wife." I waited and then continued, "He said you complete me and I complete you." I stopped and looked at her.

A look of amazement crossed her face. "The stranger who came to visit you two days ago spoke to me just as he was leaving. He said to me, 'Leah, you would be good to marry Zimri-Ruel when he asks you.' And then he left."

I watched her carefully and said, "Tell me about this visitor. Who was he?"

I could see the confusion in her face. She began, "It has been a week since you were found under the dead body of the great cat. There was only the slightest sign of life when the shepherds brought you here. I cleaned you and dressed your wounds. I have sat beside you ever since, barely taking time for a light meal. Two days ago, while you were lying here close to death, a man entered, apologized for surprising me, and asked if Zimri-Ruel was here. I told him, 'Yes, come and look upon him.' He came and sat beside you, whispering over your ear."

"What did this man look like?" I interrupted.

"He was dressed in fine white robes, middle-aged, and stately in appearance, though he had no airs about him. But there was something different about him; there was a warmth and an authority. He never said who he was, but he sat beside you for hours. After a time, he leaned over, kissed your forehead, and held your hand close to his heart. He stood up and lightly touched my shoulder. That's when he said, "Leah, you would be good to marry Zimri-Ruel when he asks."

Leah continued, "I thought that very strange. When Dov came by yesterday, I asked him about the stranger. Dov replied he knew of no strangers visiting the village. He asked everyone. No one sent him to my house. I don't know who he was, where he came from, or where he went. I don't know how he knew my name, but somehow I will never forget him. He was unlike anyone I have ever met."

I smiled at Leah and said, "You have met King Melchizedek. He came upon you just as he came upon me that night on the road to Salem. He was here speaking to me, and I heard his voice in my dream. His word is true. He is the priest of the Most High God and intercedes for us. Marry me, Leah. King Melchizedek rightly says you complete me. I pray that I may complete you as well. The Most High God has willed that we serve Him together."

A sweet smile came across Leah's face. "Are you asking for a wife or just a fellow servant?" She teased.

"I am after your olives, don't you know?" I teased back, blushing.

Our eyes met again, and I gazed their depth, the wellsprings of all her beauty, and heard her say sweetly, "Yes, I will marry you. But only because you do complete me. And I do love you."

LEARNING TO SERVE

I replied, "Is there anyone I should ask? Is there anything I must do? This is new territory for me. I know nothing of marriage. I never thought it would happen for me. I have answered the call to serve the Most High God, and now He blesses me with the love of a woman and the joy of finding a bride."

"Zinri-Ruel," she responded, "I am a widow, and my father is buried. It is only me, and now it will be us."

Sheepishly, I asked, "What must we do to be married?"

Taking my bandaged hands, careful not to hurt my wounds, Leah said, "The custom for those to be married is to make a contract between them that assures that both agree to the marriage. It tells what dowry or gifts each side brings to the other. The village elder can witness the contract. Once the contract is made, the ceremony can be planned, which is usually followed by a feast."

As soon as Leah finished, I exclaimed, "Send for Dov at once to witness our contract!"

The pain in my body quickly left me as joy filled my heart to bursting. Leah too smiled and then began to laugh. "Be careful, Zimri-Ruel. I want you strong and healed for our wedding day."

Dov was overjoyed to see me awake and alert, but he was stunned to learn why he was summoned. "You want me to witness your marriage contract? You are lying in bed, fortunate to be alive after you were badly mauled by a lion, but you want me to witness a marriage contract?"

"Exactly," I nearly shouted. "I have never felt more alive than now. And it is my wish, that is, it is our wish, Leah and I, to marry."

Dov looked at Leah. "Is this true?"

Leah smiled and nodded her head. "Yes, it is true, this is our wish. And we need a witness for the contract."

Elated, Dov smiled and said, "As you wish. But custom demands witnesses from both families. Leah, we can ask your sister, Semira, to witness for you. And, Zimri-Ruel, I can think of no better family for you than the shepherds. We will all witness your contract. You both are sure of this? Yes, I can see by your faces that you are."

Not an hour passed before all of the witnesses were present. Dov, the village elder, presided, speaking first to Semira. "Do you, as

Leah's surviving relative, agree to witness a marriage contract on her behalf?"

The simple reply came, "Yes, I do."

And to the shepherds, Dov asked, "Do you four accept the role as relative to Zimri-Ruel and agree to act as his witness to a marriage contract?"

Hod was about to make light of his answer, but Matai cut him off. "We gladly act as witness for our brother, Zimri-Ruel."

Dov then asked Leah, "What gifts do you bring to the betrothal?"

Leah quickly answered, "I bring my house, my pen, that is, the new house Zimri-Ruel built. I bring my olive grove and press. I bring my grain field, and all that I own, I will gift to my husband."

Dov turned to me. "Zimri-Ruel, what gifts do you bring to this betrothal?"

I own nothing, I thought, *except the clothes on my back*. The cloak, the rug, the blankets were all gifts from others. I nearly panicked—I had nothing! But I realized I had the one true thing that a man could give his wife. I had love, and all those years ago, it was Leah who showed me what love looked like—a warm cooked cake, a blanket for a cold body, provisions to survive a cold stay on the mountain, and a meal when I returned and repented. I replied humbly, "I gift Leah all that I have, meager as it is. But more than anything, I gift Leah my love, service, and support. I will be faithful to her and love her all her days until we are called to walk with the Most High God."

Dov paused for a moment and said, "Leah, do you accept these gifts from Zimri-Ruel and agree to marry him?"

Leah replied, "I do."

Dov continued, "Zimri-Ruel, do you accept the gifts of Leah and agree to marry her?"

I replied, "I do."

To the witnesses, he then said, "By your presence here, you are witnesses to the marriage contract and that this man, Zimri-Ruel, and this woman, Leah, are now betrothed to be married."

Then to us, he asked, "When do you intend for the marriage ceremony?"

Leah answered for us, "As soon as Zimri-Ruel is up and walking!"

LEARNING TO SERVE

Dov then announced, "Under the circumstances, there is no possibility and no need for you, Leah, to live in the house of the groom's father before marriage. I pray blessings and happiness for you both. And, Zimri-Ruel, my brave friend, rest and heal!"

After two months, I was walking, though not well and certainly not without pain. I had no shortage of visitors in my small house, and I heard over and over the story of the shepherds finding the dead lion lying on top of me. Each said they were sure I was dead, but after dragging the great cat off of me, they detected the smallest of breath still in me. They were amazed that the staff of my shepherd's crook had impaled the beast, and yet he still continued to maul until his throat was cut. I was praised over and over for my bravery. They would not hear that I was caught by surprise, and only the mercy of the Most High God saved me. I had no memory of any plan to fight such a great cat. Throughout my recovery, Leah provided meals and insisted all the planning for the wedding feast was taken care of; my only task was to recover. I never saw her without a smile—a beautiful smile that I will never forget.

The marriage ceremony was simple. At the appointed time, Leah came to live under my roof in accordance with tradition. Dov and the witnesses asked if the terms of the contract had been met, and we were acknowledged as husband and wife. The feast, on the other hand, was a wondrous event. Everyone from the village attended. The men and women feasted separately on roast lamb, raisin and fig cakes, small cakes cooked in oil, fresh fruit, and wine! I don't know how Leah put everything together, but it was a joyous occasion, and she was honored by everyone. Only when the food and wine were gone did the wedding guests reluctantly return to their homes. After the feast, we quietly returned to her house, now our more comfortable house. The time of great blessing and peace began in my life as Leah and I began our life together. I learned to tend the olive trees, to press the oil, and to milk the goat. I learned that tilling the soil was, indeed, hard work. Keeping the small grain field free of weeds was a constant chore. I still took my turn at the sheepfold, and I was very happy.

After the harvest, I led the village in sacrifices of thanksgiving. All the village joined in the ceremony and a special feast. I taught the people all that King Melchizedek had instructed me. We learned to sing together praises to the Most High God. I observed a change in the village life. People were smiling, and offers of helping one another were common. A sweet peace and unity was holding us all together. It occurred that this is what men look like when they do not chafe against the will of the Most High God. Man can learn to love the Most High God with all his heart and all his soul, and indeed man can love those whom God loves. I felt loved by my brothers and sisters and loved and fulfilled by my wife.

My joy was multiplied when Leah gave birth to our son. I proudly named him Adniel, meaning "of God's flock." What better name, I thought, for the son of a shepherd called to serve a flock of the Most High God! I do not have words for the happiness Leah and I shared. My nights on the mountain watching the sheepfold had changed, and try as I did, I could no longer find the total peace and focused observation of God's created order. I knew it was there. I knew it was true, but my thoughts would always turn to Leah and little Adniel.

As Adniel grew, so did our prosperity. The entire village became prosperous. The weather remained remarkably good. The rains came in the appointed time. The grain, the grapes, the figs, and the olives surrounding the village yielded good and dependable crops. The sheep and goats multiplied. The wool yield grew, and meat became plentiful in our diet. When Dov would lead villagers to market in Khalab, our crops and wool fetched good prices. We were told how remarkable our crops appeared since the surrounding territory was suffering drought. I remember the day Dov returned from Khalab with a yoke of oxen and a young bull. The oxen made the tilling of every field less laborious, and they could tirelessly turn the olive press. We had, indeed, become a prosperous village! Adniel was joined by a sister, Deborah. Leah glowed. I grew contented.

I cherished the time of blessing. Such joy could be found in the most humble of houses if it was filled with love. My children! Oh, what a sweet blessing from the Lord! Even my work brought me joy.

LEARNING TO SERVE

My fellow shepherds were brothers indeed. And Tizvi and Guri were always ready to help in the olive grove or grain field. Elder Dov, such a dear friend, we would talk for hours. His concern for everyone in the village was most genuine, but I believed it was Leah's cooking that brought him most days before supper. My service as priest to the people I loved was truly a service of joy.

The days of blessings became years of blessing, but in the back of my mind, I remembered the words of Melchizedek. What did he say? "You must prepare your flock. There will be troubles ahead. Your flock will be scattered, but they will hear your voice, and you will gather them together again." *How do I prepare them? I have not been diligent in my duties. I must prepare them. They are happy. They see all this prosperity coming from the Most High God. Will they hold steadfast in the troubles that are surely coming? Troubles worse than a preying lion?*

After one of Dov's trips to Khalab, I asked him, "Elder Dov, any news from Khalab?"

Dov looked at me and answered, "Zimri-Ruel, how strange it is that you ask me for news of Khalab! You are the one man in this village least interested in anything outside of the village! There is always news in Khalab! Every caravan that stops at Khalab bring news. I don't take it to heart. The squabbles of the kings of Egypt and Mari of Khalab and Ebla or this new king of the Amorites have no interest to me. There are always stories of new wars and attacks and fighting among the city states. But as you ask, I was told of recent attacks on caravans and small towns near Khalab. Bands of raiders from the north and the east have tried to steal from the caravans. But the caravans have added the numbers of their trained men. Now the raiders look for undefended villages and easy flocks. All the kings complain to the great kings, but the great kings do not send their armies out against the raiders. It is said they are too busy fighting among themselves. You look worried, Zimri-Ruel. Do you have a word from the Most High God? Are we no longer safe?"

I studied the face of Dov, now my most trusted friend, and replied, "I did not wish to alarm you. Before I even returned here, King Melchizedek gave me a word. He said, 'Your sheep will be scattered, but they will hear your voice and follow you.' And again, I had a vision when the lion mauled me, before I recovered, King Melchizedek came to me and said, 'Prepare your people. Hard times will come, and your sheep will be scattered, but they will hear your voice and follow you.'"

A startled look crossed Dov's face. "That was over ten years ago! And you never shared it with us? You never thought to warn me, the village elder? I don't understand. Did not King Melchizedek say in the vision prepare?"

I cast my eyes down, sighed, and said, "I know, I know. The vision and the words have never left me. I wanted you and our village to understand the love of the Most High God and to love Him as well. I first wanted you to trust Him. I know you trust Him as much as I do. And then things went so well. The blessings. Leah came into my life and then my son, Adniel. I never imagined such blessings could be. Yet they came to me and not me only but all of us. You are right to be angry with me. It is not yet too late. We can prepare for the hard times and still know the love of the Most High. We are strong enough, I am sure, with help of the Most High God, to live in His power. His mercy is forever!"

Dov called the men of the village together. He soberly addressed the potential for danger. "Brothers," he began, "as any of you who have travelled to Khalab or beyond well know, raiders from the north have been active not far from Khalab. The king of Ebla, overlord to our king of Khalab, has not pursued them or forced them from the land. His army stays in his city, while the king quarrels with his vassal kings. The Most High God has blessed us with good harvests and fine flocks. Our growing wealth has not gone unnoticed by the merchants. It is, therefore, wise that we prepare lest we become the prey of the raiders. We must not speak of our village to the traders. We must not tell outsiders how to find us. We must be able to defend our families. Every man should have a sword and a knife. He should have a spear or a bow. Our priest, Zimri-Ruel, has received a word from the Most High God that hard times are coming, and we should prepare. The word to our priest, Zimri-Ruel, is, 'Your flock shall be scattered, but they will hear your voice and follow you.' The Most

LEARNING TO SERVE

High God has blessed and made us wealthy. Now we must trust Him and prepare for when the hard time comes!"

Hod spoke first. "What you say is good. I have heard of these raiders. We should have a plan if they come up our mountain."

Matai added, "We should keep a watch on the path from well above."

"Yes," added Rouvin. "And we can store supplies in caves above the village if we must flee. There are many small caves, none are large enough for all of us, but we can disperse among them. We can appoint a captain for each cave."

Dov nodded. "Yes, these are good plans! Flee if we can, but fight if we must! But we must have a meeting place for the captains. Some place each can find without being seen from the village. And we must carefully select our watch station. Two men must wait there. One can return with the warning, while the other watches the way of the raiders."

Jachin was listening intently but finally spoke. "We shepherds can do this while tending the sheep. We will lead the flocks close by the watch station and establish sheepfolds at the caves."

Dov again nodded his approval and then asked, "How do we warn those in the fields and the groves?"

I answered, "We must watch for each other. Each household can send word to those in the fields and groves to meet at the safe haven. But we must make sure no one is overlooked. We must love each other enough that no one is overlooked. The Most High God has made us strong. He is the God who saves! He will direct our paths if we trust Him."

Dov told the shepherds to find the best watch station and caves and take him there for his inspection.

That night, Leah listened quietly as I told her of the meeting with Dov and the village men. She said nothing as I explained that caves will be found for all of us. I explained that food and provisions will be stored in the caves and that the sheep would be folded nearby. I repeated the plan for warning and the duties of the cave captains. Through the whole discourse, she said nothing.

When I finished, she glanced at Adniel sleeping nearby and asked, "How long have you known we were at risk?"

"Since my time in the garden of King Melchizidek and again in my vision when he told me not to fear taking you as wife," I answered.

"I would have hoped for more trust on your part," she replied. "What else have you withheld from me?" she ventured. "What word has the Most High God spoken of me or of Adniel?"

I softly answered, "He spoke as I told you that you complete me and I complete you, and so it will ever be. And it is true today as ever. I have been contented by the blessings of the Most High God. I have been contented with the joy of seeing His flock prosper. It must be His will that I now warn You and Dov and all whom we love. I should have trusted you. But now I somehow know that our trust in the Most High God will be tested. I am commanded to be steadfast when the attack comes. God will be with us."

She sat quietly gazing at me and then leaned over and gently kissed me. "Come to bed," she said.

In the weeks that followed, a new routine was established. A watch post was set on a cliff side perch just above the village. Most of the path up the mountainside was in view. In the far distance, the city of Khalab could be seen with its fortress rising from the table rock. With the village below the watch post, a runner could quickly descend with the warning. Six caves were identified that together could accommodate all the villagers. Each of the four shepherds plus Dov and myself were appointed captains. It was thought as shepherds, we who were most familiar with the mountain, could find our way in the dark and could gather the sheep to the new folds as well. Everyone brought what they could to the caves—grain, oil, raisins, figs, water, and wine. Blankets and utensils were at the ready. Families had practiced responding to the alarm, running first to the fields and groves to warn those tending crops and retreating by the most covered and protected route to the family cave. Dov and the shepherd captains were satisfied with the preparations. I could not help but worry about this flock, all of whom I have grown to love.

The questions came back: have I prepared them? Is this in response to the will of the Most High God, or is it folly born of the guilt and worry of a man grown too contented? Am I trusting in the Most High God, or am I trusting in the plans of men? O God, shepherd Your sheep!

As the questions and doubts swirled about my head, the words came softly across my lips.

> O God, I know of Your love for Your sheep!
> Great Heavenly King, Your loving-kindness
> Brings blessings to all the sheep of Your flock.
> With every good thing, You have blessed us.
> We know Your love, O Most High God,
> Now help us to trust in Your saving arm.
> Be our Shepherd and sit before the gate of the fold.
> Watch over us, Your flock, in the dark of night.
> May every lamb be secure.
> Save us from the bear, the wolf, and the lion.
> Let no thief or robber enter the fold.
> You have made us content in Your goodness.
> Now make us strong in our faith.
> We praise You, for who can deliver us but You?
> Praise the Lord, the Most High God!

Chapter Twenty-one

*"Save Your people and bless Your inheritance;
be their shepherd and carry them forever."*

—*Psalm 28:9*

As the days of watching turned into weeks and then months, the signs of doubt began to appear. Was all of this really necessary? The joy of contentment in the blessings of the Most High God gave way to stress and worry. "Why are we doing this?" they asked. "Rumors of war and stories of raids are not new. No one ventures up the small path to our village. What could be found here? Zimri-Ruel, are you certain this is necessary? Elder Dov, must we continue this watch? It wears heavily on us." In my head, their questions were difficult to answer. I tried praying, but I heard no new word from the Most High God. I prayed that King Melchizidek would visit me with insight, but he did not. Yet in my heart, I remembered the command to prepare my people! Yes, in my heart, I knew we must stay vigilant.

One cloudless afternoon, I was weeding the wheat field when I saw Leah running towards me with a bag over her shoulder, Deborah in one arm and pulling Adniel alongside her by the other hand. "Come," she cried. "We must hurry to the cave! Warriors approach quickly. There is little time. Everyone has dropped everything, they are all gone ahead of us!" I dropped my hoe, gathered Adniel in my arms, and rushed with Leah and Deborah up the hillside to our mountain cave.

LEARNING TO SERVE

When we reached the cave, I was out of breath, and I found myself trembling. I put Adniel down. He kept asking, "Papa, what is happening? Why are we here? Why can't we go home? I am frightened, Papa, very frightened! What is happening?"

I looked at my son and saw the confusion in his eyes and panic in the eyes of Deborah. I picked up Deborah and held her close against my chest. Leah gently hugged Adniel and quietly said, "We are all safe Adniel. We will all stay here for a while. Everything will be fine. You must be brave for your sister. It will be fun to stay on the mountain. Your father will show you stars of night sky and tell stories of his days as shepherd on the mountain." I could only smile tentatively.

I looked about the cave. I could see Leah's sister, Semira, and her husband, Tizvi. Their children were all there, and old Guri, weak and nearly blind, was also there. Safe. Everyone appointed to the cave was there.

I looked to Tizvi and asked, "Did everyone get out of the village safe?"

Tizvi replied, "I think so. I gathered up Guri and helped him along. I saw everyone rushing about. I think everyone is safe."

"Did you search all of the houses?" I asked.

"There was so much confusion, some of the cave captains were there, running about. I did not search every house. There was so much confusion. I think everyone is safe, but I cannot be certain." Tizvi explained.

I answered, "Yes, you did well, you remembered Guri. After dark, I will meet with the cave captains at the appointed place, and we know of everyone in the village."

I took account of the provisions in the cave, the food pouches, the water, the rugs, and the blankets. Yes, I thought we can survive here for a time. Then I saw the swords and the flint-tipped spear. I picked up the spear and remembered what Zadok had said all those years before of the superiority of the bronze spearhead. As I held it, Tizvi commented, "Think of it as a pruning shear. It will become familiar in your hands."

I gave each man his sword and told him to keep it in his belt at all times. I spoke to everyone in the cave. "We must remain quiet. Comfort the children that they not be anxious or alarmed. We do not know where the soldiers are. It will soon be dark, and I will meet with Elder Dov and the captains. I will learn of all that has happened. We will talk of what to do next. Rest now but stay away from the entrance of the cave. Have someone keep watch at all times. But now, rest. Thank the Most High God that He has kept us safe. Pray for His deliverance."

After dark, I carefully and as quietly as I could made my way to the appointed meeting place. Hod was there ahead of me. One by one, each captain arrived. Jachin came. Then Dov appeared followed by Matai, and finally Rouvin slipped silently in among us. Dov immediately took charge. "Is everyone safe? Did all make it to their cave," he first asked, looking to each of his captains. All nodded yes. "Praise God!" he exclaimed. "Who gave the alarm? Tell us what you saw."

Rouvin answered, "I was at the watch post with Matai. We saw soldiers unlike those of the guard in Khalab. There were five in all coming up the path. They traveled quickly, like ones accustomed to the hills, not stopping to rest along the way. Matai went to alarm the village. I stayed and watched them as they made their way up."

Rouvin paused, and Matai spoke. "It is as Rouvin says. I counted five among them moving quickly. I ran to the village. Every house was warned. There was confusion, but everyone did as they were taught. Then I went to my cave as we planned."

Rouvin then continued, "I watched the five soldiers enter the village. They looked in every house. They drew water from the well and drank of it. They then went to the grain fields, the vineyard, and the groves. They looked carefully at the crops and the tools and returned to the village. As I left, they were in Dov's house. They lit a fire. I believe they will stay the night there."

"Well done, Rouvin. Well done, Matai," said Dov. "We will watch them both day and night. I will take the night watch tonight. Zimri-Ruel will take the morning watch. Jachin will relieve Zimri-Ruel and then Matai and then Rouvin. Go back to your caves. Tell your brothers and sisters what you have learned. Keep them out of sight for now. They are not to leave the cave. They are not to light a fire. We will meet again tomorrow night."

At dawn, I found Dov in his perch between two boulders on the rock face above the village. The weariness could be seen in his eyes. He slid back away from the narrow opening. We retreated out of sight, and he softly said, "Nothing all night, but they should be about soon."

As he finished, we could hear water being drawn from the well. Sliding back into position, we could see one man drawing water, while two others adjusted the straps on their armor. A water bag was filled and then another. After some conversation, four of them walked out of the village. They made their way back to the path and started down the hill towards Khalab. We watched them for a while. It was clear they were heading back the way they came. The remaining soldier carefully scanned all around the village. We slid back and lowered our faces as his sight moved towards us. As he momentarily went back into the house, I said to Dov, "Only one man to watch. Why don't you get some sleep? I will keep him in sight and report to you." Dov nodded and silently slipped away.

As I slid back to look again, he was gone! I heard the sound of a stone kicked, but I could not see. He was on the move, but where? Finally, I caught a glimpse of him through the pine trees. He was on the path to the sheepfold heading up the mountain. I hurried to find another safe place to watch him. He was surely following the path to the sheepfold. They had already visited the fields and the grove. I closed my eyes and walked the path in my mind. *The path will bring him up to the right side of the gate*, I thought. *I could try getting on the rocks above, but my views would be restricted. I need to get over on the left but somewhere with a safe escape.* I didn't have much time. I made my way down from the rocky perch and across to the rocky top of the sheepfold walls where I could work my way down to the left. I moved cautiously, careful not to dislodge a single pebble or stone to betray my presence. I came down a narrow path from one of the high pastures. I quickly turned and went up the mountain. I lay motionless behind a patch of small pines and waited.

It seemed like a very long time had passed since I last saw the soldier. I tried to time his steps in my mind but could not. *He was heading to the sheepfold?* I questioned myself. *Where is he?* I listened but heard nothing. Then I heard what seemed a very loud bang against a stone. Startled, I turned and saw the armored soldier with the butt of his spear planted firmly on rock, clearly waiting for my attention. Looking me square in the eyes, he said, "Where are the sheep? You have a large sheepfold, there are many paths to pastures. We will have your sheep."

I said nothing. I just stood up and stared.

"I know you have been watching us. You fled in a hurry. Your whole village is still nearby. How many are you? Twenty? No more than thirty, I am sure. Bring us the sheep and you might live."

"You are one man," I said.

He looked at me and laughed. "Are you going to fight me, shepherd? You showed your bravery when you fled from five soldiers. No, you will not fight. My comrades will return soon with more men, scouts, and spies for our attack on Khalab. No, you will not fight, and you have nowhere to run. We know about your village. The merchants in Khalab told us you had grain and crops when all other villages were in drought. Your path was easy to find. Do not think that you can flee to the fortress in Khalab. You will soon see Khalab sacked by the combined armies of the King of Ebla and the mighty army of the Amorites. With the foolish help of your king, first we take Khalab, and then we take Ebla as well! So now we will take everything you have, your grain, your oil, and yes, your sheep. I am growing impatient. If I must run you through and search under every rock on this mountainside, I will show no mercy on any I find. Bring your people to me and gather the sheep in the sheepfold. Do as I command, and we may let you live."

The soldier began to raise his spear. Time seemed to stop. My eyes fixated on the spearhead. It was identical to the ones Zadok and Obed showed me in their forge and Jared carried to Damascus. I noted the warrior before me wore leather strap armor, and in his belt was a long, curved sword. He wore a helmet of leather with bronze staves culminating in a bronze point. Wooden sandals with leather straps protected his feet. I just stood, unable to speak, as he lowered the point of the spear towards me. And then I saw, as if in a dream, the flint head of a spear come through the chest of the soldier. The silence was broken with his scream of agony as he fell first to his knees and then forward on his face.

Dov was holding the other end of the spear and pinned the Amorite soldier to the ground. "Is that how you fought the lion?" Dov asked. "It was a good thing for you that I saw the soldier leaving the village before entering my cave. We don't have much time. The others will return, and finding him dead, they will search for us. As quickly as they move, they are sure to overtake us as we have our women, children, and the old blind man."

Coming to my senses, I replied, "If they find him, they will search. If they don't find him, they will also search. Maybe we can let him tell a different story, one that will, at least, delay their search."

Dov asked, "What is your plan?"

"What if the Amorite tells his comrades he was dragged off by the great cat? We gather sheep into the sheepfold, build a small cook fire in front, and lay out a rug next to it. We remove the Amorite's armor and set it next to the rock by the gate with his spear. The warrior's story is he found the sheep and secured them. Taking ease in front of the sheepfold, he is caught unaware by the great cat and is dragged off."

Dov replied, "It is a good plan! We leave a bloody scrap of clothes and sandal. We drag the body to a rocky area to account for prints if they think to look for them. We throw the body into a deep ravine with heavy underbrush out of sight and very difficult to search. Hod and I can do this as you and the captains start our people moving up the mountain and to the south. Let Rouvin lead. He knows the best way to travel."

I started up towards the cave. "I will start our people moving and send Hod to lead some of the sheep to the sheepfold and help you here."

Within an hour, Hod and I had gathered about twenty sheep and led them to the sheepfold. We took care to herd the sheep over the place the Amorite was killed. Dov had prepared the scene and set a small fire that would soon burn itself out. Dov recovered the warrior's food pouch and water bag along with a small rug from his house in the village. The small rug and several raisin cakes were left next to the fire. The spear and armor neatly sat alongside the rocky wall next to the food pouch and water bag. We slaughtered one of the sheep near the entrance to the fold. We splattered blood over the rug, the armor, the food pouch, and the ground around the fire. Finally, we carefully dragged the bleeding sheep and the dead Amorite soldier, erasing our footprints. It was only twenty or thirty yards to barren rock. We then carried the Amorite and sheep into the hills. Hod knew of the perfect place to throw the body—a steep cliff over a deep cleft with the bottom not visible from the rocky ledge.

Dov then draped the dead sheep over his shoulders and said, "We may not have meat for some time. We must not waste it."

We then ascended the hillside, staying on rocky ground, and moved to join our wives, our children, our brothers and sisters as we began our exile from the village—the only home the rest of them ever knew.

Dov was right about the slow progress of the villagers. We soon saw them walking south, in the direction of Ebla, just above the tree line. It was clearly visible from above but well hidden from lands and roads below the mountain and rolling hills. Within two hours, we had joined the group. We agreed that all rest stops would be made under the cover of the forest. Rouvin suggested we travel alongside the tree line until we come to the first gap. He knew of a clearing near the bottom of the gap where we could spend the night before deciding whether to follow the gap down or continue up along the tree line of the next mountain.

It was dusk when we reached the bottom of the gap between the two mountains. Darkness was setting in when the small clearing appeared just as Rouvin described. A river ran down the gap between the mountains. Being late summer, the water level was low, and crossing would not be difficult. Dov believed we could chance a fire and roast the sheep. It had been a very hard day, and many hard days remained ahead. The roast meat would restore our energy and prepare us for what lay ahead. While the sheep was roasting over the fire, we took account of the provisions we had. Our intent in stowing provisions in the caves was to be sufficient for one month. But as we looked again at what was left after two days away from the village, two weeks was more likely unless we rationed more carefully.

The captains sat with Dov and discussed our options. Dov began, "We could follow the gap down the mountain. The river would clearly lead us down, but there is certainly a village at the base where the river runs to the plain below."

Hod wondered, "Would it be safe? There would be better chance for finding food. Perhaps we could even glean from the fields. But didn't we hear in the market of drought outside of our village? And can we be certain the Amorites haven't occupied that village as well?"

Rouvin spoke up. "Do we continue along the tree line of the next mountain? How far to the next gap? And then what? Another stream down the mountain to another village? Do we know if the Amorite soldiers are following us?"

Matai ventured, "Maybe they believe the soldier was dragged off by a great cat. They took the sheep and all they could steal and left?"

I interrupted. "Did not the Amorite say that the four went to lead other scouts and spies to our village? And that the combined armies of Ebla and the Amorites were about to attack Khalab? We must remain hidden until the Amorite army attacks Khalab. Only then will the soldiers leave our village and any other village they might occupy. Is there a safe place we can watch Khalab and not be found?"

"Zimri-Ruel is right," Dov said. "We must find somewhere safe to watch Khalab and await the Amorite army."

"Shouldn't we warn Khalab?" Rouvin wondered.

Dov answered, "They have their army and their watchtowers and trained men. They watch for themselves."

As the captains continued to discuss how to watch Khalab and yet provide a safe place for the people, I quietly left and returned to Leah, Adniel, and Deborah. As I wrapped my arms around them, my body began to shake, and I started to weep.

Leah, who knew me better than anyone except the Most High God, squeezed me tightly. "We are safe. God is our shield. Has He not blessed us? Why do you weep? You of all men know the Most High God has set you upon His path."

I sighed and held both of them tighter. Adniel bravely said through his weariness, "It is all right, Papa. We are together. As Mama says, God will keep us well." Deborah just looked meekly for reassurance with large doe-like brown eyes.

Looking at the sky above, I said mostly to myself, "Did God love the Amorite? He was one of God's creature. Surely God loved him? And now he is dead at our hands."

Leah answered, "All will die. Was not Abel a righteous man who made an acceptable sacrifice to the Lord? Yet God permitted him to die an innocent death."

"Yes," I answered. "And God protected Abel's brother, Cain, the very one who slew him. Yes, this world is made corrupt by sin. Who understands God's ways? Who can know His plan? I want to do His will, but I do not understand His plan."

Leah replied, "God never asked us to understand His plan. As you have taught us, He commands that we love Him with all of our heart and all of our soul and that we love all whom He loves. It is our duty only to love Him, trust in His abiding love for us, and obey His commands. I trust that the Most High God is working His will in all that is happening now. Husband, have faith. You are our priest and intercessor. Never forget that."

In Leah's wisdom, I prayed for my sheep.

> O Lord, how great is the work of Your hands.
> Mountains and valleys, hills and plains
> All tell of Your wonderful work of creation.
> The sun by day and the moon and stars by night
> Speak of Your glory and majesty.
> Your servant lives in the beauty of Your world
> Sustained by the mercy and love You shower on us.
> You made Your servant a shepherd over Your flock.
> I love Your flock because they belong to You.

LEARNING TO SERVE

I serve Your flock because they love You.
Forgive Your servant when I fall short in my duty.
Forgive Your shepherd when Your flock is at risk.
You, O Lord, are their true shepherd.
You, O Lord, are their creator and sustainer.
Only You, O Lord, can save them from destruction.
I know not Your plan, O Most high God.
Your ways are covered in mystery.
But I pray that Your great salvation be known by Your flock.
And we praise You for Your faithfulness.
And we praise You for Your mercy, which endures forever!

Chapter Twenty-two

"Even though I walk through the valley of the shadow of death, I fear no evil for You are with me; Your rod and staff they comfort me."

—Psalm 23:4

The captains decided that the whole village traveled too slowly and would require more food if they constantly moved about. It would be safer to send one shepherd captain to spy on the village we left, another to follow the river down the mountain, and a third to seek a safe shelter for us all. That evening, they all returned safely with their reports.

Hod confirmed that the Amorites were, indeed, still in our village. "I counted a large company of warriors, at least thirty, maybe more. The sheepfold is full. They have gathered most if not all of them. The sheepfold is guarded with two soldiers. Soldiers were reaping the grain and pressing the olives, even though some are not fully ripe. They appear to be gathering everything our village has. Soldiers with weapons are stationed everywhere they work. It is not safe to go near, but I can watch them, I believe, unobserved with the help of the Lord."

Matai reported on the way down along the river. "The river can safely be followed down the mountain. I passed several pastures but saw no sheep. The grain fields were dry with only stubble left. The olive grove was pulled out, and the trees were left uprooted and dead. There was a village near the bottom of the hill alongside the river, a village larger than our own. The river stopped before reaching the village, its rocky bottom now dry. But worse than this, the village had been burned to the ground. There was no one left, and it is now only ruin and desolation and is unfit to inhabit."

Rouvin reported last. "I made my way up the river in the gap between the two mountains. I turned and followed the tree line behind our mountain. I came upon an area with many caves. The caves are in the rock wall protected from above by steep walls and ledges. I saw no signs of paths or travel by other men, only the trails of deer in the forest and mountain goats in the rocks above. I believe we can shelter there safely until danger is past. There is water and game certainly, and some berries and wild fruit can be found. With the Lord's help, we can live there."

"We shall move our people to the cave Rouvin has found." Dov decided. "Hod, you will continue to watch our village. Once we are settled behind the mountain, Rouvin will look for the best route for you and your relief to go back and forth. You have done well, captains! We will depart in the morning. Make certain no sign of our camp is left behind."

The Most High God saw us safely to the caves on the other side of our village's mountain. It was just as Hod reported—there were deer in the forest and mountain goats on the rocks above. Small streams that fed the river we followed still flowed with cool water, and yes, berries grew on bushes in the sheltered sunlight of the forest. At Dov's suggestion, I led our people in a time of thanksgiving to the Most High God for saving us from the Amorite warriors and for leading us to safety. We prayed that His goodness would continue and promised our thankfulness for all His great mercy.

As the days wore on, I was amazed at how quickly we all fell into a routine. The men took turns watching our village. The women made daily trips into the nearby forest foraging for berries and anything edible, and the children gathered firewood. The men took to hunting for deer and mountain goat. And every day, Rouvin scouted the area for possible trails, escape routes, and hiding places. As a new normalcy settled in on us, we were amazed at how our rations stretched. We knew we were dependent on the Most High God and

THE PRAISE SINGER

His creation for our survival. Once again, we were isolated from the world.

Ten days after entering our new cave home, Hod came running back before his watch was over. "They are leaving," he shouted on short breath. "They are on their way down the mountain as I speak. All of them marching like the warriors they are in full armor as if to battle."

Dov commanded, "Hod, stay here and rest. Rouvin, you watch and make sure no one comes up the river path. Jachin, Matai, and Zimri-Ruel, bring your weapons and come with me!"

When we reached the watch post above the village, it was clear no one was there. The sheep were gone from the sheepfold as well. We carefully worked our way down the path until we had a clear view to the bottom. The company of soldiers were already down the path, and they appeared to be carrying heavy sacks. Two soldiers drove the flock of sheep behind them. We watched as they turned right and walked north. Then we saw them, a vast army of men camped just below the hillside several miles south towards Ebla. I had never seen so many men in one place. They were gathered around cook fires among row upon row of tents. Directly to our east, the city of Khalab shone in the late afternoon sun, the tower of the fortress still catching the final rays of the sun before it dropped behind the western mountains. We sat transfixed on the scene below us.

Finally, Dov said, "Matai, go inspect the village. Jachin, you go and look upon the fields, groves, and vineyard. Be careful and make sure it's safe before you enter. Then come back here and report."

As they made their way back up the path, I said to Dov, "It is just as the soldier said. Their whole army has come against Khalab. They have spied out the city and the fortress. No doubt they will stay and do battle."

"Yes," Dov replied. "No doubt the defenders of Khalab will meet them in battle tomorrow. The soldiers of Khalab are a proud and confident lot. I wonder if they have any idea how vast the combined armies of Ebla and the Amorites are. We will stay here and watch."

LEARNING TO SERVE

Matai returned first with his report. "They have all left, and the village is safe. The houses have not been burned, though everything of value is gone, including the oxen. They have filled the well with rock and stubble. It will take many days to open it again, and even then, it may be fouled."

Jachin had run all the way back and was panting for breath when he arrived. Bent over with his hands on his knees, he finally started, "The grain field is bare, not even stubble remains. The vineyard has been torn out, and the roots of the vines lie exposed and drying on the ground. Not a single grape remains. The olive trees still stand, though many limbs are broken. They pulled the branches to the breaking to harvest every olive. With pruning and time, they should recover. The small fig trees have been pulled up by the roots like the grapevines and lie dried in the sun."

Dov listened carefully and finally said, "They have dealt us cruelly indeed. We will see how the Most High God deals with them tomorrow. When you are rested, go back to the cave and tell our people to prepare to go back to the village. Draw as much water as all our bags will allow, but do not leave the caves until we know the fate of Khalab and the attacking armies."

The next morning, the great army south of Khalab formed for battle. The army waited a far way off. After an hour or so, the fortress gate of Khalab opened, and the army streamed out and formed a battle line but close to the gate. Both armies waited the advance of the other. After another hour, the army of Khalab marched to meet the army massed south of the city. The attacking army stood at its battle line and waited. Only when the army of Khalab was close did the massed army move. At the sound of a great horn, the massed army rushed into the army of Khalab. Only then did I see men, warriors—many, many warriors—come from behind the hills north of the city. They advanced towards the rear of the army of Khalab. As they approached the city from the north, they split into two groups; half rushed the army of Khalab from the rear, and the other swarmed into the unprotected city.

All day, the army of the south and the warriors from behind the hills fought the army Khalab. Outmanned and with no route of escape, the army of Khalab was slaughtered. Bodies of soldiers filled the fields south of the city. When the last of the Khalab army was gone, the warriors from the hills bowed to the army of the south and let them pass in front of them to the gate of Khalab. When the army of the south neared the walls of Khalab, shower upon shower of arrows fell upon them. When they attempted to retreat, the warriors behind them attacked in full strength. By sunset, two great armies lay dead on the plain—the army of Khalab and the army of Ebla. Khalab was securely in the hands of the king of the Amorites.

Streams of people fled Khalab only to be cut down from archers on the walls and warriors who formed perimeter patrols around the city. Fires could be seen through the night. The Khalab we knew was dying, and a new order was being established in brutality. Dov and I returned to the cave on the back side of the mountain. We would start rebuilding our lives and our village in the morning.

When we returned to the cave, we were greeted with grim faces. Every water bag was filled. The wine had been spilled out and replaced with water as well. All of the belongings had been gathered, the rugs rolled up and cloaks strung for carrying. Dov studied each villager and said, "Tomorrow we begin again. The Most High God has preserved us. He has been a true shield and protector. Who are we to question His will or His ways? Our priest has taught us to trust the Most High God. He has not abandoned us. Is not our fate better than that of Khalab? I ask our priest and brother, Zimri-Ruel. to pray for us now. Intercede with the Most High God who has directed your path. Seek His favor on us this day."

I walked towards the center of the cave and said, "Brothers and sisters, come with me outside the cave. Let us look with fresh eyes on our creator's world. The sky is the same. The sun, moon, and stars still follow their appointed route. The trees are still tall and green. The deer still run in the forest, and the mountain goat knows his rocky path. A hard thing has occurred, this is true, but our children are among us, and we have all of our brothers and sisters to help us. Do not forsake the Most High God. Now we must learn to trust Him. Now we begin our time of faith. Let us sing a song of faith in earnest to the Most High God. Let the unity of our hearts rise to Him in a sweet sound of love and trust."

One by one, everyone joined in singing a new song.

> Gather Your flock, O God!
> Return them safely to Your fold.
> Water them in the springs of Your love.
> Set Your strong arm before the gate of the fold
> That no harm befall them.
> Let the ram, the ewe, and the lamb be safe.
> No longer to hide in the crags of the mountain.
> The thief and robber has entered the fold.
> Your flock was scattered, but not one was harmed.
> You have sent the thief away
> Now bring Your flock home.
> The cloak of Your love covers us
> And we shall sleep soundly knowing
> Your loving-kindness has no end.
> We have seen Your faithfulness to the flock.
> Now supply Your flock with faith in full measure
> That we may praise Your name
> For You alone are our strong shepherd,
> You alone lead us to good pasture.
> We, Your sheep, know Your voice,
> We will follow You all the days of our lives!

After we sang our praise song to the Lord, I felt the spirit of our people lift. Dov then sent the men on one last hunt.

It was late the next day when we arrived back at our village. Although the houses remained intact, no belongings of any kind remained. Every rug, stool, garment, or tool had been cast into the well. The straw and the chaff of the wheat was also in the well. Everything cast in the well was covered with rocks and stones gathered from about the village. Each family returned to their house, spread their rug, lit a fire, and rested. All of us were reluctant to open our food pouches.

First thing in the morning, the men began clearing the well; it was tedious work, but the many hands made lifting the stones easier. A large blanket was used as a pouch, while other blankets were tied to the corners with two men on each corner and two working in the well; soon the rocks were out. The straw and chaff had drawn in much water and was heavy and wet. "Take the wet straw and use it to cover the tree roots until we can replant the fig trees and vines," Tizvi suggested.

"Do as he says," replied Dov. "With the rocks gone, some of you can begin replanting the trees and vineyard, while others carry the straw and chaff to the field. Hod and Rouvin will continue to clear the well."

By evening, the well was cleared, and we were fortunate the water was not fouled. We would have safe water to drink and could begin watering the replanted fig trees and vineyard. With the help of the Lord our God, the figs and vines would recover, as would the olive trees, which were so badly damaged in the soldiers' hurried and careless harvest. But we would see no harvest this year, and the grain would not be so easy. Nothing was left of the grain field, and no seed from the harvest remained for planting. We had small amounts of grain in our food pouches, but what would we eat? The little grain we had would not replant the fields. The shepherds searched the pastures and hillsides for any stray sheep that remained.

I asked Dov to come to our house that evening and to share what little we had for a meal. Leah took several small raisin and fig cakes from our pouch. She looked at the meager amount of remaining flour and oil and didn't have the courage to touch it. When Dov settled on a rug next to me, I said what we both knew. "We cannot stay here without food. We will not live to next harvest, and that harvest will not include grain. We must consider where we shall go and how we will provide for our people."

"The travel will be very hard on the women and children. And then there is our nearly blind brother, Guri. Perhaps someone can go and return with food?" Dov offered.

I soberly replied, "We will have to travel far. You saw what happened to Khalab. Surely we will not find mercy there. Or Ebla, their army destroyed, will they open their gate to strangers? Will they have enough to survive a siege? The other villages down the hill are likely to have the same fate as what Hod saw following the river. It will not be easy to find food and then to return with enough for our people. How would we purchase food? We no longer have crops to trade. No, I don't think we can leave our women and children here. We must all go."

Leah sat next to me and said, "We women are strong. Do not underestimate us! The children will slow us some, but we will be better together. I will not stay here and worry in doubt. No, we are stronger together. Leaving to find food will surprise no one. We all see the difficulty that lies ahead."

Dov stood up. "We will all sleep on this tonight, but if we must leave, we must do so immediately. Thank you, Leah, for dinner."

Leah replied, "You did not eat!"

"No," said Dov. "Who could eat now?"

Leah and I went to sleep understanding that we might never sleep in our house again. In my sleep, the great light appeared to me again. I heard the voice come from the light. "I have other sheep in Haran. Shepherd these sheep to fold in Haran."

In the morning, Dov called everyone to gather at the well. Hod spoke for the shepherds. "We know what you must say. We are off to search for stray sheep. We will catch up. Don't worry about us."

Dov then began, "Brothers and sisters, we still have our village, our homes, our vineyard, and our groves, and the well remains sweet. All will return to fruitfulness next year, but we cannot stay here and wait. We must find food. We cannot go to Khalab. We cannot go south to Ebla. We can go over the mountains to the coast, but the sea people continue to raid there. Or we can follow our mountain north to the great Euphrates River where rich fields abound."

Tizvi asked, "Perhaps someone could remain here until we return. One man could find sufficient game and food in the mountain and keep watch over our village."

Dov answered, "Perhaps one man could survive on the mountain until our crops can be harvested, but another year will pass before grain could be planted, grown, and harvested. I am alone. I can stay if it is the will of you, my brothers and sisters."

I spoke up. "Last night, the great light again came to me in my dream. A voice spoke from the light and said, 'I have other sheep in Haran. Shepherd these sheep to Haran.' My brother Dov, it is an honorable thing you offer, but we have lost no one. We will leave no one behind. I have been to Haran. It is on the caravan road from Carchemish. Carchemish lies to the north of our mountain at the ford of the great Euphrates river. There will be food there if the gates are not closed against invaders. Haran is across the Euphrates also on a river that flows into the great river. The land is fertile and well watered. Lord Terah met me on the road to Haran and showered me with the most gracious hospitality. He is a great man in the city and will help us. We will seek to join his fold. This is what the Most High God speaks!"

Dov then spoke. "It is agreed then, we follow Zimri-Ruel to Haran. We will all go. Zimri-Ruel hears the voice of the Most High God. The Most High God directs His path. Now gather what you may bring, all the food you have and all the water you can carry, your cloak, and your blanket. Prepare your children. We leave everything else only in the care of the Most High God."

As we each went back to our house, I could not help but look at the village differently. I lived in this village my whole life. For many years a slave and alone. For a time, I loved my small cave on the mountainside near the sheepfold; it was where the voice of God first spoke to my heart. And now I loved the whole village—the houses, the fields, the groves, the vineyard, and the sheep pastures. It had all become so dear to me, and they were now places where the people I loved lived and worked. It was where they conversed and laughed. It was the village of my friend, Dov, and the home of my dearest Leah and my children, my pride Adniel and my sweet little Deborah. Who could imagine how hard it would be to leave such a humble place?

Once we were all gathered again at the well and the water bags filled, I spoke to my flock. "My dear brothers and sisters, please accept the blessing I give you for our journey. May the Most High God bless you and sustain you. May He protect you by His strong arm and shield you. May He deliver each of you safely to the home He has prepared for you. So be it! My friends and now my family, all of you, I never heard a name for our village. If it had one, I should know it, but the Most High God reserves names for His people. And as a village of His people, let this village be remembered in our hearts as Dabar El Elyon, 'God Most High speaks.' For the Most High God surely speaks to each of us. He calls us as His own, and surely it is the Most High God who directs our path. We are the people of Dabar El Elyon!"

PART FOUR

Living in a Fallen World

Chapter Twenty-three

*"From the ends of the earth, I cry to
You when my heart is faint; lead me
to the rock that is higher than I."*

—*Psalm 61:2*

Carchemish is a three-day walk from Khalab by the caravan road, four days with children. The road followed the low hills covered by olive and fig groves, vineyards, and grain fields to the east of the mountain. The higher hills and the east face of the mountain was dry, pockmarked by small oaks and terebinth trees, little more than bushes. Travel on the east side was risky; it would be hard to hide a group of women and children traveling just above the populated hills and plain. We walked up the mountain and again swung around the peak to the western slope out of sight of the roads, villages, and cities of the eastern hills and plain.

Climbing the mountain and traveling through the pine forest on the western slope, carrying all of our earthly belongings, leading our women and children would add many days to the journey. We did not know the route. What obstructions lay ahead? Could we find our way around the mountain? Could we safely bring our women and children on such an endeavor? If the way was easy, would there not be roads or paths already? None of us were prepared for the destruction of the only life we knew and the complete uncertainty of our future survival. What would become of us? What would become of our children? What lies ahead? We know so little of this city, Haran, or the Lord Terah, a man only I had met many years ago. Was Terah still alive? Are we really following an unnamed voice in a dream? Was it not His voice that warned me of danger? Has not His voice led me so far? It was the Most High God who shielded us from the Amorites and the sacking of our village. He must hear our prayer. We must trust in His voice and travel the path ahead. We must make our way to Haran.

By noon, with the hot sun directly overhead, we heard the bleating of sheep as the shepherds caught up to us as we rested in what shade the thin pine trees could offer. Hod was first to state the obvious. "We found five sheep and Leah's milk goat. The goat must have run off on the Amorites."

"There will be milk for the children, at least," Leah replied. "Thank you for finding her."

"Perhaps we can barter the sheep for flour, olive oil, and raisin cakes at Carchemish," I offered.

Dov then added, "Be sure to safeguard them at night. We can't afford to let them wander off again, and we must guard against the great cats. They are all that we have of value to trade for food."

The steep terrain, pine forest, and uncertain path meant we could only travel in the heat of the day, for we would surely lose our footing in the dark. We walked for days, and unspoken was the worry of the limited food we carried. We made certain the children ate, and the goats' milk was a true gift from God. What would we find at Carchemish? The Amorites? A city under siege? Was the city still standing? Will our meager food rations even last until we get there? *O Most High God, You have protected us from the invader. Do not leave us to die on this mountain!*

Every day, Rouvin would travel ahead and mark the trail for us. His years of herding sheep sharpened his uncanny ability to find the best path in this unfamiliar terrain. He could move quickly and silently through the forest and stony mountainside without dislodging so much as a pebble. His habit of turning up silently, totally unheard, in our midst gave him pleasure and never ceased to unnerve us. It became a game for the children, always the first to notice him walking quietly among us, to shout out, "Rouvin's back! Rouvin's back again, and I saw him first!" Only after he was discovered would he approach Dov and report what lay ahead on the trail.

Rouvin's trail began to lead us into taller pine trees. The forest was thickening, but he kept us on a safe path. His path slowly descended as we traveled north; the dry streambeds we crossed grew wider as we went lower along the mountain. Sunset came sooner as the shadow of the next mountain to the west grew larger. The sound of a river at the valley between the mountains grew stronger. A week into our journey, Rouvin returned early in the afternoon. He did not slip in among us and wait for the children to shout his presence; instead, he marched deliberately up to Dov and excitedly announced, "We are approaching a logging camp. We will be there in a few hours. I did not see anyone about, but the logging is recent. What do you want us to do?"

Dov nervously asked, "Do you know you were not followed?"

Rouvin nodded. "I doubled back twice to be certain no one was following me."

"Good," said Dov, relieved. "All the same, let's stop here for the day. We should post a watch farther down the trail and plan for tomorrow."

Matai quickly responded, "Jachin and I will spend the night ahead on the trail. If anyone approaches, one of us will return immediately and the other watch."

I asked, "Can we risk a fire? The children have not eaten since early morning."

Dov was thoughtful and then said, "Build small fires now and cook quickly. Put the fires out before dark. Do we have any raisin or fig cakes left for Matai and Jachin?"

Matai and Jachin each took just one raisin cake from our dwindling supply. They would wait at their forward post for instructions in the morning. They moved swiftly and quietly ahead on the trail like only a shepherd can.

The meal was rushed, and the children were left with their mothers who warned them to be very quiet this night. Leah told Adniel and Deborah, "We are eating early and quickly tonight so that we can play a pretend game of hide-and-seek. It is our turn to hide here in the forest. We must be very quiet so Matai and Jachin cannot hear or find us."

Deborah assured Leah. "I can be very quiet, Mama, even more quiet than a sleeping mouse, and I will make sure Adniel stays quiet too."

At dawn, Dov and Rouvin went to join Matai and Jachin ahead on the trail. I led the rest of our people along the trail an hour later, sending Hod ahead of me just in case a runner returned with a warning. We arrived in the late morning, and Dov was seated on a stump surrounded by a collection of axes and saws. There were crude huts around a large fire pit and evidence of teams of oxen, now nowhere to be seen.

As we approached, Dov signaled for us to come into the camp where he announced, "Rest here. You can make a fire and give the children something to eat. No one is here. It appears they left days ago, but Rouvin, Matai, and Jachin are searching the area now. We will wait here until they return. I have found some flour, oil, and fig cakes left behind in a food cache. It is not much, but it's something."

Although the additional food was not much, it somehow made us feel we could eat more without guilt, and surely the children would be encouraged to eat their fill. As food was being prepared, I walked about the logging camp. I could see the cleared forest and remaining stumps; I noted large slide areas where logs were sent down the mountainside. The river below was clearly visible. There were a few axes with obsidian heads held in place by splints wrapped in leather tangs. But I marveled at the fine bronze axes mounted like Zadok's spearheads on oak knees bent at a right angle. The axes' handles were long and stout, the angle at the end from a natural bend in the oak tree. Thick bronze nails secured the sharp crescent-faced ax head to the bent oak handles. They were matched in their elegant workmanship by the bronze saws, some nearly as long as a man is tall. The saw teeth were skillfully serrated and very sharp; oak handles at both ends were large enough for two hands on each handle. "Who would leave such expensive tools unwatched? They must have left in a such a hurry. But why? If they were caught unawares by Amorites, would not the warriors take such fine tools as well as the prisoners?"

As I pondered, Dov came alongside and quietly said, "They certainly left in a hurry, curious that the oxen are gone, but the tools remain. I have searched the area and found no one. There is a trail leading down along the log slide to the river. The oxen were driven down the trail, and Rouvin is following it down. Matai is heading due north along the mountain across the cut timbered area. Jachin went up the mountain to the ridge. We will wait here."

Matai was the first to return. "We are near the end of the mountain. Soon a gap will appear, and the mountain turns to the east. I could see the river below joining a large river, which runs past the end of the mountain. I saw no one as I walked."

"Carchemish is on the great river just east of the mountain," I responded. "The city should be just beyond the end."

Rouvin was next to return. "I followed the trail down to the river. There are still many logs on the bank. It appears they float the logs down to the great river. There is a trail along the river, and we can get around the logs because the water is low. We can then return to the bank trail. It is not far to the great river."

"Did you see anyone?" Dov asked.

"There were tracks from the oxen and the loggers several days old. I saw no one," Rouvin replied.

An hour later, Jachin returned. Out of breath, he slowly spoke. "I saw the city. It is just below the mountain to the north and east alongside the great river. I could see a great many people camped outside the city. It did not look like an army, it was disorganized. There were people, a few animals, small tents. The city gates were closed. I saw no one coming or going from the city gate. I also saw the ford where the caravan road crosses the great river. The road is open, people travel beyond the city."

Dov spoke. "Perhaps there may be a reward for returning such valuable tools. We have not far to travel, and our path takes us downhill. We are strong men, carrying them will not be too demanding. But we should not cover them lest we be considered thieves. Let us start down now. Rouvin will lead us."

That night, we camped where the river between the mountains entered the great Euphates river, which watered all of Mesopotamia, and was a highway to its great cities. At the meeting of these two rivers were many stacks of logs, which appeared to be sorted by size and variety. We had just left the last great forest on the river. These logs supplied the great cities, Emar, Tuttul, Mari, Babylon and all the way down to Ur.

The next morning, it took several hours to walk downriver to the gates of Carchemish. As we neared the city, we came upon families and small groups of people camped on the plain before the gate. None spoke to us; their faces and eyes were weighed down by despair. They just sat listlessly on cloaks or dirty rugs, waiting. Waiting for the gates to open? Waiting for rescue? Waiting for food? Just hundreds of blank faces, waiting.

As we approached the gate, a guard shouted down, "The gates are closed. No outsiders are permitted in the city. You may wait outside with the others. Bread will be sent out once a day at dusk."

Dov motioned for everyone to stop. Then he and I approached the gate. Once the guard noted our continued approach, Dov shouted up to him, "We return your logging equipment left in the camp. It is very expensive bronze saws and axes. Surely they are still needed by the loggers and craftsmen of Carchemish. And we bring sheep to barter for food. We do not seek to enter your city. Just trade with us, and we will be on our way."

The guard replied, "Wait where you are."

After a few minutes, a small door opened in the gate, and a guard signaled for us to approach. When we approached the guard, he said, "One of you shall stay here as hostage until the other returns with the tools. You may bring your sheep as well."

I immediately said, "I will stay here, Dov."

Dov nodded and said to the guard, "I will return straightaway."

As Dov retreated to our people, I asked the guard, "What news of the Amorites?"

The guard looked at me and said, "The news is before your eyes! Khalab has fallen, and Ebla is burned. We are besieged by those seeking refuge. Are you not also fleeing the Amorites?"

I replied, "By the mercy of the Most High God, we saw the warriors approaching our village in the high hills above Khalab, and we hid in mountain caves. Our village was sacked and everything taken. All of our crops and animals are gone, and we have no seed stock. We were able to find five lost sheep and traveled on the other side of the mountain, avoiding the roads and the Amorites. We came upon your logging camp and saw it was deserted. We saw that the men and oxen fled in a hurry some days ago, leaving their tools behind. We return your tools in hope of reward for our goodwill. The voice of the Most High God directs us to Haran. We seek only food for our journey, but tell me, why did the loggers take the oxen and leave their tools?"

The guard looked around carefully and said, "All able men of Carchemish were called to take arms. Oxen are required for war carts. They should not have left their tools. That was very careless, and they will be punished, you can be sure."

"Then you are expecting the Amorites to attack Carchemish? All of these people in the middle of a battlefield?" I questioned.

The guard answered, "The king has sent tribute of gold and silver to the king of the Amorites and seeks peace. We of Carchemish deal in timber and fine wooden products for the great cities of the Euphrates. Tribute to one king is no different than tribute to another. If the king of the Amorites, who rules now from Khalab, replaces the king of Ebla, what is that to us? We will know when our king's mediators return, but for now, our trained men have joined with the army and wait inside."

Dov and the shepherds arrived carrying the fine bronze tools, leading our five remaining sheep. The guard said sternly, "Wait, I have sent for the captain of the loggers and a merchant to discuss trading for your sheep."

"Send at least two merchants!" Dov shouted.

The captain of the loggers arrived, surprised to see his tools. He looked at each tool carefully, examining the blades and teeth for sharpness. Then he ran his hands from the ax head down the handles, counted them twice, and said, "These, indeed, are our tools. They are all here and all undamaged. Truly, these men should be rewarded. Fine tools like these are hard to obtain and are very expensive. I will confirm this with the court officer. Wait for his reward."

Two merchants arrived to trade for the sheep. The first said, "Truly scrawny sheep, if I ever saw them, but I have pity for you. One ephah of grain."

Dov replied, "Their wool alone is worth two ephahs of fine flour, and as they are healthy sheep, also two Hin of olive oil."

The second merchant offered, "Two ephahs of grain or one ephah of fine flour and one hin of olive oil."

Dov replied, "We can drive them all the way to Haran and sell their wool for this price."

The second merchant replied, "You will starve on the road to Haran. I will give you one ephah of refined flour and two hin of olive oil. You will have food for your journey."

Dov replied, "Done. One ephah of refined flour and two hins of olive oil."

After the sheep were herded off to the market, a court official arrived and spoke with the captain of the loggers. He looked at the tools and listened as the logger explained their value and costliness of leaving them behind. The court officer then said, "The king of Carchemish seeks to reward your goodwill. I am told you seek food for your journey. You may have one basket of raisin cakes, two baskets of fig cakes, an ephah of grain, and two hins of olive oil. Your reward will be delivered here to you. You may wait here at the gate."

As the palace official left, the guard spoke to me and Dov. "I would not leave here in the daylight with your provisions. Look about you, you are not safe. Wait until dark and be careful on the road to Haran. The caravans have stopped until the Amorite king has settled his affairs. Thieves travel the roads, while armies wait in their cities."

"And what about the people waiting outside your gate? What will become of them?" I asked.

The guard only shrugged his shoulders. "They are in the hands of the king of the Amorites. They will be sent home to their cities and villages or die where they are if the army of the Amorites comes."

After dark, we filed by the gate of Carchemish, distributed our provisions, and carried them off in the darkness towards the river ford and the road to Haran. The stars above looked down on a band of God's creatures, a village moving to a new city in a new land. We numbered twelve families and two widowers—twenty-six adults and fifty-six children and one milk goat—walking silently by night on the road to Haran.

Chapter Twenty-four

> *"Surely, thus says the Lord, even the captives*
> *of the mighty man will be taken away. And*
> *the prey of the tyrant will be rescued; for*
> *I will contend with the one who contends*
> *with you, and I will save your sons."*
>
> —Isaiah 49:25

We walked through the night. As the eastern sky began to lighten and warn us of the impending sunrise, Dov and I strained to see someplace of cover near the road where we could rest out of sight. The land had become flat and featureless other than the vast pastureland and occasional squares of the fields. Ahead we could make out the small undulation of a hill and a bend in the otherwise perfectly straight road. There were a few tall trees surrounded by the scrub oaks and terebinths. Dov sent Rouvin ahead to take a closer look. As our column of refugees moved slowly ahead, I looked back to see the mountains, now far behind us, catch the first rays of the morning sun. My thoughts were subdued by the words my mouth began to sing.

> Most Mighty God on High, bring shelter to Your people
> Be for us a shaded oasis in a dry desert.
> Comfort Your little children.
> Nourish us by Your grace.

> Attend to us tenderly as a mother
> Holds her infant child against her breast.
> Provide for us as a proud father
> whose heart is to give more than what is asked.
> Shield us against all harm.
> Let us rest peacefully,
> Secure from any alarm.
> Then I will know that You are my Savior.
> I will honor You all of my days.
> I will declare Your glory to all nations.
> For You alone are God!
> For You alone have ears to hear.
> For You alone answer the prayers of men.
> I will sing praise songs to You.
> I will honor You with obedience.
> Help me, O God, to walk in Your ways,
> Strengthen me to follow all of Your commands.
> Preserve me in the time of trial.
> Your mercy endures forever!

Rouvin ran back to us with his report. "There is some shelter behind the trees. There is sufficient shade for the children and the women. There is a bend in a small waterway. It looks like the work of men. The water runs through a cut as deep as it is wide. I believe it brings the water to the fields. It is a good place to rest until nightfall."

The slow-moving column of exhausted children and weary parents made its way over the small hill and under the shade of the few tall trees and short scrub. Blankets were spread, food was prepared, hungry children were fed, and a quiet peace settled over us. Dov, as was his habit since we left Dabar El Elyon, humbly asked if he could join us. Leah smiled at him and said, "Dov, you need no longer beg our permission to join us. I have long ago given up any hope of separating you from my husband. You are family now and forever. Sit and talk, I see your heart weighs heavy. I will attend to Adniel and Deborah, and then I will see if the goat can provide some milk."

Dov sat next to me silently. After a few minutes, he spoke cautiously. "My friend, there is something I have never told you. As Leah sees, it does weigh on my heart."

I looked into my friend's downcast eyes. Clearly, something was bothering him. "Dov," I replied, we are brothers. I will always hear your words."

With his eyes still fixed on the ground in front of him, he said, "It was I who brought you to the village. I was the one who found you on the road. I did not really find you. I was told to take you. I was returning from Khalab, and as I traveled the caravan road to our path up the hillside, a trained man, a warrior, was waiting by the side of the road, seated on a donkey. I know not if he was a Hurrian or an Akkadian, an Amorite or an Aramean. I remember the sword on his belt and the helmet on his head. He held a spear in one hand and clutched a basket in the other. He watched me as I approached. I feared he was a bandit, but I determined to walk on by. As I passed him, he shouted, 'Come back here! If you value your life, do as I command!' Well, I was unarmed, and you know I am no trained man, so I turned and went back. He presented me the basket and said, 'Take this child and raise him. See to it he is well cared for.' And then the trained man rode off north."

Dov paused and glanced at me. He resumed his gaze upon the ground. "I took the basket and walked to our pathway. Only once I had ascended a little way up the hillside did I stop and look in the basket. Inside I saw a child swaddled tightly and asleep. I was both amazed and pleased. A son was the very desire of my heart, and there lay a healthy young boy asleep in the basket. I sprang up the path to my house. I could not contain my joy when I told my wife of all that had happened.

"But she did not share my joy. She coldly said, 'For years, you have wanted a son, and my womb has been dry. Your desire for a son has brought only guilt and shame upon me, and now I am to raise the son of another woman? I will not raise another woman's child! Send me off I know not where, for my father is dead, and I have no brothers. Send me off to beg in Khalab.'"

Dov sobbed briefly. "I could not send her away. I knew her heart was broken. I knew she felt scorned in the village, but I could not give you up. That is when I suggested the village raise you. I always hoped she would change her heart and accept you as well. She did not."

Growing more composed, he went on, "What I foresaw as an opportunity to keep you in the village and someday make you my son, the others saw the benefit of your service. If you were to cost them the food and the effort of your upbringing, they expected a benefit. I foolishly went along, hoping I would find a way to make you one of us, not a stranger but a villager. Then in the course of time, I would give you a double share of my inheritance and accept you as my son, but events have made it all impossible. You are a man, you are a friend of the Most High God. You are God's priest, and you have truly become father to me, and now I have no inheritance to pass along to you. Please forgive me. Please know that you always brought me pride, though I could never speak. You saw the love of Leah, and the Most High God has joined you to her. Watching your family grow has been my great comfort. Although God has loved you and you did not need my love, know, my friend and brother, I have loved you every day. Forgive me if you can."

I sat stunned. I did not know what to say; we sat quietly next to each other. Finally, my thoughts turned into words. "I forgave you the day I prayed in the garden of King Melchizedek. I gave you my forgiveness the day I returned to our village. Why should I not still forgive you? The Most High God has brought us together, and we are still together. Indeed, we are closer than brothers. You are father to me, even as I shepherd our people. You lead our people, you decide our ways. You, Dov, speak with authority, and our people follow. You teach me the responsibility of leading. God has, indeed, brought us together. The Most High God has worked His will. He directs our paths. He has made us strong shepherds for hard times."

Leah had returned. She sat quietly, listening. "Dov, you never spoke against my concern for little Katan or careless Ben Kefar or withdrawn Jael. I knew you felt as I did. You have always been welcomed in our home. You could never hide your pride for my husband in your eyes. I am certain all our village knows this as well."

We shed tears and loved each other greatly, thanking the Most High God for His mercy and love that brought us together.

Well before the sun reached high in the sky, our camp was quiet. All fell asleep.

Chapter Twenty-five

*"I will sow her for Myself in the land. And
I will have mercy on No Mercy, and I will
say to Not my people, 'You are My people,'
and he shall say, 'You are My God.'"*

—*Hosea 2:23*

I awoke to screams and shouts. Springing to my feet, I saw men—strange men—all around us. They carried slings and spears, and I saw knives in their belts. Their leader was seated on a donkey, banging his sword against the shaft of his spear. Children cried, and our men stood in front of their wives and children in a futile attempt to shield them from harm. The one on the donkey rode slowly into the center of our camp, his eyes looking at us one by one. He rode slowly through our midst, occasionally glancing down at our pouches of food, baskets of cakes, and jars of wine. He bent over and picked up a grain of sack and examined the flour inside.

I stepped forward and said, "We are passing through this land. We will take nothing from it."

The leader rode up to me and stopped; he slowly looked at me, head to foot, and spoke. "You enter the plains of Nahor. We do not abide robbers and thieves. These jars and baskets bear the markings of the king or Carchemish. Return to his city with your plunder and face his wrath. The king of Carchemish is not known for his hospitality. Everyone knows how the refugees of Khalab and Ebla slowly perish outside his gates, but you hide here with his food, oil, and baskets of fruit. Return the way you came."

I answered, "It is true our provisions come from Carchemish, but we are neither thieves nor robbers. We have left our village in the high hills above Khalab as the Amorites have taken all of our flocks, all of our grain, all our olives, all of our grapes and figs. They took everything, and they filled our well. Yes, we traveled to Carchemish but not by the road, fearing the Amorites. We traveled behind the high mountains. There we came across the lumber camp of the king of Carchemish. As all his men who could carry a weapon were called to Carchemish, the camp was abandoned, and we found all of his tools of bronze. Very fine tools. Very costly tools. We carried his tools to the city and were rewarded a ransom for their safe return. We travel to Haran to seek the favor of Lord Terah, a great man in the city. We will not take from your fields or your flocks. We will travel to Haran not turning to the right or to the left."

The man on the donkey asked, "How would a man from a village in the high hills above Khalab know the Lord Terah?"

"Many years ago," I began, "I ran off from my flock, my people, and my village, and I came upon the gates of Haran. Fearing to enter, I stood before them. Lord Terah passed me, but turning back, he surmised I was a shepherd and a foreigner, and he bid me to follow him and accept his hospitality. I told him my story, that I was seeking the Patriarch Shem in the city of Salem. Terah showed me the most gracious hospitality and took me by caravan to Damascus to meet the Patriarch Shem. The Lord Terah taught me many things concerning the Most High God, as did the Patriarch Shem. Now with no seed for grain and no sheep to herd, we can no longer survive in our village. We seek his shelter and the shelter of the Most High God."

The man on the donkey looked at each of us one more time and then turned back to me and said, "Tell your people to gather up their rugs and their provisions. You will follow me. You will be safe. I will not travel the road to Haran. We will find the flocks of Nahor."

"We seek Lord Terah in Haran," I repeated.

"Lord Terah has been gathered to his fathers and is buried. We go to Lord Nahor, his son. You may make your petition to him." The captain rode off and gathered his men.

For two days, we walked north over semi-arid grassland. We followed paths made by sheep and goats. All we saw was emptiness in every direction. Only the mountains far off to the left and the sun overhead governed our path. On the third day, I saw a great field covered with what appeared as black cocoons growing from the earth. As we drew nearer, I saw men and women entering and leaving the cocoons. I saw sheep and goats nearby as well as donkeys, camels, and some oxen. It was a large city made entirely of these strange cocoons.

We entered this strange city; I surmised that the cocoons were tents. The tents varied in size, but they were all the same shape and the same black. Black but showing gray on the very tops of some. Some of the tents were open on half of the front, and men sat at the opening. I noticed fire set at the opening. The fires were inside the base of the tent, but the smoke rose up above outside the top of the tent, which was angled back from the base. The men sitting at the openings nodded to the captain of the trained men as we passed. Each remained seated on a fine rug or cushion, and I could feel their eyes follow us as we were paraded into the city. We finally arrived in front of a very large tent, and three men were seated in the front opening.

The captain waited on his donkey while all of our people gathered in front of the tent. Satisfied we were all gathered in view, he dismounted his donkey and said, "These are the refugees who seek Lord Terah. You may hear for yourself their story."

The captain led his donkey away, but his trained men stood around us. One of the seated men spoke. "Who speaks for you? Come forward and make your petition known."

I stepped forward and said, "I am Zimri-Ruel, a shepherd calling to the flocks and to the people of Dabar El'Elyon, our village in the high hills above Khalab. We have been driven from our village by the Amorites, who have carried off our flocks, our crops, and everything we own. We have come seeking the aid of Lord Terah, who showed me great hospitality many years ago. He taught me to follow the Most High God and led me to the Patriarch Shem. We seek refuge until we can support ourselves, until we can replant our fields and rebuild our flocks."

Another seated man, older than the one who first spoke, said directly, "We do not often hear the name of the Most High God. The people of Haran, the people of the road, carry other gods with them. They have forgotten the Most High God."

The younger man, the first to speak, commanded, "Tell me how you know Lord Terah."

I started, "As I told your captain—"

The young man interrupted. "You are not speaking to the captain, you are speaking to the elders. Tell me how you know the Lord Terah."

I started over. "My lord, your servant met the Lord Terah outside the gate of Haran many years ago. I was a young shepherd seeking the Patriarch Shem in the city of Salem. I was following the voice of the Most High God, but I shamefully ran off, abandoning my sheep. The Lord Terah saw me standing before the gate, too frightened to enter. He recognized that I was a shepherd and a foreigner, and he brought me to his house and showed me the most wonderful hospitality. He listened to my story and took me by caravan to the Patriarch Shem. Terah and Shem taught me much about the Most High God. They taught me to make a sacrifice. The Patriarch Shem told me the story of his salvation by the Most High God on the ark his father, Noah, built as commanded by God. The Patriarch Shem told me there was more for me to learn and directed that I go Salem. He spoke a word from God over me, and he blessed me. In Salem, king Melchizedek heard my story and told me all that Shem said I would learn. I then returned to my village where I serve my people in the fields, shepherding flocks and intervening for them as a priest."

Waving my arm towards my people, I finished, "These are the people of my village. We are the people of Dabar El Elyon, every one of us saved from the Amorites by the Most High God."

The three elders spoke quietly among themselves, and then the young one, who spoke first, said, "You shall know our hospitality. You will be provided a place to rest, food, water, and shelter. In the morning, your men shall return here, and we will discuss your future."

Motioning to the captain, he said, "Find them shelter and give them clean water and food. The people of Dabar El Elyon are our guests."

We were taken to a tent near the edge of the city. Several of the trained men brought more tents, one for each family. I was amazed by the speed and efficiency at which the tents were erected. Each tent had nine poles; three poles were higher than the stretched-up arm of a man. Each pole was spaced the stature of a man; these were set as the middle poles. They were joined across the top by a strong rope, the ends of the ropes secured to pegs set deep in the ground. Next three shorter poles, taller than the height of a man, were set in a row the span of a man behind the center poles. They too were joined by a top rope and secured to the ground with pegs. Three more of the same shorter poles were set, again the span of a man, in a row in front of the centerline poles. Again, they were roped together across the top and secured to the ground. When the nine poles were set, new ropes were run across the tops of the poles front to back—that is, from the short front pole to tall centerline pole and on to the rear short pole. These ropes were secured to pegs in the ground. All the ropes to the pegs were angled out to provide a secure hold. The poles, once set, were strongly joined and quite secure.

Once the men were satisfied with the poles—that is, they were straight and secure—they took a panel of black goat hair woven in panels about half the stature of a man wide. They hung it from the rope joining the center front pole to the center pole. Once it was in place and the bottom folded and rolled out as a carpet, other goat hair panels were laid across the rope and pole framework, covering and fully enclosing the tent. The ends of the panels were folded on the ground, so nothing could come under the side. Only half of the center was left open, as was half of the front of the tent where the elders sat. A lighter curtain was hung across the front and across the back half of the interior divider. It occurred to me that the women and children remained inside on the other side of the divider—the men occupied the side with the open front. They could entertain other men separate from their wives and children.

We quickly set about making small fires in the open doorways as was the practice of those in the tents we observed. Water and milk were brought to our tents as well as wine, small cakes, and cheese. We spread out our rugs and slept secure.

I awoke in the morning as pinpoints of light appeared in the black goat hair tent cover. I was reminded of the night stars overhead when I slept under the open sky in front of the sheepfold. Leah prepared cooked cakes for me and gave me a raisin cake as I left to see Dov. She then turned to prepare breakfast for Adniel and Deborah, still asleep in the inner room. I walked across a short clearing to where Dov shared a Beyt (tent house) with Guri. One by one, each of the men assembled.

"Do we wait to be summoned, or do we just go over there?" Dov wondered.

As we started to walk back to the Beyt of the elders, I saw the captain of the trained men approach. "Good, I see you are on your way. They have asked for you." Then trying to be polite for the first time, he added, "I hope you have found your beyts comfortable. You have enough food and are well rested after your journey."

"Yes, Captain," I replied. "Your hospitality is most generous."

We arrived at the tent of the elders and were greeted out front. The young one who spoke bowed slightly and motioned for us to come in. "Please come in, you are welcome. Sit and talk with us."

I was surprised at the elegance inside the tent; rugs every bit as fine as those of Terah and the Patriarch Shem covered the ground and the goat hair walls; copper bowls and bronze spoons were also set about. Embroidered robes and cushions were neatly resting along the side of the tent and a fine but light curtain was hung across the entrance to the inner room.

The third man spoke for the first time. "I am Huz, eldest son of Nahor, and this is Bethuel, my brother," he said, pointing to the old man and young man in turn.

"My grandfather, Terah, was an unusual man. You will find life here much different than Haran. Much simpler, I'm afraid, and lacking the activity and the variety of the marketplace."

"Terah spoke fondly of his home here," I answered. "He told me he was the 'goat who always goes astray.' He told of his past travels and wanderings. Forgive me if I am too familiar, but Terah still grieved the death of Haran and longed for his son, Abram. He confided that he traveled to trade and bring comforts for you but came to realize that you, his family, were the true source of comfort."

Continuing, I said, "I saw Abram when I was in Salem. He had returned from rescuing Lot and came to Salem to present a gift, a tithe, to King Melchizedek, priest of the Most High God. Abram led a large host and presented a great treasure. King Melchizedek blessed him, and Abram returned the hostages and treasures of Sodom and Gomorrah to their kings before returning to his people and his flocks at the Oaks of Mamre in Canaan. Melchizedek had much other to say concerning Abram's future."

"That had to be over a dozen years ago," said the old man. "Abram is now called Abraham, father of nations. The angel of the Most High God gave him his new name when he promised him a son and descendants as numerous as the stars in the sky. And Sarah, his wife, called by Terah, her father, Sarai, has indeed given him a son in her old age. We are told his name is Isaac. Servants of Abraham brought the news to Damascus, and the news was brought to us."

The old man paused and then said, "Terah was, indeed, the goat that always went astray, but he always served and loved us. He is buried alongside his father, Nahor, my grandfather and the namesake of this place. The Patriarch Shem lives yet in Damascus, and to this day, he tells of his salvation on the ark. His memory is still clear, he speaks of the voice of the Most High God, and his eyes are ablaze as he speaks. I will never forget his eyes."

The old man stopped and then said, "We are not here to remember my family, my clan, or my tribe. We are here to speak of your needs, though I feel a strong connection between us. We are careful who we permit to dwell with us, but you too do not carry detestable gods of stone and wood but follow only the Most High God.

Therefore, you can live among us and earn what you need to return to your village. We are shepherds, and your men who are shepherds can work with our shepherds. We do not till the soil or tend groves and vineyards, but those of you who tended fields and crops can learn to make tents of goat hair or become trained men to protect our people and our flocks."

I quickly replied, "What you say, my lord, is good. We are honored to serve such a noble clan and tribe that follows the Most High God."

"And you, Zimri-Ruel, is it, you are a priest and a shepherd?" the old man, Nahor, asked.

"Yes, my lord. King Melchizedek, priest of the Most High God, commanded I intercede for the people of the high hills above Khalab. Of late, we have named our village Dabar El Elyon because the Most High God spoke to us and saved us from the Amorites."

"Then you shall be priest here as long as your people are here. Who are the other men with you?" Nahor inquired.

Signaling to step forward, I introduced, "This my father, Dov, our elder. He found me and brought me to the village. To my great honor, he has adopted me as his son. Elder Dov is a strong leader and a great shepherd. You will find him a most capable man. I only speak for our people out of acquaintance with Terah"

Dov, clearly startled, stared at me for a few moments and then found his voice and said, "I am honored to serve, my lord. It is true I am a shepherd and village elder. I am willing to become one of your trained men if you desire."

I stepped back, and Dov called out to Rouvin, Matai, Jachin, and Hod. Each stepped forward at his name. "These men are shepherds—finer shepherds—you will not find in all the hill country."

Dov waved, and they stepped back. He continued with Guri, Tivzi, and on he went until every man and his skill were made known.

When the introductions were complete, Huz smoothly added, "You should hear the terms. Each of your families has been given a tent. They are very expensive, and you shall work two years to repay your tent. I will keep account of your provisions, and once your tent is paid, you will work to repay your provisions. I will be fair, of course."

Nahor looked at his elder son and said, "It is also fair that the people of Dabar El Elyon receive some compensation to prepare for their return. They shall be given every twentieth lamb and every twentieth goat born into the flocks they tend. They can establish their own flock and teach their sons to tend it. If that is all, Huz, let these people get about their work."

As we turned to leave, Bethuel spoke up. "Zimri-Ruel, please stay for a moment. I would want you to walk with me to my tent."

As we walked, Bethuel spoke. "It is not only Haran that forgets the Most High God. Some of my brothers and many of our young men do not consider the Most High God. They no longer make sacrifices for sin or thanksgiving. I will ask my father to provide what you need to sacrifice to the Most High God. I will ask him that you teach our people what they have forgotten. It is my hope you will intercede for us and the people of Dabar El Elyon. Surely the Most High God has brought you here."

Chapter Twenty-six

*"Why, Lord, do You stand far off? Why do
You hide Yourself in times of trouble?"*

—*Psalm 10:1*

The years went by. Old Guri died and was buried in Nahor. The son of Rouvin married the daughter of Tizvi; they were given Guri's tent. I purchased additional goat hair tent panels and added a third chamber to our tent; Dov moved in with us. Children of Dabar El Elyon grew up and married; more children were born. Some young families stayed in expanded tents of the groom's family, while some purchased new tents. The two-year repayment was now closer to five years; Huz kept a strict accounting. The flocks of Dabar El Elyon grew, much to the jealousy of Huz. I made sacrifices for the atonement of sin and sacrifices of thanksgiving when the sheep were shorn or the goats slaughtered for meat and hair. The people of Dabar El Elyon prospered in their work despite the creeping tent debt.

Always true to his word, Bethuel saw to it that bulls, sheep, and goats were provided for sacrifices. He listened to my story of Melchizedek and the truth of his words to me. Many of the clan of Nahor joined in the sacrifices and worship; Bethuel was always there. Huz always had a reason to be absent; some urgent duty would call him away. Afterwards, he would apologize to his father, the aging Nahor; no apology was so earnest that he actually came the next time.

Soon I learned why the Canaanites called Abraham "the Hebrew." A Hebrew wanders like a nomad and lives in tents as he travels. The tribe of Nahor moved frequently, sometimes after only a few months. They followed the flocks; when the grass ran out, they moved on to greener pastures. The difference was while Abraham moved to Canaan and Egypt far from home, the tribe of Nahor just moved about the plains of Nahor in Padan Aram in the vast openness between the rivers above the great cities of the Euphrates. Of the tribes of Shem, only the tribes of Abraham and Nahor held to the old ways, dwelling in tents and following the flocks. The others settled in cities, their sons marrying the daughters of other nations, their daughters being taken in marriage with the sons of other peoples. They forgot the Most High God; they served other gods. They did detestable things in the sight of the Most High God.

The people of Dabar El Elyon became comfortable on the plains of Nahor. Their flocks increased, their tents provided comfortable shelter, and the trained men provided vigilant security.

We had followed the flocks to the east of the plains of Nahor, near the banks of the Tigris River. Adniel, now a young man and confident shepherd, was leading the Dabar El Elyon flock to water late in the afternoon. He had hurried to arrive first, intending to water his sheep in clear water, unmuddied by the feet of many sheep. It had become a competition between us to see who would be first to the water; I could see his flock ahead, but they were not moving into the water. As I approached, I could see two trained men—no, they were warriors from Assur, a great city farther downstream on the Tigris.

I heard Adniel shout, "There is no tax, no tribute to water sheep. The tribe of Nahor has watered here for generation upon generation." He whistled and called his sheep, leading them into the shallow water. Then I saw one of the Assyrians draw his sword come behind Adniel and strike him across the back of his neck. I stopped and stared in horror as Adniel fell headlong into the river; the water was red around him. He lay there still, dead among the sheep. I screamed in agony, frozen in place. I fell to my knees and wailed. My heart was torn within me.

As I knelt, several trained men came running. They ran past me, straight for the Assyrians, whirling their slings as they ran. Soon the Assyrians lay dead on the riverbank. I ran to the river and clutched Adniel's lifeless body in my arms. I wailed in agony I had never known. I held him tight against me, crying out his name.

Weeks passed. I still mourned my son, Adniel. He was my joy. He was my pride. I never could imagine such pain. Dov could not stop me from mourning. Months passed, Leah could not console me; I could not accept that Adniel was gone. I would never again see his smile. I would never again hear him say, "Father." I would never again laugh with him. Does no one else see my pain? How can you ask me not to mourn him? His goodness and gentleness were unquestioned. Why did the Most High God not shield him? Why let him be taken? He was innocent! He honored the Most High God. He walked always according to the commands of the Most High God. Did I not name him Adniel, meaning of God's flock? Why was he taken? Why my Adniel? Why? Broken in heart, I lamented:

> Are You not righteous, O God?
> Are You not a savior for Your people?
> Have You abandoned justice?
> Do Your eyes not see the innocent lying bloody on the ground?
> Do You abandon Your watch in the hour of danger?
> If I have sinned, O God, punish me.
> If my sacrifices do not please you, chastise me.
> If I have forgotten You, slay me among the wicked.
> Take my life, O God, for my pain is beyond what I can bear.
> Did not a tender youth, an innocent, die cruelly?
> I do not see Your purpose in this.
> Are You not the Almighty God?
> Do You not love those who praise Your name?
> Do You not remember those who seek to follow You?
> Tell me the errors of my understanding.
> I have lost my son, O God.
> Have I lost my God as well?
> You alone are God, O God, make me understand.

God did not reply to my lamentation, but Leah did. "Who are you to say God is deaf? Who are you to claim God has abandoned us? You who teach the love and power of the Most High God! You who speak words of comfort to others when they are touched by death. You hypocrite! Did you alone see the death of a son? Did I not lose Adniel as well and a husband too? Did not Deborah lose her only brother and has no father to console her? Would you call God a liar? Did King Melchizedek, priest of the Most High God, not warn you? Have you not taught everyone in Dabar El Elyon that God watched the death of the righteous Abel and still protected his murderer Cain? Have not your own words taught that sin has corrupted all of creation, but the Most High God still loves his people and works His will for salvation to wash us clean by atonement to stand righteous in His presence? Is not His desire for us to walk with Him once more? Does not righteousness bring peace? Does not faith bring obedience? This is what you teach us. Did not King Melchizedek say the tithe of Abram did not accord righteousness, rather it was his faith, and he would become the father of all who have faith in the Most High God? Do you walk away from faith in the Most High God because death has touched one you love? Without faith, you can have no righteousness and no peace. Death touches all! Do you not know that the love of the Most High God does not keep anyone from the sting of death? Do you not see that death does not stop the love the Most High God has for us?"

Leah paused and, softening her tone, spoke again. "Listen to my faith and my hope. The Most High God is the Almighty God. Nothing is impossible with my God. You have said, 'The patriarch Enoch walked with the Most High God and was no more.' If Enoch can walk with the Most High God, cannot all who love the Most High God also walk with Him? If God has a place for Enoch and the heart's desire of the Most High God is to walk with those He loves, my faith assures me that Adniel can walk with Him as well. As you say, God loves us, and He can do no other. He has made a way of salvation. Is this not the will of the Most High? Is this not the final salvation? Is not our Almighty God powerful enough to work His will? As you teach, nothing is impossible with God."

Leah's words cut to my heart. I lowered my face in my hands and wept. Leah wrapped her arms around me as I wept. "Yes," I muttered. "And I thank God for giving me you. You complete me. Your faith brings strength to my soul. Pray with me that the Most High God forgives me. Pray that my doubts are taken away forever. I do love the Lord with all of my heart and all of my soul. What would I be without my God?"

The Most High God answered our prayers. I trusted the will and the work of God. My mourning ceased, though I cannot but feel the pain of loss when I think of my son. It is pain borne of separation but covered in the hope that I will see him again. I thought deeply of all that King Melchizedek told me of the Most High God's plan of atonement. God is working out His revelation to men, showing their need for salvation, revealing the cost of sin. Men must live out this revelation to understand their sin, the cost of sin to them, to other men, and to God. Men must be reminded of God's dilemma, of His work to save men from the sin He abhors and allow His love and fellowship to be restored. All of this must be done gradually that men might see the heart and purposes of their creator. But Melchizedek offered me a glimpse of the completed revelation; he told me of the final sacrifice of atonement by a Great High Priest—a sacrifice made once and for all time. Those final words stuck in my mind: once and *for all time*!

There is reason for Leah's hope in God's power to bring men to Himself, to walk with Him just as He took Enoch to walk with Him. If the sacrifice of the Great High Priest will atone for all sin, for all time, then this atonement to come will atone for my sin and has atoned for the sin of Adniel. Adniel has only gone before me and Leah, called to a restored fellowship with Almighty God Himself. Adniel can now, and we can be certain that we too in the future will, walk with the Most High God. Oh, what a glorious hope!

Chapter Twenty-seven

*"An excellent wife, who can find? For
her worth is far above jewels. The heart
of her husband trusts in her."*

—*Proverbs 31:10–11*

Leah was well known in Nahor; the women watched her. She was different than every other wife. She never broke the rigid rules of separation. There was never any hint of dishonor, but she sensed she was different. She was aware she was watched. Leah more than completed me; she shared my love for the Most High God and shared my commitment to make the message known, understood, and obeyed in Nahor just as she did in Dabar El Elyon. I had no secrets from Leah; I fully trust that she withheld nothing from me.

We talked about this. She shared her desire to raise up women unafraid to live in obedience to God, not loving their husband less but loving God more and trusting Him to lead their household. She saw the Most High God as speaking to women as well as men. She saw women as entrusted with training children. By the time children were of age to sit with their father, too often their character was already set. Yes, the Most High God can change a man's heart, but why not make it tender for change?

Milcah, the wife of Nahor, saw the strength of Leah. Leah always had an authority of her own, independent of me. Milcah saw this and admired her for it. She bore Nahor eight sons plus daughters. Bethuel, her youngest son, was a compliant boy, honored his mother as well as his father. After he was born and she could no longer bear him children, Nahor took Reumah as his concubine and fathered four more sons and more daughters. This was common for the patriarchs. There was no dishonor in a man of wealth fathering many sons. Milcah knew this, but to her, it was unjust. She saw in Leah's authority this would never happen between us; we were always one, and there would never be another to disrupt our union and harmony.

Milcah told her husband, Nahor, that the women and children could more fully worship the Most High God if Leah would teach them. This, she told Nahor, would keep dishonor from coming to the wives and maintain an honorable separation from other men, including the priest. Not, she assured Nahor, that I was a danger to the wives, but the separation must be maintained. Nahor, seeking to please Milcah, said this was good. About this time, Bethuel's wife was with child; it would be her second. Laban was an energetic and difficult son, perhaps Bethuel's wife could be helped with her children? Perhaps Milcah could find someone to help his wife? Bethuel, who deeply loved and honored his mother, quickly and earnestly sought her help.

Milcah summoned Leah. Leah went to Nahor's tent at the appointed time; she was met at the opening and ushered past the public men's chamber where I first met Nahor and two of his sons. She was ushered through the curtain to the private area reserved for family. Milcah herself led Leah into her private chamber of Nahor's beyt, the largest and most extravagant in the lavish tent. Milcah enjoyed every luxury available; she was dressed in a finely embroidered robe of many bright and vivid colors. She had the best carpets, even smooth silk-covered pillows. Upon entering, a flick of her wrist told all of her attendants and wives of her sons to leave. They filed out silently before her. She wanted Leah to be impressed; Milcah wore the wealth and authority of her husband, Nahor.

Once seated, Milcah praised Leah. "Know, Leah, you are honored as wife of the priest and provide a respectful role model to all the women of Nahor for supporting your husband."

Leah, never one for flattery, abruptly but respectfully asked Milcah, "Why have you sent for me? What is it you want?"

Milcah, apparently pleased with Leah's assertiveness, replied equally directly, "I want your help in raising stronger women. The Most High God has given you the opportunity to show strength and authority. Will not our children, our husbands, and our people learn to obey the commands of the Most High God if women too are accountable to God? They must own their own accountability and not be held to the accountability of their husband."

The thought that accountability to God did not fall on every person, man or woman, never occurred to Leah. Leah answered, "Milcah, we all have our own accountability. Our mother, Eve, was fully accountable for what she did, and her husband, Adam, listened to her and was held accountable for what he himself did."

Milcah replied, "Need I remind you, wife of our priest, that Adam had only one wife, only Eve. Never did he take another wife or concubine. Adam listened to his wife, they were both accountable. Your husband has not taken another wife. He has not taken a concubine. Do you believe he ever will? Look at me. Do you think Nahor asked me if he could take Reumah as concubine? What authority did I have in this decision?"

Leah was speechless; this thought was new to her. She grew up in a poor village where no man could afford two wives or concubines. But there was more—she never considered what it meant for a wife to step aside of or behind a husband. She considered Adam and Eve when they walked in the garden. Adam and Eve were one, and they walked as one with God, their creator; God said this was very good! Was this union between man and wife and communion with God not the perfect plan of the Most High God?

Leah slowly answered Milcah, gathering her words as she spoke. "I find truth in your words. Adam and Eve were one. They were united and joined as one. As one, they enjoyed communion with God and walked together with Him in the garden. They may have worked separately, but they were always one in their desires and determination. A second wife or concubine would break this union, a union that was the very heart of God for man and woman. I do not hear the patriarchs or the priests teach this. I will help you, Milcah. It is the very will of God."

When Leah returned to our far more modest tent, she recounted her talk with Milcah. She told me she agreed to help Milcah teach women. Then she asked, "Why have you never taught God's perfect plan for husband and wife, the marriage He gave Adam and Eve before sin corrupted them, the order God declared very good?"

I asked Leah, "Are we not one, Leah? Do we not complete one another? I will never have another wife, There will never be a concubine in my tent!"

Leah smiled and then turned serious. "I know we are one. This is not about you and me, but is not Milcah right to ask these questions? Is she not right that the heart of the Most High God is that man and wife become one flesh? Is she not right that both husband and wife have accountability before our God? Consider our daughter, Deborah. Is it not your will that she walk with the Most High God? Is it not your will that she be taught to ask the questions you have asked and find the answers you have found? And is it not your will that her husband, when the time comes, walk with her in communion with our God? Is Milcah not right to see she is harmed, marriage is harmed, when Nahor takes a concubine? Adam and Eve, though different people who lived different lives, walked as one in union. As one, they walked in the garden in communion with God. How could that union survive a concubine? You have not taught this. You cannot teach this to the wives and daughter and, yes, the young boys of Nahor, but I can."

I considered the wisdom of Leah and the wisdom of Milcah. I had not taught these things. I had not considered these things. I pondered them at night in our bed.

Asleep in bed alongside Leah, I dreamt. The bright light returned. I recognized the voice of Melchizedek; I will always recognize the voice of Melchizedek. With all of his unchanging compassion, I heard him say, "The wife of Bethuel shall bear a daughter. She has been set aside for God's purpose, for she shall be the mother of two great nations. She shall be the one wife of a chosen patriarch. They will love and be faithful as husband and wife all the days of their long lives. Bethuel will ask you to send Leah as a teacher and a helpmate for his wife. You shall send Leah and Deborah. Leah shall prepare mother, daughter, and Deborah as strong servants of the Most High God. Deborah will be the tent peg that secures God's mother of two nations through days of storm. Deborah will be honored to serve alongside God's chosen all the days of her long life until she walks with her brother, Adniel, in communion with the Most High."

The wife of Bethuel did bear a daughter. He named her Rebekah, meaning "captivating." Once the child was weaned at the urging of his mother, Milcah, Bethuel came and struggled to ask me to send Leah to his wife. "Zimri-Ruel, I know you are a man of God, a priest who intervenes and teaches all Nahor to walk in the ways of the Most High God. My wife could benefit from the help of a strong woman of God, to instruct her and help train up our children. Laban is a good boy but sometimes difficult. He is too young to sit with the men, and now with Rebekah, well, she needs help and guidance. Deborah is nearly of age, so perhaps Leah can now sit with my wife and…"

Not wanting Bethuel to struggle anymore, I interrupted him. "Master Bethuel, what you ask is good. A mother of a very active young boy and now an infant girl needs another woman, maybe a wise woman who has raised her children, to come alongside as a friend and helpmate. I have heard it said by some of the women that I cannot instruct them as I do men. Leah, indeed, knows my heart and has heard my words such that she knows them better than I do myself. Leah could teach as they attend the children, but I would ask that my Deborah come along as well to learn what awaits her in motherhood."

Milcah was pleased that Leah attended Bethuel's wife and children. Bethuel was, therefore, pleased as well.

Leah sat with the wives in the tent of Bethuel every day. Never did a day come when another wife did not sit with them as Leah told all of what she learned of the Most High God. Milcah would often come to look in on her daughter-in-law and grandchildren. She would question Leah about God's intent for Adam and Eve in the garden, always pointing out they two alone were one flesh and it was very good. Deborah was always at Leah's side, never missing a word she said. At home, when I tried to offer advice or teach Deborah something I remembered from the patriarchs or Melchizidek, Deborah would stop me and say, "I know, Papa. Mama has told me that many, many times. Love you, Papa."

She would always leave me, saying, "Love you, Papa."

Rebekah grew up adoring Deborah.

Leah saw her service to the house of Bethuel and the young Rebekah as an opportunity, or even a calling of the Most High God to pour her life and vision of strong women ready to walk alongside their husband as Eve did with Adam before sin corrupted the world, women of faith and strength. She believed it was by the grace of God or by His own calling that she grew strong and independent and married a man she completed, a man who completed her. She considered carefully what made that possible.

Leah recognized the value of work. If a woman was to be as strong as her husband, she must be confident; confidence, she reasoned, came from proven ability. Cooking and attending children would be expected, yes, but that would not show confidence to a man. These things were taken for granted. A girl should see men in their world safely yet clearly enough to understand their work and daily life outside the tent.

Now Bethuel owned large flocks tended occasionally by Laban but also hired men. Bethuel enjoyed visiting his flocks and working with the shepherds. He found great satisfaction in the proper care of his sheep and goats. He enjoyed the fellowship of the shepherds, and he enjoyed being away from his mother, brothers, and the noble family. He was proud of his flocks.

Leah instructed Rebekah with the help of Deborah to visit her father and brother with the flocks. They carried jugs of water, small cakes they had cooked for them, and raisin cakes. Bethuel was pleased with the attention of his daughter and friendly Deborah, her chaperone. Rebekah was told to ask her father about the sheep; are there any new lambs? Is the grass still sufficient? Will they move to a better pasture? Who watches them at night? Why do they always follow the shepherd? Bethuel enjoyed answering Rebekah's questions. They made him adore her even more.

As Rebekah grew older, she lingered longer in the pastures. She asked permission to help with the sheep, she loved them so much, she said. She insisted sweetly with watering the flock in the afternoon before they were gathered for the night watch. It concerned Bethuel that Rebekah was more interested in the flocks than Laban, though Laban was an excellent herdsman. Deborah was always alongside Rebekah; they were inseparable. Out of earshot, they could be seen talking with each other, laughing and being animated.

Leah never neglected instructing the girls and any visiting women in the stories of the Most High God. While they prepared the small cooked cakes each day, Leah would give a lesson; it may be the salvation story of Noah, his family, and the remnant of every living animal on the ark and the rainbow, the sign of God's covenant. She would tell the story of Babel, where God confused the language of all men. She also told of Enoch, who walked with God and then was no more, for God took him unto Himself. She taught the creation story, of Adam and Eve in the garden, told of sin and the consequences of sin for all time, and explained why I sacrificed the sheep, bulls, and goats. She helped them understand their need for atonement. She told the story of my meeting with Melchizedek, priest of the Most High God, and why I am called to do what I do. She listened to their questions and thoughtfully answered. She reminded them over and over what God expected of them. Again and again she would tell them, "Rebekah, Deborah, you shall love the Most High God with all of your heart and all of your soul, and you shall love all those God loves." She would then ask them, "Who does God love?" They would answer, "God loves all people, He loves all of His creation." Leah would ask, "Does God love the just or the unjust?" They would answer, "It is the heart of God that all people would walk with Him. He loves all."

One day, when Rebekah was nearing womanhood, while they prepared the small cakes, Leah told the story of Cain and Abel. She asked Rebekah, "Why did God not stop Cain from slaying his brother? Is not the Most High God all powerful? Cannot he do all things?"

Rebekah had no answer, and she turned to Deborah, who also remained silent.

Leah then asked, "Why did God protect Cain?"

Still, the girls remained silent.

Leah stopped cooking and knelt beside the young women. "This is a hard thing. Our world is not as it was in the garden. Sin has corrupted it. You know that God gave us atonement to deal with our sin. But God is patient, so patient it is hard for us to understand. You know His heart is for all to walk with Him. He is the God of second chances, sometimes third chances, or even more. God does not stop evil things from happening to the innocent, or even to the righteous. God knows they love Him, and He loves them. They will walk with Him. But God wants the guilty to one day walk with Him as well. That is why God let the innocent Abel die."

Turning to Deborah, she said, "That is why the Most High God let Adniel die."

And then Leah wept.

Chapter Twenty-eight

*"Your eyes have seen my unformed substance;
and in Your book they were all written,
the days that were ordained for me, when
as yet there was not one of them."*

—Psalm 139:16

Now Rebekah became a beautiful young woman. She became the strong, confident woman her grandmother, Milcah, wanted her to be. Some would describe her as headstrong and determined to do as she pleased. She was not known to be disrespectful and certainly not dishonoring to her father, but she pushed, pleaded, or cajoled her way beyond what women had been permitted to do before. She was very much like Milcah but in a sweet and engaging way. Deborah was always at her side, joining Rebekah as they ventured out of the tents and off to the pastures, the sheepfold, the wells, the flocks, and the shepherds. Deborah would sometimes caution Rebekah about going beyond the limits of respectability and safety. Both girls were well taught by Leah, but Deborah was the more disciplined in reasoning the consequences of their actions. In that regard, she resembled more her mother, Leah, though Leah often thought both girls a little too assertive. Bethuel would rarely correct the daughter he adored; he commanded Laban, her brother, to watch after her in the pastures.

The tents of Nahor were pitched at their summer pasture near the road to Haran. There was good grass and a large spring-fed well. Troughs were set up at the well to water the camels, oxen, donkeys, and nearby flocks. In the early evening, after the animals were watered, the women would go to the well with their jars to draw water. Rebekah, always happy to get out of the tent, gladly assumed this chore. One evening, Rebekah had gone to the well as usual but had run back to her tent and excitedly told her mother and Deborah about a man she met at the well.

"Mother," she said, almost out of breath, "a man at the well asked me, 'Please let me drink a little water from your jar.' And I said, 'Drink, my lord.' I lowered my jar and gave him a drink. When he finished drinking, I said, 'I will draw also for your camels until they have finished drinking.' So I quickly emptied the jar and went back to draw water for his camels. Meanwhile, the man was watching me in silence. But when the camels finished drinking, he gave me this gold ring and these two gold bracelets. Look! Then he said, 'Whose daughter are you? Tell me, is there room for us to lodge in your father's house?' I told him I am the daughter of Bethuel, the son of Milcah, whom she bore to Nahor. And I said we have plenty of straw and feed and room to lodge in. Then the man bowed low and worshipped the Lord. And he said, 'Blessed be the Lord, the God of my master Abraham, who has not forsaken His loving-kindness and His truth towards my master. As for me, the Lord has guided me in the way to the house of my master's brothers.'"

After seeing the ring and bracelets on Rebekah and hearing her story, Laban ran outside to the man at the well.

Laban told the man, "Come in, blessed of the Lord! Why do you stand outside? I have prepared the house and a place for your camels."

So the man entered the tent. Then Laban unloaded the camels, and he gave straw and feed to the camels and water for the man and the men with him to wash their feet. But when food was set before him to eat, he said, "I will not eat until I have told my business."

Laban replied, "Speak on."

The man said, "I am Abraham's servant. And the Lord has greatly blessed my master so that he has become rich, and He has given him flocks and herds, and silver and gold, and servants and maids, and camels and donkeys. Now Sarah, my master's wife, bore a son to my master in her old age, and he has given him all he has. And my master made me swear, saying, 'You shall not take a wife for my son from the daughters of the Canaanites, in whose land I live, but you shall go to my father's house and to my relatives and take a wife for my son.' And I said to my master, 'Suppose the woman does not follow me?' And he said to me, 'The Lord, before whom I have walked, will send His angel with you to make your journey successful, and you will take a wife for my son from my relatives and from my father's house, then you will be free from my oath when you come to my relatives. And if they do not give her to you, you will be free from my oath.'"

Abraham's servant continued, "So I came today to the well and said, 'O Lord, the God of my master Abraham, if it is Your will to now make my journey successful, for I am standing by the well, may it be that the young woman who comes out to draw water and to whom I say, "Please let me drink a little water from your jar," and she will say to me, "You drink, and I will draw for your camels as well," let her be the woman whom the Lord has appointed for my master's son.' Before I finished speaking in my heart, Rebekah came out with her jar on her shoulder and went down to the well and drew water, and I said to her, 'Please let me drink.' And she quickly lowered her jar from her shoulder and said, 'Drink and I will water your camels also.' Then I asked her, 'Whose daughter are you?' And she said, 'The daughter of Bethuel, Nahor's son, whom Milcah bore to him.' I put the ring on her nose and the bracelets on her wrists. And I bowed and worshipped the Lord, the God of my master Abraham, who has guided me in the right way to take the daughter of master's kinsman for his son. So now if you are going to deal kindly and truly with my master, let me know that I may turn to right hand or to the left."

Then Laban and Bethuel answered, "The matter comes from the Lord, so we cannot speak to you bad or good. Rebekah is here, take her and go and let her be the wife of your master's son as the Lord has spoken."

Hearing this, Abraham's servant bowed to the ground and worshipped the Lord. He then brought out articles of gold and rich garments and gave them to Rebekah. He also gave precious things to her brother and to her mother. Then Abraham's servant and all the men with him ate and rested, spending the night in Bethuel's tent.

In the morning, Abraham's servant announced, "Bring Rebekah, we are returning to my master."

But Laban and his mother said, "Let the girl stay with us a few days, say ten, and then she can go with you."

Abraham's servant said, "Do not delay me since the Lord has prospered my way. Send me away that I may go to my master."

They replied, "We will call the girl and consult her wishes."

They sent for Rebekah and asked her, "Will you go with this man?"

Rebekah replied simply, "I will go."

Rebekah returned to the women's chamber to gather her things. She called for Deborah and said, "Come with me. I will make you my nurse. You shall have fine clothes, the best things, and we will be together."

Before Deborah could speak, Rebekah added, "I always depend on you to see I do not stray too far. Come with me."

Deborah replied, "The Most High God has chosen this path. I will say my farewells to my father and mother."

When Deborah announced she was leaving with Rebekah, Leah and I could not speak. Deborah said, "I go with Rebekah to be her nurse. The Most High God has chosen this path."

I remembered the dream so many years before. Melchizidek had prepared me for this day. Leah remembered as well. I said simply, "It is the path chosen by the Most High God. Go with my blessing."

Deborah prepared her things for travel, and as she was about to leave, I asked, "Let us bless your journey ahead."

We walked to the line of ten camels being loaded with provisions and the garments, goods, and belongings of Rebekah. Rebekah was still adding to their number when we approached the men and the camels.

"Who is this?" a middle-aged man asked.

I spoke. "This is Deborah, Rebekah's nurse."

"I will speak with Eliezer," the man replied.

Abraham's servant walked over and said to the young man, "Abiel, load her belongings. Rebekah has required her nurse to come along as well."

Surprised to hear these names after so many years, I loudly asked, "Eliezer, brother of Keshet? Abiel, son of Jared and Abaigael?"

Both men looked surprised and answered in unison, "Yes."

Wide-eyed and grinning, I said, "My name is Zimri-Ruel, father to the nurse Deborah. I traveled with Jared and Abaigael from Salem to Hazor and then to Damascus. We were returning after meeting King Melchizidek, priest of the Most High God. Abiel, your mother, Abaigael, was carrying you at the time. Melchizedek prophesied your birth, your name, and your service to the Most High God. And you, Eliezer, I received the hospitality of Keshet when Jared brought Abaigael to Damascus for safety and to begin a new business relationship. Zadok and Obed settled there as well. And, Shem, I know Keshet reconciled with the Patriarch Shem. It was a hard thing to say goodbye to friends, no, brothers who walked with the Most High God."

Both men looked at me in amazement. Abiel deferred to the senior, Eliezer, who answered, "My brother speaks with great love for you, Zimri-Ruel. He too now follows the Most High God. He spent many years with the Patriarch Shem. He dotes on the patriarch, who was confined to his bed when we last passed through Damascus. It was my brother, Keshet, who taught Abiel the skills of trading and sent him to me as my assistant. My master, Abraham, is very old, as am I. Abiel will take my duties when Abraham is gathered to his fathers. As I served Abrabam, Abiel will serve Isaac, his son and his heir."

When Eliezer finished, Abiel spoke. "I have heard your story many times, Zimri-Ruel. My father and mother refer to you as the brother they love. They live yet in Damascus. Zadok walks with the Lord, and Obed has hired men to work the forge. Keshet still joins them for sacrifices of atonement and thanksgiving. Others have joined them and followed the voice of the Most High God."

"And Abaigael," I asked, "does she still speak the words of the Most High God?"

"Yes," he answered, "and my father, Jared, stays by her side. There is so much to tell you, but here is Rebekah, and we must soon take our leave."

"Do you follow the caravan road through Haran, Carchemish, Khalab, Hamath, and Damascus?" I asked.

"Yes, and from Damascus to Hazor and then Dothan, Shechem, Bethel, Salem, and to the tents of Abraham at the Oaks of Mamre," Abiel replied.

"Consider the amazing plan of the Most High God, that He should put my Deborah, my daughter, and Rebekah on the path I traveled so many years ago. The caravan to Damascus and the road to Salem bring so many memories to an old man. The lessons of Terah, the blessing of the Patriarch Shem, and King Melchizidek coming alongside me on the road by night. What a glorious walk that was! And I recall your master—Abram he was called then—leading his host to the gates of Salem and offering a tithe. I still remember as if it were yesterday, the blessing he was given by King Melchizidek, priest of the Most High God."

Turning to Deborah, now perched high atop a spitting camel, I softly said, "May the Most High God walk beside you and keep You on His path. May your journey open your eyes as my eyes were opened all those many years ago. Take the blessings of your father and the love of your mother with you always. May the Most High God be a shield over you and comfort you. May you find wisdom and faithfulness in your service to Rebekah, whom you love so dearly. The Most High God be with you. His mercy is forever!"

Deborah looked down on us and said, "Love you, Papa. Love you, Mama."

Rebekah was astride her camel. Bethuel, his wife, and Laban and their whole household were assembled. Laban motioned to speak as Eliezer saw everything was ready. They said, "May you, our sister, become thousands of ten thousands. And may your descendants possess the gate of those who hate them."

The voice in my soul sang out;

> I will exalt my God and my Sovereign.
> I will bless His name this day and forever
> How great is My God on high?
> His greatness is unsearchable.

THE PRAISE SINGER

His mind is ever unknowable.
One generation shall praise His name to the next
Succeeding generations shall declare His salvation!
I meditate on His great splendor
And remember all of His great works.
Let our sons and our youth be as the tall cedar
And our daughters as splendid pillars adorned for the palace.
Let their flocks bring forth thousands and ten thousands.
Let their cattle bear without loss.
Call our children to bless and serve the Most High God
To walk with Him all the days of their lives.
How blessed are the people who hear His voice.
How blessed are the people whose God is the Lord!

The train of camels moved slowly and regally despite their individual ungainly appearance. All who would see this train pass would know they were witness to a mighty and noble lady on a historic journey.

Chapter Twenty-nine

"A friend loves for all times, and a brother is born for a time of adversity."

—Proverbs 17:17

With Rebekah no longer in her tent, Bethuel's wife no longer saw the need for Leah to attend her household. The women of Nahor had all heard the lessons of Leah many times, and their talk returned to family matters, gossip, and the daily life in the great city of tents. Even Milcah, now the aged grand matriarch of Nahor, remained in her magnificent chamber of Nahor's tent. All of the enthusiasm and excitement of raising up strong daughters had been poured into two daring young women who were now gone. All were proud of the girls—Rebekah to be wife of the wealthy chief of a great tribe and Deborah, her best friend and confidant and now her honored nurse—but they knew somehow things were no longer the same. No longer would the forward, even daring exploits of these two strong, confident young women dominate the talk at the well. The young women that remained in the village would have to struggle on their own, knowing that Nahor and Bethuel's tolerance of Rebekah and Deborah's strong independence, challenging generations of tradition, would not fall so lovingly on them. And Milcah's retreat to her chambers left them without their most persuasive defender. A melancholy pervaded among the women of Nahor.

Nahor and Bethuel deeply loved Rebekah and were truly saddened by her departure. They were proud of her, of course, and most pleased that Deborah, whom they adored and admired as the voice of caution and reason for their strong-willed Rebekah, would be with her as she adjusted to the role of a great lady. The men of Nahor would also miss the two young women who challenged the rules, for deep down, they were attracted to the girls' strength. They were drawn to the two beautiful young women—women who were a challenge; women whose affection needed to be won, not purchased by a marriage contract. In their hearts, they longed for strong wives to support them and understand the challenges they faced.

Leah and I shared the unspoken melancholy of the city of Nahor. I continued to lead the people in sacrifices and praises to the Most High God, supported as ever by Bethuel. It seemed, however, the voice inside of me became silent. New songs of praise did not cross my lips. I knew the Most High God could not change, but I did not dwell on the changes within me. Dov, now old, continuously reminded me of my duties. He talked again and again of the faithfulness of the Most High. My old shepherd friend, Hod, would visit often, retelling stories with Dov and reminding me of the great adventures on the mountainside above Khalab. Hod began to include his son, Jael, in his visits. He always claimed Jael needed to hear from the elder and the priest to know his father's stories were true. The young Jael was told that the priest, Zimri-Ruel, was once known as Jael, the mountain goat, and he too was a shepherd. Hod longed that his son, Jael, would know the beauty of the mountain pastures, far greener and majestic than the semi-arid plains of Nahor. "Jael," he would say, "we need to put the mountain in you if you are to be truly the mountain goat like your namesake Zimri-Ruel."

Hod and Dov spoke longingly for the village in the high hills and wondered if it was still as they left it so many years ago. They spoke of the lost vision to return to Dabar El Elyon with our restored herds. But for many years, the sons of Dabar El Elyon had married the daughters of Nahor, and the sons of Nahor had married the daughters of Dabar El Elyon. There was no longer a sheep herd and goat herd of Dabar El Elyon. The herds divided among the families and now intermingled with the great flocks of Nahor. The people of Dabar El Elyon were one with the people of Nahor. Only the old remembered the mountain village, but they longed to see it again.

I could not stop wondering about my first friends, Jared and Abaigael, the houses of Zadok and Keshet, and the Patriarch Shem. What a wonder that the Most High God would send Eliezer and Abiel, son of Jared, to Nahor and choose Rebekah as wife to the son of Abraham, father of nations. And I considered the wonderful plan of God that my sweet Deborah would go with her as her honored nurse and friend. My heart pulled at me to follow the caravan road to Khalab where I could climb to our hillside village and on to Damascus for a visit with the Patriarch Shem and my first friends and brother and sister followers of the Most High God. But I could never abandon my sheep. No, a shepherd's place is with his flock always and forever.

Leah knew my heart; Leah always knew my heart. Always having strength when I struggled with doubt, she told me simply, "Husband, ask the Most High God. He knows your heart. He has set you on His path. You have been faithful. You say the Most High God loves his people, would he withhold the desires of your heart? Seek Him and ask him the desire of you heart."

I considered Leah's words, her simple wisdom. That night, in the silence of our tent, my precious Leah asleep beside me, I remembered walking the road first with Terah, then king Melchizedek, and finally with Jared and Abaigael. I remembered the excitement of learning the truths and faithfulness of the Most High God. I remembered the joyful songs of praise that lifted my soul to soaring. I determined I would sacrifice to the Most High God and then pray and seek His will in this longing inside me. Resolved to put the matter before the God who always led me, I fell asleep.

The next morning, I went out to the flock and chose the best lamb, one without blemish to the shepherd's eye, and offered it up as sacrifice to the Most High God, confessing my sin, acknowledging my doubt and loss of zeal for praising my creator. After the sacrifice, I sat beside the altar, remembering the blessings of the Lord in my life. Finally, I stood with arms stretched out and prayed, "Most Holy God, my love for You is unending. I have walked in Your ways and sought Your will. I have obeyed all that You have commanded me. Know, Most High God, my heart grieves to see the Patriarch Shem and my first friends in my walk with you. If it pleases You, send your servant, Bethuel, to ask me to travel with him to Damascus. If my lord Bethuel asks Your servant, saying, 'The Lord has put it in my mind to journey to Damascus, as my father, Terah, was accustomed, to sell our tents and buy comforts for our people and to comfort Milcah and my wife, who long for Rebekah. I would have you come with me and share again the lessons of your journeys, and we can behold the wonders of the night sky together,' then I will know that this is your will, and I shall go with him and with Dov and with Hod and with young Jael."

As I finished my prayer and stood beside the altar, Bethuel walked up behind and said, "Zimri-Ruel, it is good that I find you before the altar of the Most High God. I have a request for you, and if you agree, we shall make a sacrifice to the Most High God and seek his protection on our endeavor. The Lord has put it in my mind to journey to Damascus as was the custom of my father, Terah, to sell our tents and buy comforts for our people. I seek comfort for my mother, Milcah, and my wife who long for Rebekah. I would have you come with me and share again all that you have learned when you traveled the road set before you by the Most High God. We should bring with us the elder Dov and the shepherd Hod and his earnest son, Jael, who yearn to see again the high hills above Khalab. Will it not be good to sleep under the night skies and behold the wonders of the Most High?"

I smiled broadly and answered, "Truly, this is of the Most High God! For it is my heart's desire to journey to Damascus to visit one more time with the Patriarch Shem and my first friends I met on the road. I have sacrificed unto Him and asked Him to send this sign, 'If it pleases You, send your servant, Bethuel, to ask me to travel with him to Damascus. If my lord, Bethuel, asks Your servant, saying, "The Lord has put it in my mind to journey to Damascus, as my father, Terah, was accustomed, to sell our tents and buy comforts for our people and to comfort Milcah and my wife, who long for Rebekah. I would have you come with me and share again the lessons of your journeys, and we can behold the wonders of the night sky together," then I will know that this is your will, and I shall go with him and with Dov and with Hod and with young Jael.'"

Bethuel answered, "Gather Dov, Hod, and young Jael, and we shall go."

I replied, "What you say is good! And Leah will travel with me and share in my joy of seeing once more the Patriarch Shem and my first friends."

Bethuel's servants completed loading the ten, pack camels with their sacks of goat hair tent panels. Two more camels carried food, water, and provisions for the journey. Dov, Hod, young Jael, the two servants, and three trained men were to ride camels, while Bethuel chose a reliable riding donkey. Remembering the advice of Terah, I chose donkeys for me and Abaigael. The morning sun was not yet high in the eastern sky as we made our way towards the caravan road. The camel's ungainly appearance was now supplanted with a smooth measured gate as they made their way over the sparse grassland. Hod, clearly enjoying himself, could be heard saying, "Not quite the view from the high hills and mountains, but all the same, a much finer view than on foot."

Turning, I could see the city of gray topped, black tents of Nahor shrinking. I remembered my sighting of Nahor three decades earlier. The cocoons of the plains had been my home the greater portion of my life. My son was buried there. Some dear friends and their children remain—the sheep of my fold. I wondered if I would ever see them again. That was all of Nahor that I missed.

Bethuel's servants and the trained men were accustomed to travel, though their most frequent trips were to Haran, centered on the plains of Nahor. Like the great caravan Terah joined, we soon fell into a routine. As the day wore on, we each focused on protection against the sun. Covered in light robes and head scarves, talking was difficult. We rode mostly in silence, captive to our own thoughts, occasionally shaking the dust off our head scarf to take a drink of water from the water skin slung forward of the saddle. As we intersected the caravan route, we headed south towards Carchemish, only two days' journey.

We stopped briefly in the early afternoon for light food, raisin or fig cakes, and water. The servants tended the camels and donkeys while we stretched out on cloaks spread out on the hot, dry ground. It was too hot to talk, so we took the food and water with only the most perfunctory words exchanged. We tried our best to rest enough for the long afternoon ahead. Night camp was made about an hour before sunset. Again, the servants tended to the animals. Fires were started, and one of the trained men took the first night watch. A small tent was prepared for Leah, the rest of us determined to sleep under the stars. Leah insisted on preparing the meal for everyone; no one objected. The animals tethered and bedded for the night, and the servants brought food and wine from the provision supply. Once the sun set, everyone's mood improved. Hod was his boisterous self and immediately began telling his favorite stories of shepherding the flocks in the high hills and mountainside.

Young Jael heard all of his father's stories many times, but for the sake of everyone else, he asked, "Please tell how Zimri-Ruel killed the great lion."

Hod looked over at me. I nodded and then he began, "It was not long after Zimri-Ruel returned to our village after running off to follow the voice he always speaks of. To me he was still Jael, but he was, indeed, different than before he left us. For one thing, he could actually speak in whole sentences."

Glancing at me, he returned to the story. "But he insisted on serving us and insisted on taking his turn watching the sheep at the night fold. We had seen footprints of the great cat earlier, but that had been some days. Zimri-Ruel took only his shepherd's crook and a knife in his belt and set his rug across the gate of the sheepfold. Zimri-Ruel, you can tell your story better than I can."

"No," I said, "I am anxious to hear what happens next."

Hod said, "Well, Zimri-Ruel will have to say how the great cat got the jump on him, but when we found him in the morning, the great cat lay dead on top of him, impaled by the staff of Zimri-Ruel's crook. The knife that cut the lion's throat was still in his hand. Our friend and priest was badly mauled, some took him for dead, but the faintest of breath could be heard from his mouth. Such a great cat it was! Claws as large as a camel's foot! Such bravery and strength! Well, Zimri-Ruel is a true shepherd, indeed! A defender of the flock until the end! And Leah, Leah nursed him for many days. By the grace of the Most High God, Zimri-Ruel is a shepherd to the shepherd. He will always be a wise old mountain goat watching for danger and ready to move us from the threat below."

Bethuel had been listening carefully. When Hod finished, he spoke. "Perhaps I should use our priest to lead our trained men! I never heard this story before. But I see the steadfast spirit the Most High God has poured out upon you. And Leah could do none other than to nurse you back to health. Surely God blessed us when he sent you to our camp. And now Deborah serves alongside my Rebekah as well. Truly, we are blessed."

The two trained men and the servants gazed closely upon me and spoke quietly to each other. I could see Leah smile as she sat quietly in her tent.

We arrived at the gates of Carchemish just before sunset the next day. Bethuel took us along with him to an inn he knew in the city. The trained men and servants led the camels and donkeys to stalls where fresh straw and fodder awaited them.

The inn was different than those of Haran and Damascus. The interior was crafted with panels of wood, brightly painted and richly carved. Even the ceiling was paneled in boards of aromatic cedar. The tables were solid and intricately carved. Rugs and embroidery were hung on the walls, but it was the wood paneling that showcased wealth and beauty. The skill of the craftsman in wood was on display everywhere I looked in this enticing city. Bethuel provided us with the finest food the inn could offer. We enjoyed his company and goodwill and then went to bed. It was strange seeing neither the dark goat hair of a tent or bright stars of the night sky over my head; instead, I looked up to see a brightly painted wood ceiling.

The road south from Carchemish to Khalab skirted along low hills, rising steeper to the west and flanked by tall mountains. There seemed to be less dust in the air, and fields of grain and groves of trees could be seen clearly in the hills. The early afternoon stop was much the same as the previous ones—simple food, water, and rest. That night, we stopped just off the road sheltered behind a hill covered with oak and terebinth. Again, the fires were lit, and Leah assumed responsibility for the meal. Hod settled comfortably into his role as chief story teller, the men of the camp now content to listen.

Bethuel walked up beside me and asked, "Walk with me, Zimri-Ruel. We have a fine canopy of stars above and a good moon to give us light. Come, walk. I would have your ear on a matter."

"Of course, my lord, it is, indeed, a fine evening."

We walked a few moments in silence, and I could sense the unease in Bethuel's manner. After a few minutes, he began, "I am afraid this journey will not lead me to what I seek." He paused again.

"What is it that you seek, Lord Bethuel?"

Looking up into the clear night sky, Bethuel quietly said, "I seek to bring comfort to my wife. I seek to ease her fears and unrest."

I said nothing. Bethuel continued, "My dear wife fears that I shall do as my father and take a concubine or another wife. He has said several times, 'You have but one son and heir. You have sent off your only daughter, should not you, a wealthy man, have many sons?' My wife knows of the pain of my mother, Milcah, when Nahor took Reumah as his concubine. Eight sons plus daughters were not enough? None of Nahor's expensive gifts to Milcah have removed the hurt. There is no happiness in the tents of my father. I know he is a great man and righteous, but his tent has no peace."

I answered, "And Leah has taught Milcah and her daughters and daughters-in-law that this was not the Most High God's chosen path for man, for it was not so in the garden when God walked with our father, Adam, and mother, Eve. The Most High created Eve from Adam and said they were one flesh."

"It as you say," Bethuel replied. "My dear wife has told me this as well. I have told her I will have no other wives or concubines, but she says we have only Laban, and wealthy men forget the wives of their youth and beget sons as they do flocks and cattle. It is always this way with great men. And rich embroidered robes and rings of gold did not satisfy Milcah. They will not satisfy your wife either. They are as tassels and richly appointed bridles on a camel, decorations on a rich man's property. No, gifts alone will not satisfy her, just as words alone have been to no avail. She will know the truth of your words by what you do, not what you say."

Bethuel stopped and looked at me. "I have always loved my wife. I honor her. I do whatever I can to please her. Do, you say? What else can I do?"

I asked Bethuel, "Has Nahor ever sworn an oath?"

"Yes," Bethuel answered. He is a righteous man. His word is true, but he has sworn an oath."

"Why?" I asked.

"Well, to show the matter is most important to him, he would place all of his honor and very life against his word on the matter."

"And you, Bethuel, have you sworn an oath? Would you swear an oath for your dear wife? A public oath before the household of Nahor that you will love only your wife until death takes you or her? An oath as one given against all of your honor and very life?"

"An oath to my wife? A public oath before the whole household of my father? Yes, she would find comfort in such an oath and a gift, a token to carry as a sign of my oath. Yes, dear priest, what you say is good."

As we walked back towards the fire, I asked Bethuel, "If you would hear me on another matter, my Lord Bethuel, I do not see Laban when I offer sacrifices for atonement or for thanksgiving. He shows no interest in the stories and worship of the Most High God. From my first day in Nahor, you have sought me to be your priest, to intercede for Nahor just as I intercede for my sheep, Dabar El Elyon. If I am to intercede for your son, Laban, I would know his heart. Laban is under your household, how would you have me intercede for him?"

Bethuel sighed. "Yes, Laban, my son, cares little for the sacrifices and worship. He does not object that we worship, that would show great disrespect. My son, Laban, follows the ways of my brother, Huz, his uncle. They always speak of more."

"More?" I asked.

"Yes, more—more sheep, more goats, more cattle, more donkeys, more camels, more tents, bigger tents, more gold, more silver, more rugs, and more embroidered robes. And still more, more wives, more concubines, more sons. They live only to have more."

I asked Bethuel, "Has great riches brought peace and happiness to the tent of Nahor and Milcah?"

"Not to Nahor and Milcah or to my tent either. No, Terah's words were true. Comfort cannot be found in treasures but in a happy household."

Bethuel stopped and paused before asking, "Does not sacrifice atone for our sin? Will not the Most High God show us mercy if we sacrifice to Him? Laban tells me that the bulls and sheep of my sacrifices come from his inheritance. The Most High God will accept these sacrifices on his behalf, though it pains Laban to see them destroyed. And Laban would have no idols in our midst as an offense to the Most High God."

My heart went out to Bethuel; I could feel the pain in his question. "The Most High God does not desire sacrifices of bulls and sheep. They are but a sign and a reminder to us of the cost and penalty of our sin. Is it not said, have you not heard, that Abraham, your uncle and father-in-law to Rebekah, trusted God? And God gave Abraham a son, Isaac, in his old age when his wife, Sarah, was well beyond the age to bear a child. Is it not true the word of King Melchizidek, priest of the Most High God, when he received the tithe from Abraham, for he told me that Abraham was made righteous by his faith, not by sacrifice and not by tithes. And Abraham will be the father of nations and the father of all who trust the Most High God in faith."

Bethuel was listening carefully, so I continued, "The Most High God's desire is for us to walk with Him in righteousness as He did with our father, Adam, and our mother, Eve, in the garden. Have I not taught you what God commands us? You shall love God with all of your heart and all of your soul, and you shall love all whom the Most High God loves. Should we not love our God in whom we can place all of our trust? A God who made us and loves us? A God whose mercy will endure forever?"

Bethuel replied, "What you say, I know to be true, but it does not lift my burden for my son. How does a father direct the path of his son?"

I answered truthfully, "I know not if he can. He can train up a child in the ways of righteousness. He can teach his son what is expected of him. He can live righteously himself, and he can intercede for his son. He can remind his son to listen for the voice of the Most High God, but a father cannot atone for the sins of his son. A father cannot purchase the mercy of God for His son. A father can only direct his son to the right path."

Then encouraged in my soul, I added, "Take hope in this, the Most High God does not need to be instructed in mercy and patience. By his mercy, He provides atonement. By His mercy, He sends His voice to speak to our mind and soul. It is His nature to love, and His patience is great. The Most High God's will for Laban is as your will. He desires to walk with Him. Take hope, Bethuel. We shall both stay steadfast in this hope and pray for Laban. Who knows the path laid before him?"

Chapter Thirty

*"The house of the wicked will be destroyed.
But the tent of the upright will flourish."*

—*Proverbs 14:11*

As we approached the walls of Khalab, Bethuel determined to enter the city and sell some of the tents. He sought to visit the marketplace and perhaps find a special gift for his wife. I begged leave to take Leah, Dov, Hod, and young Jael up the path to the village we called Dabar El Elyon. Reckoning the many years that had passed since fleeing our homes, Bethuel warmly insisted we go with his blessing. He insisted he would wait for us whatever time we required.

We declined Bethuel's offer to send his trained men with us and left the camels with his servants. Leah and Dov rode the sure-footed donkeys while Hod, Jael, and I walked alongside. We had no problem in finding the path off the caravan road. It had not changed in all the years that had passed. We walked slowly up and over the small hills, past the groves of olives and figs, and we climbed higher into the scrub oaks and terebinth trees. As we walked, we watched Khalab grow small and the ridge of the mountain come closer. The rocky ledges and cliffs were in view. The thin pine trees separating high pastures told us we were near the village. When I first saw a mountain goat gazing down on us from only sling stone away, I could not help but think Matai would have spotted him from far below. The path, the mountain, the sky, all were the same, as if the last three decades were but a dream.

Young Jael was the first to announce we were being watched. Scanning the fields above, I saw him, no, two and then three men watching us from the far grain field just below Leah's olive grove. They stood and watched. Just before we came in view of the village, a man approached us.

"Friends, you have lost your way. You can go no farther. There is no road over the mountain. It is best you go back down the mountain and follow the caravan road."

Seeing the pain in Dov's eyes and anger in the eyes of Hod, I replied, "The walk was hard, would you deny us the hospitality of water and rest for our journey?"

The man appeared reluctant. I determined to go on. "Many years ago, we fled over this mountain at the sacking of Khalab. We traveled this very path. The village just above was also sacked and plundered. We found our way over the ridge and through the forest on the other side, down to a river between the mountains, which led north to the great river. We now follow this path to thank the Most High God for His great salvation. I see groves and grain fields before us. Surely there is water, a well where we may be refreshed?"

The man relented. "You may, indeed, refresh at the well and your donkeys also. And then you may go about your pilgrimage."

As we walked the final length of path into the village, I asked our guide, "Do you have a name for this village? I see it is well tended with grain, groves, and hillside and mountain pastures."

The villager replied, "We are a poor village. We do well to supply our needs. We are not like the cities and villages on the road where hospitality can be shown at no cost. Our forefathers built this village, planted the groves, cleared the fields. and established the pastures and fold many generations ago. It is called Beth Sadi, 'Mountain House.' Here is water you may drink, and here you may rest."

We stopped in front of the well in the center of the village. As we looked upon our former home, strangers stared back at us with hostile eyes. Dov's house, directly across from the well, looked just as it did the day we left. Leah's house was still there, also untouched by time. I saw that the house I built and the shepherds finished for me had been opened up on one side and once again provided shelter to the goat.

Dov and Leah looked around silently. Neither said a single word. Hod could be seen pointing and speaking to young Jael. The eyes of every villager followed Hod's gestures. Once water was drawn, the animal's watered, and we had drunk our fill, the unnamed villager returned to us. He spoke to me impatiently. "You have your water, should you not be on your way down the mountain while the light of the day is good?"

I answered him, "We will not impose any more on your hospitality. Thank you for the water. But as I said, we seek to remember our salvation by the Most High God and ask only that we go higher to the ridge of the mountain. We will take nothing from your fields, from your groves, or from your flocks. We will follow the path to ridge, not turning to the right or to the left. We will worship our God, and then we will go as we came."

"We do not know this Most High God you worship. We worship Amurru, known as Belu Sadi, 'Lord of the Mountains,' and his wife Belit-Seri, Lady of the Desert. Do not offend our gods with your worship in sight of this village. But you may go in peace as you wish."

I helped Leah onto her donkey. Dov climbed on his donkey, and we walked slowly out of the village, up the path towards the sheepfold. The stares of inhospitable eyes burned on our backs as we went. Out of sight and out of earshot, the others began to speak.

Dov remarked, "There was no hospitality, none. They live in our houses, eat our figs, cook our grain in our olive oil, and feed their sheep on our pastures!"

Hod could not contain himself. "Their forefathers built this village generations ago? They dug the well? They planted the groves, terraced the fields? Lies! And they are unwilling to share with the foreigner or traveler? Has there ever been a people of less honor?"

Jael remarked, "They call Dabar El Elyon after a god made of stone? A deaf and dumb idol and command we not offend it? Take our worship out of its sight? A stone idol has no eyes to see, no ears to hear, or mouth to speak!"

Leah spoke last. "It is good to worship the Most High God on this mountain. For, indeed, he did lead us to salvation from the Amorites and from poverty. Yes, I desire to worship Him on the mountaintop."

After a few moments of silence, Leah added, "Husband, your goat pen is back as it once was." Then she laughed lightly.

As we walked, we came upon the sheepfold or what once had been the sheepfold and now a deserted, stony enclave surrounded by rock. Nearby was the cave that sheltered me as a slave shepherd. I had forgotten how small it was, barely long enough to lie down. I instinctively looked up from the cave at the sky above and thanked the Most High God for finding me in this small hidden place.

We continued up the path to the high pastures, above the thin pine trees to a wide rock at the ridgeline. The village below was hidden by the pine trees; Khalab was just visible far below to the east. The next ridge of mountains rose as a sentinel to the west. It was a good place to worship the Most High God. We each fell first to our knees and then lay prostrate on the ground, our arms outstretched, and thanked the Most High God, our God and savior, for His mercy and our salvation. I led our small band in a song of thanksgiving, singing one praise phrase at a time, which was repeated by Leah and my brothers of Dabar El Elyon.

How good it is to sing praises to our God on the mountaintop!

> With thankful hearts, we praise our Savior!
> Hear, O God, our cries of thanksgiving!
> Listen as we praise Your holy name.
> We are a small people of no account to kings and princes.
> But You found us on this mountain.
> You heard our cries for help.
> By Your mighty hand, O God, you sheltered us.
> By Your mercy, you led us from danger.
> Even our little ones were protected by Your shield.
> You have loved us with Your tender mercy.
> As the shepherd leads his flock,
> You, O God, have brought us to new pastures

> You led us to green grass
> You draw for us cool water from Your well.
> The whole of creation is but a pebble in Your hand.
> The mighty sea, the mountains, and the plains
> Are as sand shaken from a sandal.
> Nations stumble and fall before You.
> Kings and princes will kneel before Your name.
> They are no more than a tuft of wool in the wind.
> Your voice we have heard, O Most High God,
> We will follow You all the days of our lives.
> We will thank you forever.
> We will serve You always.
> Keep our hearts tender in love for You.
> You have showered us with tender mercies.
> Keep us in Your path of righteousness always
> Walk beside us in love.
> Guard our hearts with praise
> To Your glory, O God, forever!

Our praises to the Most High God lifted our spirits. We began our walk down while the sun was still above the western mountain. Refreshed in our souls, we talked of our children who never knew this mountain, and marriages, and new families. We spoke of our freedom of want and growing wealth of all who left this place; we thanked God for his many blessings and prayed for more blessings to come. Our talk and laughter must have been curious to the Amorites now inhabiting our homes, but we walked by them, giving them no thought at all.

As we reached the low hills, the sun was behind the mountain, and darkness quickly enveloped us in its shadow. It was our boisterous laughter that betrayed our presence and the rising moon above that revealed our approach as Bethuel's hired men waited for us where the path met the caravan road.

The leader of the hired men asked, "Is all well up in Dabar El Elyon?"

Elder Dov spoke for us. "Dabar El Elyon walks before you and walks among Nahor. Up there is only a poor Amorite village."

I entered Khalab for the first time that dark night. It was strange, having looked down upon the city from the high hills, to enter its walls and see its people. It had none of the fine carvings of Carchemish or the wealth of Damascus. The buildings within the stonewalls were common mud brick. The streets were narrow and dusty. We passed by the market, but the merchants were home and their stalls hidden behind closed curtains. We passed by the temple, still lit by torches in the late-night hour; a great stone idol was seated under its massive roof, its blind stone eyes fixed out towards the square in front. Beyond the temple, a street could be seen rising to the citadel built on the rocky tel or hill in the center of the city. The fortress and the palace rose high above the tel. We followed a side street beyond the temple to the inn where Bethuel was waiting for us. It amazed me that the king of the Amorites chose this dusty city as his capital. But I considered the security provided by the citadel on the tel. Opulence took second place to security in the mind of the king. Dov told me the only change he noticed was the idol in the temple.

The inn was busy; men were seated at every table. Some were eating, others seated with a bowl of wine in front of them in private conversation with those nearby. Bethuel was expecting us, and when we entered, he immediately came over and beckoned us to join him. As we sat at his table, he summoned a steward to bring wine and the food he asked to have waiting. We had barely filled our cups from the bowl of fine wine set before us when three servants filed in with the feast he had ordered for us. It suddenly occurred to me how hungry I was. The others appeared as I, as they quickly filled plates with roast lamb, bread, figs, and raisins. The emotions of the day were pushed to the back of my mind as I ate and enjoyed the company of my friends.

The trained men came in while we were eating, having taken the donkeys and camels to the stable. The leader could be seen speaking in Bethuel's ear. "I am sorry to hear you did not find your old homes as you wished," he began. "But the Most High God has surely blessed you as he has blessed me with your company." Then he added, "My search today was also disappointing. Eat well, rest tonight, and we travel on to Damascus tomorrow."

"My Lord Bethuel," I replied, "indeed, today we thanked the Most High God for his salvation and his blessings upon our people as we live as one with Nahor. As you say, it is surely by His will we prosper among you."

Chapter Thirty-one

*"Behold, how good and pleasant it is for
brothers to dwell together in unity."*

—*Psalm 133:1*

As we approached Damascus, several caravans were reforming outside the city gate. There was an air of excitement to see groups of laden camels coming and going between caravans and in and out from the city. Merchants could be seen going back and forth through caravans speaking with travelers from many nations. It was just as Terah had told me to expect all those many years before.

As we came near the gate, I heard Bethuel say to himself resolutely, "If I can't find it here, it probably doesn't exist."

I came close alongside Bethuel. "My lord, when we enter the city, ask for the house of Keshet. It was he who showed me great hospitality when I arrived here with my dear friends, Jared and Abaigael. Keshet can help you."

"I had planned to stay at the inn as is my practice," he replied.

"Keshet once told me his business is to know who to know. He is very well known in the city with every merchant and man of influence and is a disciple of the Patriarch Shem. And Keshet is the brother to Lord Abraham's steward and servant, Eliezer. He may have news of Rebekah. Keshet is a righteous man who can be trusted, my lord."

"What you say is good, Zimri-Ruel. We will seek the house of Keshet."

We entered the city through its wide and welcoming gate. We followed the merchants and traders to the market. Such a large market! There was nothing to compare with it in Haran, certainly not Khalab, or even the elegant Carchemish. We passed row upon row of stalls filled with every treasure imaginable; we passed exotic foods I did not recognize, and people in every manner of dress. The noise! Men were shouting and haggling over price, and women at the food stalls were quieter than the men but animated in their business. I could see the excitement in Bethuel's eyes. We asked after Keshet and were led down a short street off the center of the market to the compound I remembered. I dismounted my donkey and knocked on the small door in the gate to his compound. A servant opened the door.

"I am Zimri-Ruel, a friend to Lord Keshet from many years ago, about the time Lord Keshet became a disciple of the Patriarch Shem. I came with my friends, the household of Zadok, workers in bronze. Would you announce my presence to your lord?"

The servant closed the door. Soon the large gate opened, and he motioned for us to enter. The compound was as I remembered it; inside, I saw the warehouse and storerooms and a large stable. The house of Keshet was beyond through the inner gate. Immediately, several servants appeared who went about helping Leah, Bethuel, Dov, Hod, Jael, and the trained men and servants dismount. The Camels and donkeys were led to the stable, watered, and given fresh straw.

The gatekeeper once again spoke. "My master, Lord Keshet, is at the house of the Patriarch Shem. The patriarch is near death, and my master comforts him. I will send someone to tell him you are here. The sons of Zadok wait with him also. Please come inside. Wash the dust of travel. Be refreshed while you wait."

We were ushered into the inner compound, the house of Keshet. The peace and serenity came upon me again just as it did those many years ago. The contrast to the noise of the market was striking. The only sounds were the songs of the birds and the muffled low voices of the household servants. Small trees, palms, aromatic flowers, and blooming bushes surrounded the outside wall and framed small tables and benches. A half roof covered the compound, and shade awnings of fine linen were draped across outstretched beams. Water ran continuously in a small pool. The shade, the water, and the songbirds all spoke of peace, tranquility, and comfort. It was a safe refuge from the outside world.

Leah was led to the women's courtyard where she could wash and refresh privately. The servants and trained men were shown to the courtyard of the servants. The chief servant told us, "Your servants and trained men will be treated well and with the greatest hospitality and will join you later after they too have been refreshed." Then we were led to an inner room open to the magnificent courtyard.

Dov was shaking his head in unbelief, his mind unable to fathom what his eyes were seeing. All he could say was, "Such beauty, so much beauty."

Hod's eyes were as large as the full moon on a clear night. "I did not know such a house could be! Is the Master Keshet a king? Surely this is a palace!"

Jael ben Hod was speechless. His jaw was dropped open, and his eyes scanned everything in sight. I saw the water set before us and clean tunics. I motioned for him the wash and change.

Bethuel was smiling. He immediately began to wash. As he put on a clean tunic and was handed a fine embroidered robe by a household servant, he said, "Zimri-Ruel, I shall let you arrange our lodgings in the future! This is, indeed, finer than any inn. Lord Keshet is, indeed, a great man in this city."

I replied without thinking, "His greatness lies not in his wealth. His greatness lies in his love for the Most High God!" Thinking my answer harsh, I added, "The Most High God has blessed the Lord Keshet. He is truly a gifted man, a man of great honor and ability as is his brother, Eliezer."

We were led to another room opening onto the courtyard. The three-sided room was painted in bright colors with a roof painted as the night sky over the desert of Aram. A fine table was set before us in the center of the room. Ripe grapes and olives, cakes of figs and raisins, and a bowl of wine were set on the table. Leah joined us. Once she arrived, the head servant said, "Please eat. Take comfort.

The courtyard is before you. My Master Keshet has been told of your presence." Then he quietly walked off.

After about an hour, Lord Keshet came into the courtyard. A smile came across his lips as he saw me, but his eyes and countenance were heavy. He approached me straightaway and hugged me firmly. "My good friend and brother, Zimri-Ruel, it is truly a blessing form the Most High God to see you again. You and your friends are most welcome. Have my servants treated you well? Please introduce them. I would honor the friends of my friend and brother."

"Lord Keshet, this is Lord Bethuel, a son of Shem by Nahor. He is a great lord of the plains of Nahor and father to Rebekah, taken by your brother, Eliezer, to be wife to Isaac, son of Abraham."

"Welcome, Lord Bethuel. I have news of your daughter, Rebekah, wife to Isaac. She is well loved by her husband and a most happy wife. Truly, the Most High God has called them to be one."

"And this is Elder Dov, my father who adopted me out of slavery to be his son and heir, though he is dear to me as a brother and friend."

"You are honored, Elder Dov. Your son should bring you honor, joy, and pride! You chose well your son and heir. Accept my hospitality."

Keshet motioned to Leah. "Who is this noble woman? I would know her name."

"Pardon, Lord Keshet, this is Leah, my wife. Truly the Most High God's greatest blessing to your servant! A more loving and honorable woman cannot be found! She is mother to our daughter, Deborah, who serves Rebekah as nurse."

"Welcome, Leah, wife of Zimri-Ruel. It is good that my brother, Zimri-Ruel, does not walk his paths alone. Whatever you ask is yours. Deborah is safe and honored as she serves Rebekah."

"And this a shepherd friend, Hod, and his son, Jael ben Hod. It was Hod who first told me the promise of the Most High God in his sign of the rainbow. He is a shepherd's shepherd and a constant source of joy."

"Welcome, Hod and Jael ben Hod. I suspect Jael honors our good friend, Zimri-Ruel, with his name. I have heard of the bond between shepherds. As for joy, it is a hard thing for me as I return with bad news."

"Yes," I replied. "I see a weary sadness in your eyes. Is all well with the Patriarch Shem?"

"The Patriarch Shem has breathed his last and has gone the way of his father, Noah. I heard him say at the last, 'His voice! His voice! Yes, it is clear and unmistakable! The Most High God calls! Yes! I come! I come!' Then he was gone. Jared and Abaigael and Obed were with me at his side when he breathed his last."

Keshet paused with his eyes cast down to mask a tear. Then he said directly, "Zimri-Ruel, I require your help tomorrow morning."

"Of course, Lord Keshet. I am in your debt and in debt to the Patriarch Shem. I am honored to serve as I can."

"Now, my friends and honored guests, what brings you to Damascus and my house?"

I answered first. "My Lord Keshet, after our daughter, Deborah, departed with Rebekah, our house was empty. Our only son, Adniel, was taken from us years ago. Our hearts longed to look upon our mountain village one more time and to see once again our friends here in Damascus. Your brother, Eliezer, and his aide, Abiel, told us you served the Patriarch Shem and that the household of Zadok still worships the Most High God with you. It is a blessing of the Most High God to be under your roof again."

Keshet nodded, and I pointed to Dov, Hod, and Jael. "These, my brothers, also longed to see our village, Dabar El Elyon, one more time and to journey beyond the plains of Nahor."

Keshet replied, "It is a hard thing to lose your only son and also bittersweet to watch your daughter travel afar. I am glad that you have come. We will show you the hospitality of a brother. Jared, Abaigael, and Obed will rejoice to see you. Abaigael will honor Leah as a sister."

He then turned to Dov. "Tell me, Elder Dov, was it good to see Dabar El Elyon once more?"

"Our journey brought us only to a poor Amorite village, where no hospitality was shown to the stranger. We met only rude men, liars, who worshipped the idol Ammur, whose cold stone eyes see nothing. We worshipped the Most High God on the mountaintop and thanked him for our great salvation from the Amorites. No, Dabar El Elyon is no longer in the high hills above Khalab. It is here in the house of Lord Keshet and lives among Nahor on the plains of the patriarch."

"The people of Dabar El Elyon are always welcome in the house of Keshet."

Bethuel finally spoke. "It is a hard thing for me to say. I come seeking something of comfort for a wife whose heart despairs the loss of a favorite and only daughter, Rebekah. I have but one son and heir, Laban. It is the fear of my wife that I will take another wife or concubine and her grief will become greater still."

Keshet listened patiently, and after a brief pause, Bethuel continued, "Zimri-Ruel has shown me that comfort cannot be bought. My tent will know no peace until my dear wife is assured of my promises to her. I have determined to make an oath to her. A public oath at the well before all of Nahor to love only her, to seek no other wife or concubine as long as we both shall live. I seek a token of my oath to her that she shall always have as a sign and remembrance of my oath. I have searched the markets of Carchemish and Khalab and have found nothing. It is my prayer that in the market of Damascus, such a token can be found."

Keshet looked warmly on Bethuel. "What you determine to do is a wise and good thing. I know of a man who may help you with what you seek. I will arrange for you to meet him."

Then Keshet said to all of us, "Rest from your journey. You will eat at my table this evening."

That afternoon, as Leah and I rested alone during the heat of the day, she said to me, "Husband, you advised Bethuel to make an oath to his wife. Such a noble thought! Yet you never offered to make a public oath to me, not before the well in Dabar El Elyon when we wed and never before the well of Nahor. Is not every wife in Nahor and every wife in Dabar El Elyon worthy of such oath? Am I to be less honored than the wife of Bethuel?"

I sputtered to reply, "Yes, I mean no. Of course, you are worthy, I just thought, I mean Bethuel asked me, and I… I…"

"Husband, I tease. What you advise is a good thing. I know that the Most High God has made us one more than any marriage contract witnessed by the village elders. What Bethuel does for his wife will be a sign unto all the tribe of Nahor of God's perfect plan for man and wife. You are a good man, a good husband, a good father, and my closest companion. Oh, how I am blessed by the Most High God."

In the cool of the evening, we enjoyed the table of the great and noble Keshet. Even Lord Bethuel had never beheld such a fine table. After the meal was finished, Keshet spoke of the arrangements he had made that afternoon.

"Lord Bethuel, I have arranged for you to meet with a man gifted in his craft. He will make for you the perfect tokens you seek. His gift is with his hands, yes, but more so, he has a gift of understanding. He will know the desire of your heart and capture it in beauty."

"Leah, I have need of your husband. I pray your permission for his company for a few days. I believe you would enjoy the company of Abaigael, wife of Jared and mother of Abiel, the servant of Isaac. I believe you will find her a most extraordinary woman and like-minded to yourself."

Leah nodded her agreement and turned to me with her inquisitive eyes. I softly said to her, "I will explain all to you."

To Dov, Hod, and Jael, he said, "I would welcome your help as well, but you are free to stay and wander the streets and markets of Damascus if you desire."

All three responded, "We are your servants, Lord Keshet. We will go with you."

Keshet then finalized the conversation. "Good. We will depart at sunrise, before the day grows too hot. Good night, my friends. The Most High God keep you until tomorrow."

Turning to me, he said, "Come walk with me in the garden."

The others rose from the table and returned to their rooms. I walked with Keshet into his garden. "Let's go where we can see the night sky," he said.

Once in the darkness of the outer courtyard, looking up, he said, "I remember our last walk in the night together. Remember the comet? Your words burned within me, and the Most High God affirmed them forever."

Looking into my face, he grimly said, "Tomorrow we go to bury the Patriarch Shem. It was his desire to be buried with his father, Noah. He has told me alone where to find the tomb. He wants his resting place to remain a secret. He would have no pilgrims searching for his tomb. The Patriarch Shem would not have his bones be venerated. Only the Most High God is worthy of worship. Can I trust you and your friends to honor this command?"

"It is an honor to help you carry out this command. I only regret that I did not meet with the Patriarch Shem one more time, but I will carry his teaching in my heart always. Tell me, Lord Keshet, were his eyes as bright as ever?"

"The Patriarch Shem was blind for years, but his eyes shone bright to the very end."

Chapter Thirty-two

*"These are the records of the generations of
Shem. Shem was one hundred years old, and
became the father of Arpachshad two years
after the flood. And Shem lived five hundred
years after he became the father of Arpachshad,
and he had other sons and daughters."*

—Genesis 11:10–11

The next morning, Keshet provided an early breakfast. We followed him to the outer courtyard where camels awaited us. A pack camel had been loaded with packs of provisions for our journey. Another pack camel adorned with a fine blanket and a bridle festooned with ribbons and tassels of braided wool of many colors stood in the middle, carrying only a rolled rug across its back. We did not have to be told that the camel bore the body of the Patriarch Shem; no words were necessary. We each mounted a camel. The leader of Keshet's trained men led the way. Another trained man followed behind us as we ventured out of Damascus.

I will not say which way we went or how far we traveled. We followed Keshet and his trained man. I will speak only of the sky above, as it cares not if it covers mountain, plain, desert, or sea. The heavens of the Most High God kept watch over us. Nothing is hidden from His eyes.

Lord Keshet knew the place—a lonely place but not unknown to the Most High. When we came upon the place, Keshet led us in worship to our God and creator. We fasted that night, tasting only water. In the quietness of the night, sitting before the watch fire, I asked Keshet about the kings and tribes and peoples of the land.

"Lord Keshet, you are a man of great wisdom and knowledge. You deal with men of every nation. How can men be so different? Are we not all sons of Noah, just as the Patriarch Shem? Should cousins quarrel and war against each other? My people of Dabar El Elyon were driven from our home by Amorites who say the land has been theirs for generations. I do not understand all this warring."

Keshet kept looking at the low flames of the fire. "Noah lived many years ago. His three sons raised many sons and daughters. Most men have forgotten we are all cousins of one patriarch. Others remember but say that was many years ago, only my tribe are my people."

The fire crackled as a burning log split. "Do not even brothers fight just as Cain killed his brother, Abel. What reason more than the sin of an evil heart."

I thought and then answered, "Perhaps I am blessed having no genealogy. I can love the people of Dabar El Elyon and of Nahor and of my friends from Caanan and Damascus."

"You, Zimri-Ruel, needed a tribe and a people. You found them in Dabar El Elyon and in our friends. The Most High God's intent was for man to be in communion with Him and with each other. When man could no longer walk the garden with our God, his heart still longed for fellowship, so we look to tribes and families for fellowship. You of all men should know the pain of walking alone. Fellowship is a good thing. It comes from our desire to walk with the Most High God. It is good thing that also was corrupted by sin."

"Corrupted by sin?"

"Yes, men with evil intent find others of the same mind, and something created for our good is made evil. Tribes intended to support, nourish, and protect now attack and destroy. Is there anything under the heavens not corrupted by the sin of man?"

We sat and listened to the fire crackle. Then I asked, "Terah visited Shem, but is he not of another tribe than you, Keshet?"

"Terrah, son of Nahor, descended from Shem's firstborn, Arpachshad. His other sons were Elam, Asshur, Lud, and Aram. The sons of Aram were Uz, Hul, Gether, and Mash. Just as the plains of Nahor are named for a descendant of Shem, so Aram and the great desert of Aram are named for a son of Shem. Damascus is the city of Aram as Haran is to Nahor. But the Patriarch Shem welcomed all men. All were kin in his eyes, even the Canaanites, sons of his brother, Ham. The Most High God is God of all men. Our brothers and sisters of the household of Zadok are children of Canaan, but they walk in the ways of the Most High God as we do. The Amorites who pushed you from your village are Canaanites, kin to the house of Zadok. Do you love your friends any less?"

I watched the sparks of the fire rise into the clear night sky. It seemed each spark sought its way to become a star in the firmament above only to burn out and fall, blackened, back into the fire and ashes.

We sat in silence, and our eyes danced back and forth between the fire and the stars above. A camel snorted, and then there was silence again.

Keshet said slowly, "The Patriarch Shem was one hundred years old when he left the ark and lived five hundred years more. He outlived all of his sons and daughters. He outlived his grandsons and great-grandsons. He lived only to tell the salvation story of the Most High God, and he told me over and over how it was a love story of our God and father. He told the story to any and who would hear. Was not his long life a blessing and a gift of God for his faithful remembrance? But men no longer want to hear his story. Damascus, the city of Aram, home to the patriarch, forgot him or ignored him."

"Yes," I replied. "And tomorrow we place him alongside the bones of his father, Noah. My Leah has shown me that if Enoch walked with God and then was no more because God took him, then our hope is that all who serve the Most High God will be taken to walk with our God just as Adam and Eve walked with him in the garden. Was this not the intent of the Most High God in the beginning?"

I could see Keshet smile by the light of the fire. "Yes, I too have the hope that Most High God will make us righteous to walk with Him again."

As Keshet and I sat silently by the fire, Dov, Hod, and Jael Ben Hod came and sat beside us in silence. The fire crackled. The night grew cold, and the stars were bright in the heaven above.

The cold of dawn soon gave way to the warming sun above. We carefully carried the wrapped body of the Patriarch Shem to the humble tomb of his father, Noah. Opening the tomb, we saw a small room, just big enough to lay the body of our patriarch. Above the floor of the tomb, a shelf was carved from the rock. Three stone boxes were on the shelf. There was room for only one more.

As I stared at the stone boxes, Keshet said, "Noah, Ham, and Japheth."

We resealed the tomb such that it will never be known, sang a psalm of thanksgiving, and started for Damascus.

>Most High God and Savior of our Patriarch Shem
>He has heard Your voice and has obeyed Your command.
>He has walked in Your way to the glory of Your name.
>You have honored him with long life.
>He has seen his sons and daughters to many generations.
>But his heart was always towards You.
>The desire of his soul was to walk with You.
>We listened as he told of Your call.
>His desire was to come.
>Shem has gone to You.
>Receive your servant, we pray.

Chapter Thirty-three

"Immediately the boy's father cried out and said, 'I do believe; help my unbelief.'"

—Mark 9:24

When we returned to Damascus, Keshet determined we should wash, refresh, and visit the household of Zadock, now the house of Obed and Jared, where Leah awaited our return. I asked after Bethuel and was told by a servant that he was in the market as was his habit during our absence. Servants saw to the camels, and we straightaway sought water to wash away the heat and dust from our journey. As I poured the last of the water over my head and watched the dirty brown water puddle at my feet, I remembered my first washing at the house of Terah and the beginning of my journey to the calling of the Most High God.

Now cooled, washed, and dressed in a clean tunic, I joined the others in the courtyard where a table was set with fresh fruits, wine, and water. Our task completed, the mood of the others had lifted. Hod was his talkative self, reminding Dov and Jael of the cool streams of the mountains and the shade of the trees and the comfort of a cool cave on a warm day.

Keshet was the last to join us. "It is but a short walk to the compound of Zadok. I will show you there myself."

When we left Keshet's compound, we turned left, away from the market, and followed a narrow street towards the city wall. It seemed an entirely different city without the noise and crowd near the market. As we walked, we could hear the sound of slow heavy blows of metal on metal. We could smell the acrid air of the forge. At the end of the street was a large wooden gate with a smaller wooden door. Keshet rapped the door twice quickly, and it opened.

"Lord Keshet," the worker said, "come in. I will send for Obed at once."

The worker who opened the door was only one of a dozen or so shirtless men whose torsos and waists were covered with heavy leather aprons. Leather gloves nearly to the elbow protected hands and arms, and leather-topped sandals protected the feet. Bins of coal, copper, tin, and ores were filled near capacity. Storerooms abutted the mineral bins. In the far corner was the large oven and forge. The heat in the courtyard was equal to the hottest day on the desert of Aram. Just inside the large gate was another smaller gate in the wall opposite the storerooms and bins. The door opened, and Obed, dressed in the leathers of the forge, welcomed us in.

I was amazed at how much older he looked. His skin was as leathery as his apron. His hair was white against his red brown skin, and his eyes seemed tired, betraying his words of welcome. "Keshet, welcome, my friend. And you must be, yes, it is you, Zimri-Ruel. It has been many years. Welcome, and these your friends…"

"Obed, it has been my great desire to see you and the household of Zadok again. This is my father, Dov, who has adopted me out of slavery, and this is my friend, Hod, a shepherd's shepherd, and his son, Jael."

"Welcome, friends of Zimri-Ruel. We have been expecting you but not knowing when you would return. Your wife, Leah, is here. The three of them have become inseparable."

We entered the inner compound, a handsome and comfortable courtyard with fountain, garden, and apartments. The difference between the working compound and the inner courtyard could not have been more surprising. The acrid smell was gone, the air was much cooler, and the tranquility of the shaded courtyard was only interrupted by the soft laughter of women.

"Three of them?" I asked.

"Yes, Leah, Abaigael, and Namaah. Please take refreshment in the cool of the garden."

"Your garden seems to me a miracle. How can it be cool here next to the great oven?"

Obed smiled, and a hint of pride brightened his eyes. "The courtyard abuts the north wall of the city, the coolest wall. And below your feet, a branch of the river from the mountains enters the city to supply all of the city's water needs. The water keeps our stone cold, and the sun does not warm it. The great oven is downwind of the courtyard. You may know the ways of a good sheepfold, but we know how to arrange a forge."

Moving towards the courtyard door, Obed said, "The others will join you soon. I am needed in the forge. You will sit at our table this evening, and we will share our stories."

As Obed departed, Leah, Abaigael, and Namaah emerged bearing a basket of fruit, a bowl of wine, and fine copper and brass drinking cups.

Abaigael was the first to speak. "Brother Zimri-Ruel, so many years! Abiel told me he met you in Nahor, and now the Most High God brings our paths together once more. Such a great blessing! Jared attends to trades for the forge. He will join us at the table this evening. Leah has spoken much while we awaited your return."

Addressing Dov, she said, "Father Dov, you are most welcome. God's blessing be upon you! Both father and brother to my brother and friend, Zimri-Ruel."

Turning to Hod, she said, "Welcome, Hod, a shepherd's shepherd. We will hear of your many stories during your stay!"

Finally looking at Jael, she said, "Welcome, Jael ben Hod, you are blessed to walk with such strong and faithful men. Learn from them and walk in the ways of the Most High God for many years to come."

"Brother Zimri-Ruel, you remember Namaah, widow to Jared's cousin, Baram from Bethel. She now lives with us. She walks in the ways of the Most High God."

Namaah replied, "How well I remember your bold story to my husband. Your faith in the Most High God was unshakable! Baram was astonished by the strength of your belief. It is a blessing that we are all brought together again, and Leah, we marvel at her wisdom and love. Truly, she is a blessing from God."

I replied, "I am saddened to hear Baram sleeps. Your children, Namaah, they are well?"

"Like you, Zimri-Ruel, I have mourned a son. The others remain in Canaan. They do not walk in the ways of the Most High. They worship the deaf and dumb idols of Canaan as did Baram their father. That is why I find comfort here with Jared and Abaigael."

Namaah's face brightened, and she said, "Truly, I am blessed to be here with friends who love me and love the Most High God. Your coming brings me added joy, and Leah has become a great help and friend."

We gathered that evening at the table of Obed and Jared. The brothers were very close, and each knew their strength. Obed was a large man and very strong. His years of beating metal into shape chiseled his muscles and toughened his face. He was by nature a quiet man and sensitive. His gentleness was hidden behind his forceful figure. Jared, the younger brother, was much smaller, outgoing, and likable. He exuded enthusiasm and optimism. While Obed ran the forge, Jared made the trades and handled the money. The love and trust between the brothers was evident to all who knew them. At the table, Obed sat quietly, listening to the conversation. Jared was the able host, bringing everyone into the conversation and ensuring an enjoyable evening.

Hod insisted on retelling my encounter with the lion and how Dov saved me from the Amorite warrior. We recounted Eliezer's and Abiel's visit to Nahor and God's selection of Rebekah as wife for Isaac. Leah told of Deborah's decision to serve Rebekah. Keshet made mystery of Bethuel's daily visits to the market. Bethuel would only smile and say nothing. When I spoke of my love for Zadok, how blessed I was to witness his strong faith and leadership, I noticed Obed's face drop, his eyes closed and looking down. I saw a tear fall on his hardened face.

Jared replied, "We miss Papa very much. Obed especially grieves and yet mourns him. They were together every day in the forge, never seeing one without the other."

Everyone could see the pain of loss and respectfully honored Obed and Jared with silence.

Seeing his brother's anguish, Jared said simply, "Papa was so very proud of you, Obed. Did he not say that your skill in bronze was far better than his own? I heard him say many times you were the teacher and he just your apprentice. Were you not the first to find new methods and better bronze tools and wares? Know that you were loved."

Obed sighed. "Papa was so strong. I miss his strength. The workers in our forge would never cross Papa. never would he allow a detestable idol in our forge. Now it seems I find them everywhere, hidden by men who earn their food in our forge. They see I lack Papa's strength."

"But you are strong, brother. I know of your strength. You walk upright and righteous. Never tell me you are not strong!"

"Jared, I am not like you and Abaigael. God has chosen Abaigael, and she speaks His words. You and Abaigael are one and share the strength and the word of the Most High. Zimri-Ruel has heard the voice of God and dreamt dreams. God has heard his prayers. I alone never hear the voice of God. It must be that I am weak."

Jared paused and thought and then replied, "I never remember Papa say he heard the voice of God, yet he believed and led our house in worship and sacrifice. Surely you are not alone, my brother. Some men dream dreams, some men see visions, some men believe on the word of another. Did not Zimri-Ruel say he heard the voice of God with his eyes? He saw the order of God in creation…"

Namaah spoke softly. "Cousin Obed, like you, I have never heard His voice. Like your father Zadok, I believed on account of the word of Abaigael. If I were to ask how God spoke to me, I would say He spoke with comfort when Baram and my son died by the sword."

Dov spoke. "With respect, friend, I have never heard the voice of God, never dreamed dreams or saw visions but believed on the word and changed life of my son, Zimri-Ruel.

Jael ben Hod spoke, a rare event for his young self. "When crossing the desert or arid plains, sometimes a storm would come up. The wind would grow strong, and dust fill the sky. Well, man cannot breathe the dust, so we cover ourselves with our cloak or blanket. The dust is so thick we cannot see the sun. We cover ourselves, and the light of the day is gone. We go on. We know the sun is still in the heaven and God is still on His throne. I do not need to see the sun to know it is still there. And so it is with the Most High God. I know He is there, even if I do not see Him or hear Him. Was this not the strength of your father, Zadok, his faith in what he did not see?"

We sat in silence. Feeling the pain of Obed, I spoke. "Obed, you are now the head of this house. Your father, Zadok, has taught you what you must do. He has always trusted in your ability. I ask you, Obed, to lead us in worship and in sacrifice to the Most High God, a sacrifice for atonement and thanksgiving for the blessing on all in this house. I will help you if you wish, but I believe you know what to do."

Obed straightened his back, lifted his head, and said authoritatively, "Tomorrow the house of Obed and Jared sacrifice to the Most High God. We will worship Him with thanksgiving. Brother, Zimri-Ruel, I ask you lead us in a new hymn of thanksgiving. The Most High God keep you this night. Search your hearts and prepare for His atonement."

Obed rose from his seat and retreated to his room. Each of us silently followed his example.

The next morning, Obed led the sacrifice and worship as his father, Zadok, had done before him. He wore a face at once of urgency and authority. We all saw the strength of Obed that his brother, Jared, always knew was there. We sang a new song of thanksgiving:

> Show us Your presence, O God Most High
> Answer us when we call unto You.
> Hear our prayers and do not hide your loving-kindness from us.
> A gentle touch, O Lord, to keep us in Your care.
> A stern rebuke when we depart Your path.
> Lead us to good pasture.

> Accept the sacrifices we offer
> In love and praise before Your throne;
> Sacrifices of righteousness and faithfulness.
> Salvation is from You alone, O God,
> Your blessing be upon Your people,
> For our trust is in our Lord.
> May no storm or darkness hide the light
> of Your countenance from us.
> For You, O Lord, have put gladness in our hearts!
> Accept our song of praise.
> You alone, O God, are worthy of all praise.

As we returned from the altar outside the city to the gate of Damascus, our way was blocked by a royal procession. The warrior king of Damascus riding a donkey was followed by a guard of warriors. Behind the warriors was a line of priests leading six teams of oxen pulling a great cart with a massive stone. More priests followed the cart, and another guard of soldiers ended the procession. We followed as the procession made its way past the market, turned on Straight Street, and turned again in front of a new temple across from the royal palace. A great ramp had been erected, and teams of men hauled on great ropes to move the massive stone up into the temple. We watched as they skillfully moved the great stone and then lifted it erect in the center of the temple. For the first time, I saw the new foreign idol of the king of Damascus. The great stone bore a relief of a bearded figure, like a man, with a horned headdress. In his left hand, he held an axe, and in his right hand, he clutched thunderbolts. He was flanked by a bull and a lion.

The king climbed the steps of the temple and motioned for silence. "People of Damascus, Amu-pi'el, King of Quatna and new high king of all the Amorites and Arameans, seeks the favor of his god, Hadad, to be worshipped in all the cities of the Amorites and all of Padan Aram. Hadad will protect us from the Egyptians who have increased their garrisons in Canaan and from the sea people and invading tribes from the north. You shall provide the priests of

Hadad whatever they require of you. So orders King Amu-pi'el, and so order I, king of Damascus."

Abaigael could not be restrained. She made her way through the crowd, past the priests and guards, and halfway up the steps of the temple before she was stopped. Being halted by a bodyguard of the king, she shouted, "Is not Damascus the chosen home of the Patriarch Shem? Was not Aram, father of the Arameans, a son of Shem? Has not our patriarch told of the salvation by the Most High God? Has he not heard His voice? Has not the Patriarch Shem reminded us throughout his blessed long life that the Most High God is God and there is no other? And now you defile his city with this detestable image? Repent! Do not incur the wrath of the Most High God for this stone idol with no eyes to see, no ears to hear your prayers, and no mouth to speak truth."

The king looked down at Abaigael and said, "It is only one more god, the city is full of gods. Go home to your husband, woman." He turned and walked away. The soldier released his grip from her arm and said, "The king has shown you mercy. Go home."

Jared made his way to her and said, "Come home now. There is nothing more we can do. This is not the king's doing. He is compelled to show deference to the king of Qatna. It was the price of peace."

As we walked back to the house of Obed and Jared, Obed spoke. "Abaigael, what you say is true. The price of peace paid to the king of Qatna was too high. The Most High God will surely punish Damascus for this weakness and sin."

We returned to the pleasant courtyard in the compound of Obed and Jared. Our thoughts were not on the sacrifice for atonement and thanksgiving we made to God or on the refreshments set before us. We could speak only on the great idol now staring with cold blind eyes upon the city Damascus. But it was also true what the king had said. It was only one more god, and the city was full of gods. Did not Obed say last night he could not stop his workers from bringing their idols into his forge?

Abaigael was adamant. "The Most Hight God detests idols. It is the greatest affront to him man can make. What is it that God desires from us but to love Him with all of our heart and all of our soul. Can we love the Most High God and bow before detestable idols? No! And God will hold men accountable. We try His patience sorely! God is holy and righteous, He cannot abide such sin. Destruction is set before our city!"

I tried to answer her charge. "Yes, our Lord God is holy and righteous, but He is also merciful and loving. Does He not seek all men to come to Him and walk in His ways? Is He not a God of patience, ever willing to accept us as we return to Him?"

Jared answered, "Zimri-Ruel, you know well that God cannot be other than holy. He cannot abide any sin. Yes, He is loving. Yes, He provides atonement for sin, it is an unmerited gift given by God. But man must seek atonement. Man must accept God's way, His gift of atonement, or he remains condemned. You speak so well of the love of God for all His creation, but someone must warn them. Someone must tell them to seek atonement. Someone must proclaim that atonement is God's forgiveness and that it comes only with repentance. The Most High God waits for men to seek him, to hear His call to them, to repent from their sin and seek His will and walk in His ways. Who knows the mind of God? Who will try His patience?"

Abaigael told me that that night she had a dream. The bright light blinded her and said to her, "Obed and Jared will be summoned before the king. You shall accompany them and address the king and say to him, 'This is what the Most High God says to the king of Damascus…'"

Chapter Thirty-four

*"Do I not hate those who hate you, O Lord? And
do I not loathe those who rise up against you?"*

—*Psalm 139:29*

The next day while returning from a storeroom to the forge and oven, Obed saw two workers place a small object in a crevice in the wall behind the forge. When they saw Obed return, they quickly picked up their tools and resumed working without a word. Obed walked directly to the crevice and retrieved a small stone figure. Looking at the object, he instantly recognized the likeness of the new god, Hadad. He asked the two men to summon all of the workers to the forge.

When all of his workers were assembled, he spoke. "I see that someone here seeks the protection of Hadad. Is Hadad the only god protecting you? What other gods protect us? Tell me. Hadad is new to Damascus, surely other gods are here as well. Where are they? Tell me. We can gather them together, perhaps they will see our work better if they are here. Walk with me and show me your gods."

As Obed walked the compound, one by one, idols were retrieved. Most were stone, some wood, and some bronze. Obed recognized the Canaanite gods, but some were unknown to him.

"Let us take these gods to the forge. That is where protection is most needed." Obed reasoned.

Just as he returned to the forge, there was a heavy pounding on the gate. A worker walked over and opened it. Two priests and a court official entered. The court official loudly announced, "I would speak to Obed and Jared on the orders of the king."

"I am Obed. I will send for my brother, Jared."

Then speaking to a worker, he said, "Ask my brother, Jared, to come here. Tell him there is a messenger from the king."

While the worker went for Jared, Obed tossed the wooden idols into the firey furnace.

Jared arrived quickly. He bowed before the court official and, smiling, said, "Welcome, we are honored by a visit of the king's court."

The official nodded his acceptance of Jared's bow and said, "The king honors the house of Obed and Jared by permitting you to make an altar of bronze and four bronze candleholders for the temple of Hadad. These priests of Hadad will direct your work. Your work is well known, and its placement in the temple will be an everlasting honor to your name."

Before Jared could answer, Obed spoke. "The house of Obed and Jared serve only the El Elyon, the Most High God. There is no other god but the Most High God. We cannot build an altar or altar pieces for your temple."

As he spoke, Obed placed the stone image of Hadad on the anvil, picked up his heavy hammer, and shattered it with one mighty stroke. The priests of Hadad gasped. The court officer said to Jared, "Jared, reason with your brother. You work in bronze, just make what is asked."

Jared looked at his older brother, turned, and said to the court officer, "What Obed says is true. We serve only the Most High God. We will not make an altar or altar pieces for a detestable idol. Is there anything else the king may have need of?"

The court officer said, "I will give the king your answer." And to the priest, he said, "We leave now."

As the court officer and the priests left, Obed looked at his workers and said, "The house of Obed and Jared follow the Most High God. There is no other."

He then smashed every idol and calmly said, "The Most High God is my shield and defender. I place my trust in Him alone."

He set down the hammer and said, "There is much work to be done. Back to your work, everyone."

Jared smiled at his brother and said, "The forge is your responsibility, brother. I will leave you to your work."

An hour later, there was once again heavy pounding on the gate. A worker opened it, and the court officer and two soldiers of the king's guard entered. The court officer loudly announced, "Obed and Jared, you are summoned before the king."

Obed put down his hammer and told a worker, "Tell my brother, Jared, we are summoned by the king. Come immediately."

I was with Jared and Abaigael in the garden as she was telling she had another dream. As the worker brought the news to Jared, Abaigael immediately said, "Husband, this is of the Lord. I am coming with you. I have a word from the Most High God for the king's ear."

I said, "I am coming also. We are as brothers, are we not?"

As we entered the work yard, the court officer asked Jared, "Who are these?"

Jared replied, "They are of my household. They will come with me."

The court official shrugged and said, "Follow behind me."

We followed behind Jared and Obed with a guard walking along each side of us, up to the market, to Straight Street, and on to the palace. We were shown into the king's throne room. The high priest of Hadad and the two priests who came to the compound were there waiting. The high priest, dressed in his rich robes and wearing a jewel-encrusted ephod, was pacing impatiently back and forth, stopping occasionally to lecture his two subordinate priests.

The throne room was large, cold, and austere. Built of large stone blocks, the room was square, and its height equaled its length and width. At one end was a carved wooden throne covered in bright gold. A small table was beside the throne with a bowl of wine, fresh fruit, a jar of water, and a golden cup. The walls were covered with bronze shields, javelins, and spears. A golden bow and quiver of gilded arrows hung beside the throne. This was unmistakably the hall of a warrior. The only trace of opulence beside the golden throne were four crimson curtains gathered in a circle at the ceiling, guided and hanging down the four corners of the room. Large torches were lit on each side, and one wall had high windows, which leaked shafts of light onto the bare stone floor.

After a few minutes, a guard slammed the shaft of his spear on the floor and announced, "The king!"

The king of Damascus entered hurriedly. Noticing Abaigael, he said, "You with Obed and Jared? Who are you, woman?"

Jared answered, "My lord king, this is Abaigael, my wife. You summoned my brother, Obed, and me. I am Jared."

"I know who you are. Did you not hear me yesterday order all people of Damascus to provide the priests of Hadad whatever they require of you? And today you refused to make a bronze altar and candlesticks for the temple of Hadad. You should be honored that your work stands in a temple. Perhaps you did not understand my court officer. This was not a request but a command. What do you say?"

My lord king, the house of Obed and Jared, like the house of our father, Zadok, before us, has been most honored to serve the king as we have served your father before you. It is well known that our house follows the Most High God. Never have we been commanded to serve another god. We will agree that you honor another worker in bronze for this god. As the Patriarch Shem lived, never did a king of Damascus command us to adorn the temple of an idol."

The king replied, "The Patriarch Shem is dead. Did you not hear me—"

Before the king could continue, Abaigael spoke out loudly and forcefully. "King of Damascus, hear what the Most High God says to you. 'You have not listened to my servant, Shem. You have forgotten the Most High God. Drought will come upon the land of Aram and the city of Damascus. There will not remain an ox, a donkey, or any beast of four legs in the city. There will be no wheat in the market, no figs, and no raisins. Wine will be a memory. No caravan will supply you. The dead of the city will lie unburied for the weakness of the living. For the sake of my remnant who will not bow before idols and for the sake of my servant, Shem, who saw the destruction of the world, I will not utterly destroy Damascus. But the Arameans and the kings of Damascus will bow before other nations and serve other kings.' These are the words of the Most High God."

The king looked intensely into the face of Abaigael and said, "I have heard there is a prophetess of the Most High God in Damascus."

The king thought a long time before continuing, "The house of Obed and Jared shall not be compelled to provide bronze for the priests of Hadad. You shall serve the Most High God. Make sacrifices to him and intercede for your king and your city. I shall not bow before the altar of Hadad. Go in peace."

The high priest of Hadad protested. "Lord King, these men have offended Hadad. Your duty is to protect Hadad and his temple."

The king glared at them and said, "If Hadad is god, he needs not my protection. You have your god and your temple find someone else to make your altar pieces. Compel no citizen of Damascus to kneel before your god. I have kept my bargain with king Amu-pi'el."

We bowed before the king and returned to the house of Obed and Jared. As we walked, I sang a new song.

> How long, O God, will the wicked oppress?
> How long, O God, will proud men scoff?
> When we will they be cut off?
> When will their arrogant words be stopped?
> Your people, O God, seek justice!
> O that the evildoers be utterly destroyed!
> O that their ways are forgotten among men.
> Men who steal from widows
> And would put the orphan to the sword.
> Men who make war for a vineyard
> And send trained men to take their neighbor's lamb.
> Nations of evildoers send forth raiders as
> thieves among your people.
> Judge them, O God, and strike them with Your strong arm.
> Remove from us the wicked and the evil.
> Men with eyes You formed that do not see Your handiwork,
> Men with ears You gave them that do not hear Your call,

LIVING IN A FALLEN WORLD

Men whose mouths blaspheme Your name.
Men who do not love You, O Most High God
Men who show no love or mercy to those You love.
O that all whom You chasten would turn from their wicked ways!
That they do not fall into the pit You have appointed for them!
By Your mercy, O Most High God, You
will not abandon your people.
By Your love, Your remnant will remain secure.
You will judge all men with righteousness.
You will save Your children, whom You love
With upright hearts, they shall know Your
will and follow Your ways.
Your children shall have an inheritance in the land
And they shall sing praises to Your name forever!

Chapter Thirty-five

"How blessed is he whose transgression is forgiven, whose sin is covered! How blessed is the man to whom the Lord does not impute iniquity, and in whose spirit there is no deceit!"

—*Psalm 32:1–2*

Obed and Jared continued to supply fine crafted bronze to the palace of the king of Damascus. No more idols were found hidden about the forge and work compound. Keshet visited often, introducing customers to the finest bronze craftsman in all Damascus, finer than those of Egypt, Canaan, or far off Babylon. Obed was unhindered as he led the household of Obed and Jared in sacrifices to the Most High God on the stone altar outside the city gate. Because the king repented, Abaigael prophesied that God would spare Damascus from deadly drought and pestilence. But because the temple of Hadad was not torn down, Damascus would serve other kings and other nations. Many people in Damascus forgot the stories of the Patriarch Shem. They forgot the Most High God. But a remnant of faithful remained; men and women who never bowed before an altar of a detestable idol still walked in the city, and men and women who loved the Most High God told their stories to any who would listen. The children of the Most High God lived and prospered under His protection.

One afternoon, during the heat of the day, while the household of Obed and Jared enjoyed the cool of their courtyard garden, a messenger arrived. A servant of Keshet came in haste, begging the household of Obed and Jared and all the guests of their household to join his master at his table that evening to share in the good news and joy of his master. Saying nothing more, the servant departed as quickly as he came.

I joined the household of Obed and Jared and my friends from Dabar El Elyon at the home of Keshet. We were welcomed at the small door in the gate and shown politely to the inner courtyard where Keshet warmly greeted us. He was dressed in the finest of robes. A gold hilted knife in a gold sheath was on his belt. He wore a crisp white headdress held by twisted gold cord. A jewel-encrusted pendant hung from a gold chain around his neck. And he smelled of sweet perfume, which anointed his head. I had never seen Keshet dressed so nobly. I knew he was a wealthy man, but he was never one to show his wealth.

He gave each of us a kiss and said, "Welcome, friend. I'm very honored you come to my house to share in my joy. Welcome, welcome!"

"Keshet," I asked, "please share with us your news! Let us join you in the celebration of joy."

"Soon, soon, my friend, you will learn at the table with the others."

We were shown to the table of Keshet. I have never known a richer table than his, but this night was beyond imagination. The table was filled with the most enticing food I had ever seen, food that I never knew was food—roast peacock with their colorful feathers! The tongue of songbirds. Fruit I could not identify. Savory dishes with unknown aromas. Breads and cakes of every imagination. I fail to describe the wonder of his table. As we sat, Keshet could be seen chuckling with joy. Finally, he ended the suspense.

"Friends, I have asked you to my table to share in my joy. I have a guest of honor, no, a new member of my household, no, a returning member of this household, which is his and mine. Please, brother, join me at our table."

From a room just off the courtyard, an elderly man slowly walked out. He was dressed in the same noble manner as Keshet.

He came to the table and was seated in the place of honor. At last, I recognized him, Eliezer, Keshet's older brother.

Keshet spoke. "My brother, Eliezer, has returned from his service to Lord Abraham, the Hebrew. He returns as head of the household, never more to wander Canaan and Egypt in tents. My heart is full of joy, and I ask my friends to join me in joy. And news! Eliezer brings news for you, Lord Bethuel, and you, Zimri-Ruel. He has stories that even my friend Hod could not tell. Wisdom, young Jael ben Hod, you are a seeker of wisdom. You shall hear from him. But I am a poor host, dear friends. Eat, eat the finest table Damascus can offer and wine, such wine you have not tasted. This night is a joyous night! Feast and be filled!"

Eliezer sat and then spoke. "Little brother, how you go on and on! Let these dear people eat. And me as well!"

Turning to Bethuel, Eliezer said, "Lord Bethuel, Rebekah is dearly loved. She is honored by a noble house. And happy, yes, she cannot hide her happiness! Truly, she is a remarkable woman. Strong and brave. Lord Isaac can contain neither his love for her or her joyful spirit. She is strong and independent yet loving and sweet. Such honor she brings to your house!"

Looking at me, he said, "Deborah is Rebekah's source of wisdom and diplomacy. A whisper from her in Rebekah's ear and the perfect word emerges from her tongue! No sisters could be closer! Only Deborah can bridle the spirit of Rebekah. A woman of compassion and comportment. Truly, she is called by God to serve her!"

Eliezer paused to sip his wine. "Very good, brother. Very good, indeed!"

"Jared, I need not tell you of my love for Abiel, a man after my own heart. He is faithful in all that he does. His word is trusted by his lord, Isaac. He walks faithfully in the ways of the Most High God, a blessing to all who know him."

"Forgive me, my sisters, for the custom of Lord Abraham is more restricted between men and women. But we are brothers and sisters. Blessing to you, Abaigael, for nurturing a beloved son, Abiel, and blessings to you, Leah, teacher of your daughter, Deborah, and her mistress, Rebekah. Truly, they know the truth of the Most High God."

"Even before Abraham breathed his last and died in a ripe old age, he had given his inheritance to Isaac, his son."

I asked, "Abraham is dead? Abraham, father of nations, blessed by king Melchizedek?"

"Sadly, yes," replied Eliezer. It has been well over a year. It was well before I heard the news that the Patriarch Shem had died here in Damascus. Well, I could not return because I was assisting Abiel in his new duties. After all, did he not assist me in my duties?"

Sampling some of the food before him, Eliezer ate a few bites and then added, "A most remarkable event, the burial of Abraham. He is buried in the cave of Machpelah in the field of Ephron, the son of Zohar the Hittite, facing Mamre, the very field that Abraham purchased from the sons of Heth. He was buried with his wife, Sarah."

"You say remarkable?" I asked.

"Oh, remarkable, indeed. You see his sons, Isaac and Ishmael, buried him. Ishmael, his oldest son, was sent off with his mother, Hagar, many years ago with no inheritance, though Abraham did provide him gifts. Yet Ishmael, his son, honored his father and his younger brother, the son of inheritance, the son by the promise of God, Isaac. My heart was warmed by their reconciliation. I hope it lasts."

Jael, son of Hod, asked, "I am told you have many stories of your master, Abraham. Zimri-Ruel tells us he follows the voice of the Most High God. Tell a story of Abraham following the voice of God."

Eliezer laughed. "My brother would need many more bowls of wine for me to tell all of the stories of my master following the voice of God. He traveled far, sat with kings, and entertained angels sent from God. But one story truly stands out. It will tell you everything you need to know about my master, Abraham. God tested his heart like no other."

Eliezer stopped again. "Wonderful food, my brother." Then to us, he said, "Is everything to your satisfaction? This is a feast of joy, friends. Please, such a table is not set every day."

Hod spoke. "You were telling us, Eliezer, one story stands out?"

Eliezer's face grew serious. "Yes, it is a hard story. You see, God tested Abraham and said to him, 'Abraham!' And he said Here I am. And God said, 'Take now your son, your only son whom you love, Isaac, and go to the land of Moriah and offer him there as a burnt offering on one of the mountains of which I will tell you.' So Abraham rose early in the morning and saddled his donkey and took two of his young men with him and Isaac, his son, and he split wood for the burnt offering and arose and went to the place of which God had told him."

Eliezer stopped to fill his cup. "On the third day, Abraham raised his eyes and saw the place from a distance. And Abraham said to his young men, 'Stay here with the donkey, and I and the boy will go yonder, and we will worship and return to you.' And Abraham took the wood for the burnt offering and laid it on Isaac, his son, and he took in his hand the fire and the knife. And the two of them walked on together. And Isaac spoke to Abraham his father and said, 'My father!' And Abraham answered, 'Here I am, my son.' Isaac said, 'I see the fire and the wood, but where is the lamb for the burnt offering?'"

Eliezer took another sip of wine. "And Abraham said, 'God will provide the lamb for the burnt offering, my son.' So the two walked on together. Then they came to the place of which God had told him, and Abraham built the altar there and arranged the wood and bound his son, Isaac, and laid him on the altar on top of the wood. And Abraham stretched out his hand and took the knife to slay his son. But the angel of the Lord called to him from heaven and said, 'Abraham! Abraham!' And he said, 'Here I am.' And the angel of the Lord said, 'Do not stretch your hand out against the boy and do nothing to him. For now, I know that you fear God since you have not withheld your son, your only son, from Me.'"

Eliezer paused for a moment. Everyone was silent. Every eye focused on Eliezer. "Then Abraham raised his eyes and looked, and there beyond him was a ram caught in the thickets by his horns. Abraham went and took the ram and offered him up for a burnt offering in the place of his son. And Abraham named the place The Lord Will Provide as it is said to this day."

I breathed a sigh of relief and took a sip from my wine cup. But Eliezer wasn't finished with his story. He said, "Then the angel of the Lord called Abraham a second time from heaven and said, 'By myself I have sworn,' declares the Lord, 'because you have done this thing and have not withheld your son, your only son. Indeed, I will greatly bless you, and I will greatly multiply your seed as the stars of the heavens and the sand, which is on the seashore, and your seed shall possess the gates of their enemies. And in your seed all nations of the earth shall be blessed because you have obeyed My voice.'"

Eliezer finished his story and chose a ripe fig to sample. The rest of us were speechless. I heard the voice of young Jael say, "Truly, Abraham followed the voice of God in true faithfulness. All who walk after the Most High should walk as Abraham, yes, truly a faithful man. God provides when we honor Him with our faith."

As I listened to Jael, I remembered the words of King Melchizedek about Abraham. Yes, he would be father of nations, and yes, out of him will come a nation and a tribe of priests. But I clearly remembered him saying a day will come when one man will lay down his life as a sacrifice for the atonement of all the sin of man. One time and forever. Was this not a sign from God that a man will come, a son of Abraham, an only son, who will lay down his life as an atonement for sin? One time and forever. It was as clear to me as the sign of his creation in the stars in the night sky above. Oh, what love the Most High God has for His children!

> O Most High God, I tremble before Your presence.
> My sins are many, and my transgression are great.
> Though I confess them before Your throne
> I return to them as the rain returns to the sea,
> Who can forgive such a sinner?
> What is the end of a man whose testimony is false?
> What can atone for so great a sinner?
> I will trust in Your mercy, O Lord.
> You know my heart seeks Your comfort,

THE PRAISE SINGER

And my ears listen for Your instruction.
Bind my hands that they do no evil thing.
Wall the path beside me that I do not stray from Your way.
Cover my mouth against hateful words.
Bend my knees to kneel before You when You can be found.
Soften my heart to trust in Your deliverance.
Then, O Lord, my joy will overflow in praises to Your name!
In You I will have trust!
My faith will grow strong and never fail me.
It shall rise every morning as the sun in the eastern sky.
Let all who trust in Your name shout their joy,
For Our God will never fail to save!

Epilogue

*"The Lord has sworn and will not change
His mind, 'You are a priest forever
in the order of Melchizedek.'"*

—Psalm 110:4

I never made another visit to Salem. King Melchizedek, priest of the Most High God was no longer there. It is said he left as he came, unannounced and unexpected. He walked out of the city one day and never returned. For a time, his memory led the people, but a new people who did not know King Melchizedek and would not walk in his ways came into the city. The city has a new king, a leader of the tribe Jebus, sons of Canaan. The Jebus city of Salem has forgotten the Most High God. The people bow before the detestable idols and gods of Canaan. The sons of Shem and all who followed the Most High God have left the city but have taken their faith and their knowledge of God with them, and the truth of the Most High God is like the seed of grain, which is planted wherever they go. A remnant of God's people has spread throughout the land.

I did not return to Nahor, and Dabar El Elyon is no longer spoken of. You will find no Dabar El Elyon in your journeys. It is only a memory for a few old men who wait to join their father's tombs and rarely mentioned by their sons and daughters. Of all whom I led from Dabar El Elyon to Nahor, only Jael ben Hod remains with me. He tends to my needs and talks to me daily of every word King Melchizedek spoke. He tells me my story must be chronicled.

EPILOGUE

My dear Leah rests in the small cave beside the sheepfold in the high hills above Khalab, the very cave where I first studied the handiwork of God in the order of His creation and where, from the entrance, I marveled at His handiwork in the night sky above. I purchased the sheepfold and nearby caves from the Amorite villagers with the money Bethuel paid me for my flocks in Nahor. I have instructed Jael, son of Hod, to lay my bones beside hers.

My old friend, Dov, who adopted me out of slavery and loved me truer than any father, is buried in a cave beside the sheepfold. Beside him is his wife, Naamah, whom he married in his old age. Widow and widower joined in a marriage of love and communion. They became one and lived joyfully together to their very last day.

Bethuel returned to Nahor and, true to his word, proclaimed an oath to his wife that he would take no other wife or concubine. She was his one wife and only wife. He made his oath at the well before all the people of Nahor, and it is said Milcah lived to see her son's oath and rejoiced in his testimony to the people of Nahor. As tokens of his pledge, Bethuel presented his wife not one but seven proofs of his oath, a pledge of perfection as God's perfect plan for man and wife. He gave her two gold bracelets of intertwined grape leaves. He presented her two jeweled gold pomegranate earrings and two gold necklaces, one with seven suns and one with seven moons of different phases. And he placed on her head a golden crown of seven strands flowing down over her hair, each strand with seven stars studded with sparkling jewels. No queen has ever been appointed such magnificent jewels! Bethuel's wife treasured the gifts of her husband, and they lived the rest of their days in peace and joy.

Hod returned to Nahor with Bethuel. He became Bethuel's constant companion, chattering as he was wont to do, always another story for the patient ears of his aging friend, Bethuel.

Keshet yet lives and worships the Most High God. Abiel makes occasional visits to Damascus to trade for goods in the service of his master, Isaac. He always stays in the house of Jared and Abaigael, and I am their invited guest. Never would he betray the confidence of his master, but he has told me Deborah serves faithfully Rebekah, who loves her husband, Isaac, though she is said by some to be headstrong, and they favor different sons—she Jacob, the younger twin, and he Esau, the older twin brother. Surely they are one, and never will Isaac take another wife or concubine. Sweet Deborah's words still echo in my ears. "Love you, papa."

Every day I bless the Most High God for his love and mercy. He attends my soul. I consider the wonder of His calling. His voice goes throughout all the earth, calling all men unto Him. He put me on my path. He led me on a journey new in riches every day. He led me to His priest, Melchizedek, and opened my eyes to His will and His salvation for all men. Was there ever a need He did not meet? Was there ever a danger when He did not shield me? Was there ever a sorrow He could not comfort? O man, open your eyes to your creator! Open your ears to his instruction! Open your heart to His loving-kindness and mercy! He will see your need. He will hear your prayers and the cries of your heart. He will heal your wounds and comfort your sorrows. He is faithful and just and true. He will deliver you and save you. He will forgive you all your sin and blot out every transgression. He loves you and will sing songs of love over you. He will teach your lips to praise Him so your joy will be in Him!

O man, you know what the Most High God desires from you, and He will provide the strength you need to obey. What does He ask, O man, but for you to love God with all of your heart and all of your soul and to love all whom He loves! Go and do as He commands.

I, Jael ben Hod, write these words. I attest to the story of Zimri-Ruel. I have heard his words and made a careful record of his sayings. And here is the end of my friend and teacher. I was with him in his final hour. As he lay on his bed, weak and blind, I heard him say, "I see Him, yes, He awaits. I hear his voice. Do not worry for me. I just go to walk with the Most High God."

But Deborah, Rebekah's nurse died, and she was buried beneath Bethel under an oak; and the name of it was called Allonbachuth (the oak of weeping). Genesis 35: 8

About the Author

David Martyn lives in Gig Harbor, Washington with his wife Karen. Retired from a career in the Maritime Industry, he can keep watch over the ships passing to and from Tacoma and the Vashon Island Ferry. He still loves the sea, the ships, and the men and women who sail and service them. Like any who is awed by God's creation can attest, God reveals Himself and sets us on a journey of discovery that brings us by the revelation of God's Word, to the very heart of God. David's love of Scripture, has been strengthened by years of home Bible Study groups, which brought insight on Bible passages and confirmation of God working in the lives of His people. Hours of sitting with brothers and sisters pouring over Scripture helped put flesh on the bones and blood in the veins of the men and women of the Bible. Real people who struggled with sin and doubt. Men who failed God time and again, yet by the grace of God were victorious and today wear the victor's crown. It is David's hope that his stories awaken the seed of revelation God planted in the reader's heart, provides a fresh love for the fathers of our faith and brings hope to a new generation.